express:

ᵃ brief guide ₜₒ
technical
ᵃⁿᵈ business
communication

David Ingre
Kwantlen University College

NELSON
✦
THOMSON LEARNING ™

Australia · Canada · Mexico · Singapore · Spain · United Kingdom · United States

NELSON
THOMSON LEARNING ™

Express: A Brief Guide to Technical and Business Communication
by David Ingre

Editorial Director and Publisher:
Evelyn Veitch

Acquisitions Editors:
Nicole Gnutzman/Kelly Torrance

Marketing Manager:
Don Thompson

Project Editor:
Jenny Anttila

Production Editor:
Natalia Denesiuk

Production Coordinator:
Hedy Sellers

Art Director:
Angela Cluer

Cover and Interior Design:
Peter Papayanakis

Cover Images:
Jeremy Woodhouse/PhotoDisc
(commuters); Digital Vision

Copy Editor:
Sarah Robertson

Proofreader:
Erika Krolman

Compositor:
Carol Magee

Printer:
Webcom

**Canadian Cataloguing in
Publication Data**

Ingre, David, 1947–
Express: a brief guide to
technical and business
communication

Includes index.
ISBN 0-17-616758-7

1. Business communication.
2. Business writing.
3. Communication of technical
information.
4. Technical writing.   I. Title.

HF5718.I53 2000   808'.06665
C00-931318-4

Contents

Preface   xi

Chapter 1   Building a Foundation   1

The Relevance of Technical Communications   1
Characteristics of Technical Communications   1
    Necessity for a Specific Audience   2
    Integration of Visual Elements   2
    Ease of Selective Access   2
    Timeliness   2
    Structure   3
Ethics   3
    Codes of Ethics   3
    Definitions   4
    Applications   4
    Conclusions   5
Multiculturalism   6
    Cultural Referents   6
    Cultural Preferences   6
Gender   8
Case Studies   10
    Grandstone Technical Institute (GTI)   11
    Mississauga University (MU)   11
    Accelerated Enterprises Ltd. (AEL)   11
    Radisson Automobiles Inc. (RAI)   11
Exercises   12
Exploring the Web   13

Chapter 2   The CMAPP Analysis   14

Transactional Communication Models   14
The CMAPP Communication Model   16
    Definitions   17
    Analysis Tips   18
    Example   19
    Interrelationships Among CMAPP Elements   20
    Applications   21
Case Studies   21
2A Mississauga University Student Association Function   21

Situation	21
Issues to Think About	22
Revision	25
2B Reorganization Notice at Radisson Automobiles Inc. (RAI)	26
Situation	26
Issues to Think About	31
Exercises	32
Exploring the Web	37

Chapter 3   From Data to Information: Outlines and Reference Works

	38
Data versus Information	38
Process and Structure	38
Collecting Data	38
Organizing Data into an Outline	39
Refining the Outline	40
Subordination	42
Division	42
Parallelism	42
Reference Works	44
Dictionaries	44
Thesauri	44
Grammar and Usage Guides	45
Electronic References	45
Spell Checker	45
Thesaurus	46
Grammar Checker	46
Case Study	46
GTISU Facilities Leasing Report	46
Situation	46
Issues to Think About	48
Exercises	48
Exploring the Web	50

Chapter 4   Visual Elements in Written and Oral Communications

	51
Document Visuals	51
Body Text and Level Heads	51
Headers and Footers	51
White Space	52

Justification	52
Fonts	54
Other Attributes	56
Lists	56
Style Guides	56
Visuals in Documents and Presentations	57
Information and Impression	57
Considerations	58
Charts and Tables	60
Pie Charts	60
Vertical Bar Charts	62
Horizontal Bar Charts	62
Line Charts	63
Tables	66
Clip Art	67
Case Study	68
AEL Engineering Report	68
Situation	68
Issues to Think About	73
Revision	74
Exercises	74
Exploring the Web	79

Chapter 5   Complementary Attributes of the CMAPP Model   81

5WH	81
KISS	82
ABC	83
Accuracy	83
Brevity	83
Clarity	83
CFF	84
CAP	86
Concise	86
Accessible	86
Precise	88
Case Study	89
Mississauga University Registration	89
Situation	89
Issues to Think About	92
Exercises	93
Exploring the Web	94

Chapter 6   Communication Strategies (1): News, Technical Description, and Simple Instructions   95

News   95
  Conveying Good News   95
  Conveying Bad News   96
  Neutral News   98
Technical Description   99
  Simple Technical Description   100
  Complex Description   102
  Computerized Hyperlinks   102
Simple Instructions   102
  Strategy   103
Case Studies   105
6A Acceptance Letter from GTI   105
  Situation   105
  Issues to Think About   105
6B Rejection Letter from RAI   105
  Situation   105
  Issues to Think About   107
Exercises   107
Exploring the Web   109

Chapter 7   Communication Strategies (2): Persuasion   110

Persuasive Strategies   110
  Intellect versus Emotion   110
  Targeting the Intellect: Logical Argumentation   110
  Targeting the Emotions: AIDA   115
  A Note on Ethics   117
Case Study   118
Persuasive Messages from MUSAEx   118
  Situation   118
  Issues to Think About   118
Exercises   121
Exploring the Web   121

Chapter 8   Common Products (1): Letters, Memos, Faxes, and E-mail   123

Letters   123
  Block and Modified Block   124
  The Simplified Format   127

Memos   129
Electronic Communications   132
   Faxes   133
   E-mail   134
Case Studies   136
8A Mississauga University: Interdepartmental Memorandum   136
   Situation   136
   Issues to Think About   137
   Revision   138
8B Student Association Cooperation: Fax from MU to GTI   138
   Situation   138
   Issues to Think About   141
   Revision   141
8C E-mail: Personal Communication at RAI   143
   Situation   143
   Issues to Think About   143
Exercises   147
Exploring the Web   148

Chapter 9   Common Products (2): Proposals   149

Classification of Proposals   149
CMAPP Implications   150
   Scenario 1: Solicited Internal   150
   Scenario 2: Unsolicited Internal   151
   Scenario 3: Solicited External   151
   Scenario 4: Unsolicited External   151
Informal and Formal Proposals   152
General Considerations   153
Case Study   156
Proposal to AEL from Superlative Design   156
   Situation   156
   Issues to Think About   156
   Revision   158
Exercises   158
Exploring the Web   160

Chapter 10   Common Products (3): Reports and Summaries   161

Characteristics of Written Reports   161
   Response to Need or Request   161
   Rationale   161

Hierarchy 162
Level of Technicality 162
Informal Reports 164
Characteristics 164
Classification 167
Categories 168
Formal Reports 171
Structure 172
Summaries 174
Categories 174
Content and Length 175
Content Summary Process 176
Case Study 178
RAI Report on Participation in GTI Internship Program 178
Situation 178
Issues to Think About 179
Exercises 179
Exploring the Web 187

Chapter 11   Effective Presentations   188

The CMAPP Approach to Presentations 188
Audience Analysis 189
Purpose 190
Conquering Stage Fright 191
The Development Process 192
Types of Presentations 194
Manuscript Presentation 194
Memorized Presentation 194
Impromptu Presentation 194
Extemporaneous Presentation 195
Elements of the Presentation 195
Introductory Segment 195
Body 196
Concluding Segment 197
Paralinguistic Factors 198
Dress 198
Confidence and Presence 198
Eye Contact 198
Posture and Movement 199
Facial Expressions and Gestures 199
Volume 199

Speed	199
Tone, Pitch, and Intonation	199
Enunciation and Pronunciation	200
Hesitation Particles	200
Time Management	200
Visuals and Visual Aids	200
Handouts	201
Props	201
Overhead Projectors	202
35mm Projector and Slides	203
Computer Presentations	204
Data Projectors	204
Question Period	204
Case Study	205
AEL Presentation to Students	205
Situation	205
Issues to Think About	211
Exercises	212
Exploring the Web	212

Chapter 12   Seeking Employment   214

Preparation	214
Cover Letters	216
Rationale	216
Content	216
Form	217
Format	217
Résumés	217
Message	218
Audience	218
Purpose	219
Product	219
Chronological Résumés	220
Functional Résumés	220
Relevant Information	222
Electronic Résumés	226
Ethics	226
Interviews	227
Questions and Answers	228
Follow-up	228
Case Study	228

Cover Letters from MU Students to AEL   228
    Situation   228
    Issues to Think About   229
Exercises   229
Exploring the Web   232

Index   235

Preface

Rather than attempting to be everything to everyone, this text focuses on the most important elements of contemporary technical communications in Canada. For its approach and content, I have drawn on my years as a teacher of English as a second language, a public-sector manager in such areas as training and development and human resources planning, an instructional designer, an independent communications consultant and trainer, and a regular faculty member in the applied communication department of a large postsecondary institution.

Whether you're a seasoned professional or relatively new to this field, I believe the book will be of value to you and your students. It is comprehensive and challenging enough to be the sole assigned text for a college or university technical communications course. At the same time, its structure is such that you can easily incorporate complementary materials or rearrange the sequence of teaching activities.

Express is predicated on the ongoing, dynamic analysis of context, message, audience, purpose, and product (referred to in the book as the CMAPP model). The model provides thematic continuity as students learn to apply the approach in a variety of communication strategies, including good news and bad news, description and instructions, and persuasion, and in the creation of such products as letters, memos, proposals, reports, and summaries. Through their active participation in the book's interrelated case studies and exercises, students come to understand and develop the critical thinking and planning skills that are essential to effective technical communications.

The text explores the growing distinctions between technical communications and more traditional forms of writing such as narratives and essays. While it uses the increasingly informal language of today's marketplace, it offers students an additional learning opportunity by presenting them with possibly unfamiliar, though nontechnical, vocabulary. As well, students learn about the importance of ethics and multiculturalism in technical communications. Ethical dilemmas relating to various facets of technical communications are considered at strategic points throughout the book.

An Instructor's Manual is available. It contains recommendations for classroom use of the CMAPP model, a suggested course timetable, supplementary examples, sample examinations, and a broad selection of reproducible materials (such as transparencies or handouts) on such topics as the CMAPP model, reports, summaries, and visuals.

Acknowledgments

I am particularly grateful to two friends and colleagues, David Wiens and Panteli Tritchew, for their inspiration and cooperation in the initial development of the CMAPP model.

As a student, you might in the past have been assigned a textbook, asked to read long and often boring passages, and expected to memorize innumerable theories and apparently unrelated details. You might have gone to the exam expecting (and prepared) to recite everything back. Some time later, you might have realized that the exam was the one and only time you put that unappealing (and probably expensive) textbook to practical use.

Will your experience with *Express* be any different? You'll decide that as you use the book. It does have some aspects you should find appealing. To begin with, it doesn't try to be everything to everyone; it deals only with common types of technical communications, treats them from a distinctly Canadian perspective, and tries to do so concisely. Instead of the traditional, academic "third person impersonal," it employs the "you approach" typical in today's technical communications. So, for example, I'll make use of contractions (e.g., "I'll"), of the second person ("you," as reader), and of the first person ("I," as writer). Though I'll define technical terms, you may encounter other vocabulary with which you aren't familiar. If so, I suggest you look up the words—that too is part of improving your technical communications skills.

The book describes and uses a dynamic analysis model of technical communications. In Chapter 2, you'll look in detail at this approach or model, whose acronym, CMAPP, stands for its five elements: context, message, audience, purpose, and product. You might at first think that this approach is superficial or formulaic. You might also wonder how learning to use the model will help you to create particular types of letters, memos, or reports. Consider this analogy: you can learn to prioritize a set of objectives simply by numbering them in order of importance; you can then successfully apply that simple formula to your homework, your daily chores, or your workplace tasks. Applying a deceptively simple formula can thus yield a multitude of complex, sophisticated results. You should find that the CMAPP approach yields a similarly rich harvest.

Organization of the Text

The sequence of topics in *Express* differs from what you will find in many other technical communications books. You'll find an introduction to the field of technical communications in Chapter 1. In Chapter 2, you'll examine the analytical model, CMAPP, in detail, because it serves as the basis for all that follows. In Chapter 3, you'll find recommendations for organizing your thoughts, since having a clear idea of what you actually want to communicate is crucial. Within the same chapter, I'll offer some suggestions regarding the use of electronic reference materials.

In Chapter 4, you will study the visual aspects of technical communications, because the way you show and illustrate what you write or present will help determine its success with your audience. Some of those features are among the additional CMAPP attributes that are the subject of Chapter 5.

Putting all this together leads to a discussion, in Chapters 6 and 7, of CMAPP communication strategies—ways to structure information in the creation of a large variety of technical communications. These strategies allow you to generate a host of technical communications products, a number of which are covered in Chapters 8 through 10.

Chapters 11 and 12 show how the CMAPP approach is applied in two specific areas: presentations and the search for employment.

Features of the Text

Most chapters include the following features:

- *Case Study*   At the end of Chapter 1, you will be introduced to four organizations that are featured in the book's interrelated case studies. The case studies allow you to examine the application of the CMAPP approach in the real world. The sample communications presented in each case study let you analyze common weaknesses.

- *Exercises*   The exercises are based on material covered in the chapter. Some exercises help you review what you have learned. Others require you to take on roles associated with the case study organizations. Still others require you to interact with people in the real-world marketplace.

- *Exploring the Web*   Here you will find a list of URLs (current at this writing) for Web sites that relate either to the material covered in the chapter or to other communication issues.

Conclusion

I won't claim that this book will teach you to be an effective technical communicator (its underlying premise is that you have to do the work). Nonetheless, I do believe it can help you learn to apply what is largely common sense to create a variety of effective real-world technical communications.

All the material in this textbook derives from three things: the application of commonly accepted principles of rhetoric and communications; my years of experience in, and observation of, technical communications in the private and public sectors; and the successful testing, in postsecondary classrooms, of everything in *Express*. I hope that you enjoy the book and find it useful.

The Relevance of Technical Communications

Since this book is about technical communications in Canada, you might think that if you don't intend to write manuals or sell a product, it won't apply to you. But, despite the name, the field includes:

- letters or memos to, from, or between people who work in any kind of company, organization, or association, from multinational conglomerates, to home-based businesses, to charities such as the Canadian Cancer Society;
- advertising and promotional material, from magazine ads to business cards;
- a host of other documents, from the annual report of a firm like General Motors Canada to your own income tax return, and from the operating and repair manuals for specialized equipment such as CAT scanners to the last parking ticket you received;
- oral communication, from the formal presentation of a new product line to a large group of prospective clients, to the informal explanation of your opinion at a small meeting.

You'll use technical communications at school and in your career, and the more effective you can make them, the greater your likelihood of success. Suppose that you and your friend both study hard in a particular course and have some valuable ideas to contribute. If you have learned to express your ideas (both orally and in writing) precisely and effectively, but your friend hasn't, which of you is likely to get the better grades? Similarly, if you were an employer deciding between two applicants with roughly equivalent qualifications and experience, and only one demonstrated communication skills that would represent your organization the way you wanted it to be represented, which applicant would you hire?

So, as you read this book, think of it not as a complicated explanation of a subject of little use to you, but as a set of practical guidelines that can boost your chances of success in a wide range of areas.

Characteristics of Technical Communications

In recent years, the field of technical communications has been developing a style of its own. This is particularly true of written material. We can clarify some of the distinctions between technical communications and what I will loosely label "traditional prose" by examining five salient features of technical communications: necessity for a specific audience, integration of visual elements, ease of selective access, timeliness, and structure.

Necessity for a Specific Audience

Much traditional prose is what we might term author-driven. Someone makes a discovery, has a revelation, develops a theory, wants to share feelings with others, wishes to entertain, or simply believes that a particular story will generate profit by appealing to a large number of anonymous readers—and so begins to write, believing that there will be "an audience out there." But no one gets up one morning and says, "I want to write the definitive Canadian business letter" or "Today, I'll fulfill my dream of writing a lengthy report." Technical communications is audience-driven. People create it to respond to a *specific* audience's need for information. Whether you are writing a letter, a memo, a report, or an e-mail, you always tailor it to a specific audience. In fact, if you don't already know exactly who your audience *is*, you don't really have anything to say. The better you know your audience, the more effectively you'll be able to communicate. The same principle applies to *oral* technical communications.

Integration of Visual Elements

Great literature would be just as great if it were handwritten on loose-leaf pages, rather than printed in a book. By contrast, the effectiveness of advertising or promotional material such as a brochure, a flyer, or a sales talk relies at least as much on presentation as on content. The term "visual elements" refers to everything from illustrations such as diagrams or charts, to headings and type. Careful integration of ideas and presentation is essential to effective technical communications.

Ease of Selective Access

Literary authors normally expect you to read every word, rather than skim quickly, looking for the main points. They assume that you, as a reader, are willing to devote your full attention to the writing, from start to finish. At the same time, you recognize that your understanding of the text is likely conditional on your having read all of it. By contrast, technical communications writers assume that readers will have other demands on their time and, as a result, may want to quickly identify only the principal points, perhaps returning later for a more careful reading.

If you are checking your office e-mail, for example, you're likely to first glance quickly at the header to see who sent the message and what it's about. In checking your advertising mail, you'll tend to scan for headings or other prominent words or phrases, and based on what you find, either delete the item or put it aside for later perusal. Good technical communications allows the reader to make the choice without penalty. And it does so in large part through the judicious integration of visual elements.

Timeliness

The world's great books are supposed to be timeless whereas the technicians' manuals for the Apple II or the IBM PCJr are well past their expiry dates. Last year's Canadian

Tire catalogue is of little use to consumers. By the middle of January, the newspaper ad for Future Shop's Boxing Day sale has no practical value. And once you have received your merchandise, the online purchase order you filled out at *www.chapters.ca* has been reduced to bits and bytes of electronic rubbish. Almost without exception, the useful life of technical communications is relatively short: it is usually over as soon as the reality it addresses changes.

Structure

You might have been taught that a paragraph must have a topic sentence, one or more supporting sentences, and a concluding sentence. You might also have been told never to begin a sentence with *and* or *but*. In contemporary technical communications, these rules don't apply. If you can express the idea of a paragraph in one sentence, you should do so. Also in the interest of brevity and ease of access, you may replace topic sentences with headings or subheadings. And most business and technical writers accept the practice of beginning some sentences with *and* or *but*. They also vary sentence length and structure to avoid monotony of style.

Ethics

The question of ethics cannot be restricted to philosophy or religion courses. It has practical applications in education, commerce, government, and technical communications.

Codes of Ethics

The importance of ethics in the conduct of business and technology is broadly accepted. In fact, organizations ranging from businesses to self-regulating professional associations publish codes of ethical conduct. Several years ago, a group of international business leaders, primarily from Europe, Japan, and the United States, developed what they called the Caux Round Table Principles for Business. Effectively a code of ethics, it states that "while accepting the legitimacy of trade secrets, businesses should recognize that sincerity, candor, truthfulness, the keeping of promises, and transparency contribute not only to their own credibility and stability but also to the smoothness and efficiency of business transactions, particularly on the international level." The Institute of Electrical and Electronic Engineers, an international professional association headquartered in the United States, publishes a code of ethics that includes the mandate "to accept responsibility in making engineering decisions consistent with the safety, health and welfare of the public, and to disclose promptly factors that might endanger the public or the environment."

Closer to home are the following examples of public statements on ethical conduct:

- The Manitoba Association of Architects' Code of Ethics
- The Professional Engineers' Code of Ethics (Professional Engineers Ontario)
- The Canadian Association of Broadcasters' Code of Ethics, published by the Canadian Broadcast Standards Council
- The Canadian Marketing Association Code of Ethics and Standards of Practice

Definitions

What do we mean by ethics? The *ITP Nelson Canadian Dictionary* (1997) provides the following definitions:

> eth·ic. n. 1.a. A set of principles of right conduct. b. A theory or a system of moral values. 2. ethics. *(used with a sing. v.)* The study of the general nature of morals and of specific moral choices; moral philosophy. 3. ethics. *(used with a sing. or pl. v.)* The rules or standards governing the conduct of a person or the members of a profession.

Unfortunately, all but the last definition incorporate highly subjective terms. There is no consensus as to the meaning and implications of "right conduct." (Do you and your family and friends always agree on what is "right"?) Similarly, what is meant by "moral"? Does it mean the same to everyone? Has its meaning changed over time? Over the centuries, philosophers have wrestled with these questions. More recent attention has been focused on the development and meaning of medical ethics, professional ethics, journalistic ethics, business ethics (which some people facetiously consider an oxymoron), and so on. Can we derive from a confusing but important maze of ideas any practical guidance for those who engage in technical communications?

Applications

However we define ethics, most of us have a sense of what we consider right and wrong, and most of us would agree that most of the time, we should try to apply the injunction, "do unto others as you would have them do unto you." Most successful people seem to believe that treating others as justly as possible is one of the cornerstones of their success. How might this approach be reflected in technical communications? Here are a few examples.

Honesty   Many of us know someone who lied on a résumé and so got the job. We often forget that in most cases, the lie is eventually discovered, and the person loses not only the job but his or her reputation. Telling someone that "the cheque is in the mail" when it isn't may bring short-term benefits, but if you persist in this kind of deception, you'll soon come to be thought of as dishonest and will find it difficult to continue doing business. Being dishonest with others is illegal in some cases; for most people, it is always unethical.

Accuracy An important criterion for technical communicators is accuracy of information. If your document or presentation contains inaccuracies, and if someone in your audience notices the errors, your entire message—and likely any future ones—is compromised. Whenever you communicate, your credibility is on the line; and regaining lost credibility is very difficult indeed. If the lack of accuracy in what you communicate is intentional, the issue becomes one of honesty, and thus of ethics.

Exaggeration Whether you're trying to sell a product or express an opinion, you should certainly try to present your information in the best possible light. You might do this, for example, by accentuating the advantages of your brand and glossing over its weaknesses. Similarly, in describing your preferred option, you might use more forceful vocabulary than you use in describing the alternatives. Here the question of ethics tends to be one of degree. Only a technical audience is likely to be swayed by neutral facts alone. Consequently, when you wish to persuade—and technical communications certainly involves persuasion—you must in some sense exaggerate.

Communication that exaggerates beyond what is reasonable, however, may be scorned. Of course, deciding what is and is not "reasonable" can be difficult. Think of the difference between what you would consider "reasonable exaggeration" in a loan application and what you accept (despite the apparent absurdity of the claims) in advertisements for cars or toothpaste. For the sake of both expediency and one's reputation, it's best to adopt an ethical approach at all times.

Creating Impressions Whenever it conveys information, language also creates impressions. Consciously or unconsciously, audiences respond to the emotional effect of language (its connotation), as well as to its objective meaning (its denotation). Thus, the way you phrase a communication will influence how your audience responds to it. (Think of the importance of spin doctors in political circles.) Suppose that you are a manager in a company and your record shows that three-quarters of your decisions have proved to be good ones. To describe your batting average, we could say that you are right 75 percent of the time or that you are wrong 25 percent of the time. Which description would you prefer to see in your personnel file?

As in the case of exaggeration, the ethical path may be indistinct. In most cases, technical communications requires you to be as objective as possible, even though the nature of language itself makes it all but impossible to present communications that are entirely free of connotation.

Conclusions

As an ethical communicator, you have to be willing to put the needs of your audience before your own interests. Twisting language to camouflage an unsavoury truth may produce the results you want, but you should not ignore the potential repercussions. Rarely are ethical people comfortable with the rationalization that the end justifies the means. Whenever you are communicating, try asking yourself how you would react if you were the audience. Would you feel that you were being treated fairly and respectfully? If you can't honestly answer yes, it's likely that as a communicator, you haven't given sufficient weight to the ethical aspects of what you're doing.

Multiculturalism

Turning once more to the *ITP Nelson Canadian Dictionary*, we find the following entries:

> **mul·ti·cul·tur·al**. *adj.* Of, relating to, or including several cultures.
>
> **mul·ti·cul·tur·al·ism**. *n.* **1.** The condition of being multicultural. **2.** The preservation of distinct cultural identities among varied groups within a unified society. **3.** Government policies, institutions, and practices that are intended to preserve varied cultural identities.

When some Canadians hear the term "multiculturalism," they think of government policies to promote heritage activities but ignore the diversity in society those policies are designed to address. The fact that it has become one of the most distinctive characteristics of Canadian society makes multiculturalism relevant to effective technical communications.

Cultural Referents

People, ideas, and things that form part of the popular culture and become ingrained in our thinking and in our language are referred to as *cultural referents*. As a technical communicator, you must consider whether your audience will understand the cultural referents that you take for granted. For example, an audience that had never been exposed to the Grade 1 primers common in North America in the 1950s and 1960s would probably not know that a "Dick and Jane approach" is one that is overly simplistic. The multicultural nature of Canadian society means that you must pay attention to the cultural referents you use, and consider whether they are relevant to your intended audience. If your audience doesn't relate to them as you do, you are not communicating effectively.

Cultural Preferences

Just as different people respond differently to cultural referents, different groups tend to react differently to certain types of behaviour. For example, the use of first names in newly established business relationships is very common in the United States and increasingly common in Canada. Presumably, this behaviour is designed to promote an impression of friendliness and conviviality. It is not, however, universally accepted. Many cultures, and, in fact, many native-born Canadians, feel that business relationships should be more formal, and that the appropriate form of address—even among people who know each other quite well—is a last name preceded by an honorific such as *Ms.* or *Mr.* Unless you know your audience's preferences, therefore, you run less risk of being thought impolite if you avoid using first names in such cases.

Another characteristic of North American business dealings is the value placed on directness. Thus, brevity and concision are seen as desirable qualities in letters and memos. In some other cultures, these same qualities would be regarded as brusque, curt, or abrasive. In Japan, for example, tradition dictates a much more roundabout approach in which ideas are conveyed through implication rather than stated explicitly. A related issue is letter-writing conventions. In Canada, we are accustomed to ending a business letter with a phrase such as "Yours truly" (although we are certainly not swearing to the truth of what we've written). People from other cultures may consider this phrase abrupt or unfriendly. Even in French-speaking Quebec, for example, a standard complimentary close to a business letter would translate as "I would be pleased if you would accept, Madame, this expression of my very kindest sentiments."

Spelling and vocabulary must also be considered. When writing to an American business, which should you use—Canadian or American spelling? Again, consider both your audience and your purpose. You may make a point of using Canadian spelling (e.g., *favour, centre*) when you want to draw attention to the fact that your firm is Canadian; conversely, you would use American spelling (e.g., *favor, center*) if you didn't want that fact to be so conspicuous. You should also be aware of differences in vocabulary. For example, if you are writing to someone in England, you will be better understood if you use the words "lift," "boot," and "biscuit," rather than "elevator," "trunk" (of a car), and "cookie." Nor should you be shocked if someone from England offers to "knock you up" at 7:00 a.m. It's simply that person's way of proposing a wake-up call.

Although humour plays at best a minor role in technical communications, you should exercise care in its use. The same caution applies to references to religion and politics. North Americans tend to approach such references with what for some cultures is inappropriate familiarity. Unless you are certain of your audience's reaction, you should avoid potentially offensive references in your communications—in other words, stick to the facts.

The term "personal space" is often used to refer to the physical distance we like to maintain between ourselves and those with whom we are speaking. Different cultures have different norms. Many Europeans and South Americans, for example, prefer much less personal space than most North Americans are comfortable with. When you see two people from different cultures talking, you might observe one advancing to decrease the personal space and the other backing up in an effort to increase it. Although the issue of personal space does not have a direct bearing on written technical communications, it is a good idea to be aware of the cultural differences involved.

A related issue is eye contact. Most North Americans believe that looking someone in the eye while conversing is an indication of honesty and forthrightness. In some other cultures, however, such behaviour can be viewed as rude or presumptuous.

Although you should make eye contact with your audience during a presentation, you should not assume that your audience's failure to reciprocate implies shiftiness or deceit. Here again, knowledge of your audience will help you develop worthwhile professional relationships.

Gender

In the field of technical communications, we also need to keep abreast of linguistic change. Such change is dramatically evident in the increased use of nonsexist language in recent years. The article "Sexism in Our Language" (see Box 1.1), which appeared in 1990 in a Vancouver business periodical that targeted SOHO (small office/home office) operators, addresses the issue.

Box 1.1 Sexism in Our Language

In recent years, people have been focusing greater attention on a topic commonly known as "sexism." For distressingly good reason, sociologists, social reformers, activists, politicians, and others have studied and commented on the ways our society distinguishes between men and women.

Did you notice the order of the last three words of the last sentence? We have been taught that it is proper form to say "ladies and gentlemen" rather than "gentlemen and ladies," and most of us would more naturally write "men and women" than "women and men." Both practices are socially learned. Are both sexist? To what extent do societal distinctions between the sexes exist in the language itself? Can we change them? What happens to the language when we do?

These are highly complex questions. They are also very loaded ones. Few people are neutral; once they have begun to look at the issue in any depth, fewer still expect quick solutions. What we can do here is look at a few examples of systemic gender discrimination in English, and point out some of the strategies for dealing with them. Since a great deal of the problem seems to reside in the words "man" and "woman" and their compounds, it might be worthwhile seeing where these words come from.

The word *man* can mean "man" as opposed to "woman," as well as "man" as opposed to "other animal species." *Man* derives from the old Anglo-Saxon word "mann," which was originally applied to both sexes but eventually took on its modern meanings. *Woman* comes to us from another Anglo-Saxon word, "wifman," literally "wife [or "woman"] man." (Its plural, "wimmen," explains our modern pronunciation of "women.") Thus, it would seem that defining women in terms of men is in a sense entrenched in the language.

Another social issue that has affected English is employment. Until fairly recently, a number of fields were considered "men's work"; others (and, more often than not, those of lesser status) were seen as "women's work." So we get words in the language like "policeman," "fireman," and "chairman," contrasting sharply with others like "charwoman" (which is always strongly pejorative) and "midwife" (which derives from Old English, meaning "with woman").

Two other things to remember ... First, English has a number of words that don't show gender; that is, they don't tell us whether we're talking about a man or a woman. These are words like "friend," "colleague," and "person." Second, English has words that show gender in the singular but not in the plural. Among them are the pronouns *he* and *she* (as opposed to *they*) and their derivatives (*him, his, her, hers* as opposed to *their* and *theirs*).

When we speak (and often, when we write), we may not want to specify whether we're talking about a woman or a man. To avoid being forced to by the language, we sometimes take some slightly clumsy detours. For example, you may hear a sentence such as, "A colleague of mine always carries a spare key in their pocket." We find more problems with two sentences together: "I was talking to a colleague last night. They tell me there's a new contract coming." Although everyone understands what these sentences mean, the language is still often considered substandard: we are not (yet) really supposed to use a plural to refer to a singular.

One way around the difficulties in such sentences is to rephrase. For example: "A colleague of mine always carries a spare key." This revised version gives all the information that's likely necessary and avoids the problem of using a plural to refer to a singular. The other example would be a bit more formal (and acceptable in writing) if it were changed to "A colleague to whom I was talking last night tells me a new contract is coming."

Particularly in the public sector, people have been recommending ways to remove sexist language. Basically, they have tried three strategies. First is the one mentioned in the last paragraph: rephrase your sentences to avoid the problem.

Second is the use of an initial note of some kind, such as: "All references to the masculine in this document should be interpreted as applying equally to the feminine." This "solution," in fact, may be worse than the problem. Not only is it irritatingly bureaucratic, but it emphasizes the very distinction it is supposed to diminish.

Third is the substitution of words or the creation of entirely new terms. As far as the pronouns are concerned, we see slightly peculiar forms such as "he/she," "him/her," and so on. (I have also seen "(s)he," although never "her(m).") This route generates a visually curious document and causes obvious problems if you try to read it aloud.

Words like "ombudsperson" and "chairperson" or "chair" have become commonplace. Other creative substitutions include *flight attendant* instead of *stewardess* or *steward*; *server* rather than *waiter* or *waitress*; and *police officer* instead of *policeman* or *policewoman*. As well, there is a tendency for some pairs of words to coalesce. Thus, *actor* and *singer* are commonly used for both men and women, to the exclusion of *actress* and—almost never seen now—*songstress*. As our society changes, we're likely to see more and more such attempts to remove sexism from the language.

The decade since the article's publication has seen further efforts to eliminate sexist language. Many books on writing feature lists of gender-neutral words or phrases that can be used to replace gender-specific vocabulary. For example:

Instead of	Use
businessman/businesswoman	businessperson
businessmen/businesswomen	businesspeople
foreman	supervisor
mailman	postal carrier
man-made	synthetic
manpower	personnel

As well, the use of *they* when referring to a singular antecedent is gaining some acceptance. In business letters, the use of salutations such as "Dear Personnel Manager," as an alternative to "Dear Sir" or "Dear Madam," is becoming commonplace.

Whether you are dealing with issues of cultural difference or gender bias, as an effective technical communicator you are required to keep abreast of what is acceptable practice and what is not. This, in turn, means constructing your message with careful consideration of your context and your audience—in effect, applying the communication model you will examine in detail in the next chapter.

CASE STUDIES

In the subsequent chapters of this book, you will look at examples of technical communications involving one or more of four organizations that are based on real companies and institutions.

Each case study is introduced in a section titled *Situation* that presents examples of flawed communications produced by people within the organizations under consideration. The section entitled *Issues to Think About* presents questions raised by the samples. Some cases conclude with a section titled *Revision*, which lets you examine a better-constructed version of the material.

Here are profiles of the four organizations.

Grandstone Technical Institute (GTI)

Located in Langley, British Columbia, GTI offers one- and two-year certificates or diplomas in such fields as management information systems and engineering technology, as well as internship programs in such areas as automotive mechanics, electronics, and welding. GTI's reputation for excellence is such that its graduates are often welcomed by companies across the country.

Mississauga University (MU)

Situated in Mississauga, Ontario, MU offers both undergraduate and graduate degrees, principally in arts, law, and engineering. One result of the university's successful fundraising campaigns was the construction of a new Student Association Building. The Mississauga University Student Association Executive (MUSAEx) remains very active in promoting cooperation among student associations across the country.

Accelerated Enterprises Ltd. (AEL)

In 1980, two young Winnipeg engineers, Sarah Cohen and Frank Nabata, opened a small consulting practice—optimistically named Accelerated Enterprises Ltd.—in the city's north end. Over the next two decades, business prospered. Cohen and Nabata (now married) took in a number of associates and opened branches in Toronto, St. John's, Edmonton, and Vancouver. With the expansion came broadened expertise, and AEL is now involved in chemical, civil, and geological engineering, as well as software design and development. While the original partners still oversee the firm's overall strategy from their now-spacious offices in Winnipeg, they believe in allowing their branch associates significant latitude in running the local operations. As well, AEL tries to maintain good working relationships with several postsecondary institutions, viewing them as important contributors to the country's economic growth, and as likely sources for future AEL consultants and employees.

Radisson Automobiles Inc. (RAI)

Headquartered in Ottawa, and with locations in Halifax, Moncton, Montreal, Winnipeg, Regina, and Vancouver, RAI is a highly successful automobile dealership chain.

In 1970, Maurice Radisson, an energetic, successful entrepreneur who had become alarmed by the activities of the Front de Libération du Québec, relocated his auto sales business from Quebec City to Ottawa. Over the years, RAI prospered, and in 1990 Maurice turned the stewardship of the business over to his eldest son, Gilles, who held an automotive mechanics diploma from GTI and an MBA from MU. As president and chief executive officer, Gilles built his father's Ottawa dealership into a wealthy and respected cross-country network. A firm believer in federal bilingualism, he insists that all companywide announcements be presented in both English and French. To strengthen RAI's image as a good corporate citizen, he favours establishing relationships with Canadian postsecondary institutions.

EXERCISES

1.1 Give four or more examples of what could be classified as technical communications.

1.2 Describe at least one real-world situation in which technical communications skills would serve you well.

1.3 Briefly explain the significance of the following characteristics of effective technical communications:
   (a) necessity for a specific audience
   (b) integration of visual elements
   (c) ease of selective access
   (d) timeliness
   (e) structure

1.3 Briefly discuss the importance of ethics in technical communications, referring specifically to the issues of honesty, accuracy, exaggeration, and the creation of impressions.

1.4 Discuss how ethics played a role in an example from your own experience.

1.5 Talk to someone in business or government who is involved in hiring new employees, and report back to your class on what that person thinks are the most important ethical issues in his or her workplace.

1.6 Give two or more examples of cultural referents that you take for granted, and suggest alternatives for an audience that might not understand them.

1.7 Provide two or more examples (not mentioned in this chapter) of gender-specific words or phrases and beside them list gender-neutral alternatives.

EXPLORING THE WEB

Here are some Web sites you might wish to investigate.

URL	DESCRIPTION
http://www.stc.org/	The Regional and Chapter Information page of the Society for Technical Communication (STC) offers links to STC region and chapter Web sites around the world, as well as information on educational resources, seminars and conferences, and employment opportunities.
http://www.bcr.com/	The home page of the Business Communications Review offers information and links for those with an interest in the broad area of business communications.
http://www.ethics.ubc.ca	The home page of the University of British Columbia's Centre for Applied Ethics provides links to information pages concerning the Centre's activities and history, as well as links to Web sites dealing with various branches of applied ethics (e.g., health care ethics, business ethics, professional ethics, environmental ethics, media ethics, and computer ethics).

If you wanted to find out the effect on Vancouver of a two-foot rise in sea level, you wouldn't try to melt the polar ice cap and then visit the West Coast; you'd try to find a computer model that would predict the likely consequences. Similarly, when we study technical communications, we use a model.

Transactional Communication Models

Various communication models have been developed over the years. Figure 2.1 shows a simple transactional model, so called to reflect the two-way nature of communications. The model, which in principle works for all types of oral and written communications, has the following characteristics:

Figure 2.1: A Simple Transactional Model

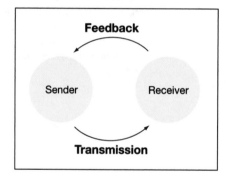

1. The originator of the communication (the *sender*) conveys (*transmits*) it to someone else (the *receiver*).

2. The *transmission* vehicle might be face-to-face speech, correspondence, telephone, fax, e-mail, etc.

3. The receiver's reaction (e.g., body language, verbal or written response)—the *feedback*—can have an effect on the sender, who may then modify any further communication accordingly.

As an example, think of a face-to-face conversation with a friend. As sender, you mention what you think is a funny comment made by another student named Maria. (Note that the basic transmission vehicle here is the sound waves that carry your voice.) As you refer to her, you see your friend's (the receiver's) face begin to cloud over, and you remember that your friend and Maria strongly dislike each other. This feedback makes you decide to start talking about something else. The model thus demonstrates an ongoing transaction between sender and receiver, conditioned by both the type and effectiveness of the transmission and the impact of the feedback.

The more complex transactional model that appears in Figure 2.2 has the following characteristics:

1. The sender has an idea, which he or she must *encode*—that is, put into appropriate language.
2. The sender uses a transmission vehicle (as in the previous model).
3. When the receiver *decodes*, the transmission is susceptible to misunderstanding of structure, differing interpretation of words, and so forth.
4. Both sender and receiver may respond to feedback.
5. Real-world communication is always subject to *interference*, which can be *external* and/or *internal.*

Figure 2.2: An Interference Transactional Model

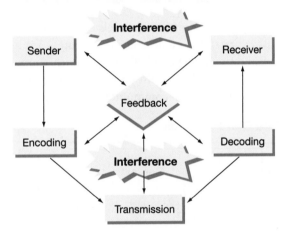

Traffic noise, people coughing nearby, a garbled e-mail file, and smudges on paper are some examples of external interference. Examples of internal interference would include the receiver's having a migraine or having a strong bias against either the sender or the topic. Interference can impede the encoding, the transmission, the decoding, and/or the feedback, thereby greatly reducing the effectiveness of communication.

Here is a simple example. In an exam, you have to answer a complex question. While you have a clear *idea* of what you mean, you have to find the right way to express it. You have to *encode* your idea in language that is logical, clear, and concise. External interference while you are encoding might include the coughing of other students and the hum of the fluorescent lighting. Internal interference could come from your nervousness during the exam or from your fatigue from having been up all night studying.

The transmission vehicle is the exam paper—the composition you are writing. An example of external interference at this stage would be your pen leaving an ink blot.

Your instructor—the receiver—will have to *decode* what you have written—that is, interpret your words and assess your knowledge. During this process, there might be external interference from other people's conversations or even from the difficulty of deciphering your rushed handwriting. Internal interference might stem from your instructor's irritation at the poor quality of the papers already marked.

In this example, feedback cannot be immediate: you will receive it only when you get your exam back. When that happens, your dissatisfaction with your mark might interfere with your understanding of your instructor's comments. Finally, the late arrival of several students might annoy your instructor and thus interfere with the delivery of his or her subsequent feedback.

The CMAPP Communication Model

The simple and interference transactional models appear to work for most types of communications. By contrast, the model shown in Figure 2.3 is designed specifically for technical communications. The CMAPP model, which you will have noted does not include the terms "sender," "transmission," or "receiver," reflects the deceptively simple nature of real-world technical communications.

Figure 2.3: The CMAPP Model

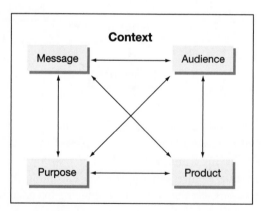

The CMAPP approach incorporates the following ideas:

■ Situations (the *context*) in which people find themselves affect their communications.

■ What people say and how they say it (the *message*) are affected by the person or group with whom they are communicating (the *audience*).

■ What people communicate is affected by their reason for communicating and their expectations (the *purpose*).

- The physical form of the communication (the *product*) affects the way in which the communication is formulated and received.
- All these ideas affect each other all the time.
- The first step in creating effective technical communications is conducting a CMAPP analysis.

Definitions

Following are explanations of the CMAPP model's terminology.

1. **Context** refers to the surrounding situation. It may include (but isn't limited to):
   (a) personal relationships;
   (b) time and place;
   (c) all circumstances that may influence the people and the communications involved;
   (d) external and internal interference that might have an impact.

2. **Message** refers to the content of the communication, and might include:
   (a) an overview of the situation;
   (b) the most significant facts, issues, and questions.;
   (c) relevant details;
   (d) a primary message (the main thing you wish to communicate) and, potentially, a secondary message (ideas that might appear in parentheses).

3. **Audience** is similar to the receiver in the transactional models. Here, however, it can include:
   (a) a primary audience, which refers to the person or people you want to reach first;
   (b) a secondary (and perhaps even a tertiary) audience, which refers to other people that you wish to reach as well (e.g., your boss's boss, the manager who receives a copy of all interoffice memos, your teacher when you are delivering a presentation to your classmates).

4. **Purpose** refers to "why" you are communicating. The concept includes:
   (a) your motive or motives—potentially, both overt and covert—for communicating;
   (b) the possibility of a secondary (and perhaps even a tertiary) purpose;
   (c) the reaction to your communication that you expect from your audience;
   (d) the response you wish to elicit.

5. **Product** is the "shape" of the communication. This can refer to the physical form (e.g., a particular appearance on paper) and/or the job it does (e.g., summarizing another product). The choice of product will affect and be affected by the context, message, audience, and purpose. Thus, the term would include (but not be limited to):

(a) memos

(b) letters

(c) reports

(d) summaries

(e) faxes

(f) e-mails

(g) telephone conversations

(h) face-to-face conversations

Analysis Tips

You should use a CMAPP analysis to plan your document or presentation. Before you begin drafting your product, ask yourself questions about the CMAPP components. Make sure that you have adequately defined the particular context, the principal message, the primary audience, and the overall purpose. Examine each of the elements closely. As you find one component affecting others, modify each accordingly until your product is ready for delivery.

You should understand that there is no predefined set of necessary questions. The ones you arrive at will be determined by the interrelationship of context, message, audience, purpose, and product. Recall, however, that the *specifics* of your message should respond to what you think your audience will need and/or want to know.

Following are examples of questions that could relate to each CMAPP component.

Context

- What is the underlying or surrounding situation?

- What are the physical conditions (lighting, noise, etc.)?

- How will the context affect how my audience responds to me or my message?

- What is my relationship with my audience?

- Are there other relationships involved that might have an impact?

Message

- What, exactly, am I trying to communicate?

- Is it a message worth communicating?

- Is my message self-contained, or is it the initial, middle, or final segment of a longer communication?

- Have I included all necessary and excluded all unnecessary information?

- Have I provided the specifics that my audience will need and/or want?

- Do I have more than one message (i.e., one or more secondary messages)?

- If I have more than one message, have I arranged them in an order that is appropriate for this context, audience, and purpose?

Audience

- Who *should* receive my communication?
- Who *will* receive it?
- What does my audience know already?
- What does my audience *need* to know?
- What does my audience *want* to know?
- What assumptions have I made about my audience?
- How specialized (technical) is my audience?
- How will my audience benefit from my communication?

Purpose

- Why do I want to communicate?
- Why do I want to communicate at this particular time?
- Why would my audience need or want this communication?
- What do I want to achieve?
- Am I trying to inform, persuade, instruct, or describe?
- Was my communication explicitly requested?
- Are there deadlines involved? Have I identified and dealt with them?

Product

- Should I be writing, phoning, visiting, etc.?
- Have I chosen a product (e.g., letter, memo, report, presentation) that is appropriate for this context, audience, message, and purpose?
- Do the wording and format of my product reflect the image I want to present?

Example

Consider the following scenario. You receive an envelope that is supposed to contain a cheque and an explanatory note. The note is there; the cheque is not. What do you do? According to the CMAPP approach, you would conduct a brief analysis before you actually do anything. Here's an example:

- *Context*   Were you expecting the cheque or was it a surprise? Was it on time or overdue? Was it a refund from Revenue Canada, a birthday gift, a student loan installment, pay for overtime work? Do you have a personal relationship with the person who was to send it? If you do, is that relationship a good or a bad one? If the note was signed by more than one person, how will you determine to whom you should direct your response?

- *Message*   What, specifically, should you say? Are you providing everything your audience will need in order to understand and respond? Should you mention your annoyance? (Think of the context.) How much detail should you include? What kind of language should you use—very simple or sophisticated?

- *Audience*   Are you communicating with a single individual, a company, a large bureaucracy? Will that audience know who you are ... or care? Do you have reason to believe your audience is competent to deal with the situation? Are you trying to communicate with the person who forgot to enclose the cheque or with that person's boss?

- *Purpose*   Are you communicating simply to get your cheque as quickly as possible, to voice your irritation, or to obtain an apology? Do you expect an immediate response? Do you want to maintain a good relationship with your audience, or do you not care?

- *Product*   Should you telephone? If so, would you be satisfied with voice mail? Would calling long-distance be acceptable to you? Should you—or can you—pay a visit instead? Would written communication be more effective? If so, should it be handwritten or word-processed, on personal or letterhead stationery? Which product is most likely to fulfill your purpose?

Interrelationships Among CMAPP Elements

Whereas most traditional models seem to be linear in the sense that they progress from A to B to C (and then, for example, back to A), the CMAPP model is dynamic: each element continuously affects all the others. In the missing cheque example, the CMAPP dynamic included the following interactions:

- Knowing more about your audience helped determine your context.

- That knowledge about your context helped you identify the particular audience.

- Knowing your audience helped you identify and refine your purpose.

- As you refined your purpose, you got a better idea of the most appropriate product.

- Your conception of the product was also dependent on your audience, which in turn affected your message, which itself affected ... and so forth.

In this dynamic, even the slightest change in one element has a ripple effect on all the others.

You may have noticed that CMAPP does not make explicit reference to a prime component of transactional models—feedback. The concept, however, is fundamental. Modifications to any one of context, message, audience, purpose, or product have an inevitable impact on the other elements, altering them over time. These shifts are, in effect, the manifestations of feedback. For example, your message affects your audience in a particular way, which alters the context, which has an impact on both your audience's reaction and your own response to that reaction. Technical communications, just like life, can get complicated ...

Applications

Is the CMAPP model likely to be of any practical use to you? As a student, you'll be communicating with your instructors, with other students, with groups to which you belong, with potential employers, with businesses, banks, government, and so on. Applying a CMAPP analysis to your communications with all these groups will undoubtedly help you obtain what you want. The benefits of understanding and using the CMAPP model could be even more valuable in the workplace where you'll be dealing with colleagues, your boss, clients and potential clients, suppliers, and consumers. It has been shown time and time again that professional success is much more likely if you can communicate well. The CMAPP communication model is designed to help you do just that.

CASE STUDIES

2A   Mississauga University Student Association Function

Situation

During construction of the Student Association Building (the SAB), the Mississauga University Student Association (MUSA) has continued to rent from the university the following premises:

- office space in the Dominion Building (main administration building) for the 10 members of the MUSA Executive (MUSAEx);

- a "student space" (a former classroom) on the main floor of Vanier Square (the Engineering building), containing several video-game terminals, two foosball tables, a Ping-Pong table, an ATM, food and drink vending machines, and several tables and chairs;

- a small editorial office in the Confederation Building (used primarily for Department of Humanities faculty offices) for the editor and associate editor of the student newspaper, *The MUckraker*.

When it wishes to put on functions such as concerts, dances, or parties, MUSAEx normally arranges to rent either Sassoon Hall, the university's main auditorium, or one of two large conference rooms named after corporate benefactors Accelerated Enterprises Ltd. (AEL) and Radisson Automobiles Inc. (RAI).

After often heated debate, MUSAEx finally decides, on September 28, to celebrate the Thanksgiving holiday on Monday, October 11, 1999, with a rock concert. On Friday, October 1, Jack Lee, the MUSAEx functions coordinator, sends a MU room booking form to the Room Booking Office; he also confirms bookings with (and sends cheques to) two popular local bands, Hodgepodge and Really Me. As usual, he contracts with a local company, Specialties, to produce and distribute posters and flyers advertising the event. He is obliged to pay extra because the work is a rush job.

Checking the MUSAEx mailbox on Wednesday, October 6, Jack is shocked to find his booking form returned and marked "rejected"; he is unable to decipher the signature on it. In a bit of a panic, and angry at MU administration, he tries to contact Dorothy Palliser, the MUSAEx president, but discovers that she is in the middle of a two-day Engineering field trip in Oshawa. Realizing that he has to take immediate action, Jack leaves a voice mail (since he is unable to reach her personally) for Kulwinder Atwal, the administration room booking clerk. (A transcript of Jack's message is shown in Figure 2.4.) As well, since he once booked the RAI Conference Room by phone and was later told there was no record of the reservation, Jack decides to hand-deliver to the Room Booking Office a handwritten memo (Figure 2.5). Finally, he pens a memo to Dorothy (Figure 2.6), and leaves it in her mailbox.

Issues to Think About

In considering this scenario in terms of CMAPP, you have to take into account the following interconnected communications involving MU and MUSAEx: the original booking form completed by Jack, Jack's voice mail to Kulwinder, Jack's memo to the Room Booking Office, and Jack's memo to Dorothy.

Booking Form

Not having seen the original booking form, we don't know if it was completed incorrectly—a possible reason for its rejection. But we do know that it was submitted less than two weeks before the planned concert—another possible explanation for its rejection, since Sassoon Hall might have already been reserved for another function. We also know very little about the relationship between MU administration and MUSAEx. Had there been problems before? Had the administration been unnecessarily rigid in its requirements? Had MUSAEx been lax in submitting rental payments?

Figure 2.4: Transcript of Lee's Voice Mail to Atwal

Hi! It's Jack from MUSAEx.

How come our booking was rejected? No one told us there was going to be a problem, and we've already got Hodgepodge and Really Me coming, and Specialties has got some stuff up already.

I hope this was like just a mistake, 'cause we've got to have the room 'cause we're really in really deep already.

Can you call me and tell me what's wrong with it?

Had there been incidences of damage to university property? Do you think that any of these details of context might have had an impact?

Voice Mail

What can you say about its content? Was it specific? Did it contain all the information that Kulwinder would have needed to look into the matter? For example, would she know that Jack is the MUSAEx functions coordinator? Shouldn't he have given his last name, too? Why didn't he leave a number and a time for her to reach him?

Was the message polite? Had Jack given sufficient thought to his audience? What might Kulwinder's reaction to the message have been? Do you think that Jack's purpose was clear to Kulwinder? More important, do you think that Jack himself had a clear idea of his purpose? Did he simply want, as his message states, Kulwinder to call him back and tell him what was wrong with his booking form? Or did he really want Kulwinder to find a venue for the concert?

What about Jack's product? Was leaving a voice mail the best way for him to communicate? Could he not have tried to reach someone else? Did he take likely delays into

Figure 2.5: Lee's Memo to Room Booking Office

MUSAEx Memo

Dominion 243   Mississauga University Student Association Executive   Local 4334

From: *Jack Lee, Functions Coordinator*
To: *Room Booking Office, Administraton*
cc.
Date: *Wednesday, Oct. 6*
Subject: *Rock Concert*

I booked Sassoon Hall for our Thanksgiving concert, and already hired the bands and got the publicity arranged. Now you've rejected our booking without saying why, and we don't have time to get our arrangements changed. I've already left voice mail for Kulwinder but can't get hold of her to do anything about it. The bands want to set up at 6pm, and we want to arrange with the caf to get food and refreshments. Would you please remake our booking.

If you have any questions, don't hesitate to call me. Otherwise, we'll just assume you made another mistake.

Figure 2.6: Lee's Memo to Palliser

MUSAEx Memo

Dominion 243   Mississauga University Student Association Executive   Local 4334

From: *Jack*
To: *Dorothy*
cc.
Date: *Wednesday*
Subject: *Amother Admin Foul-up*

We got a problem with the booking for the concert on Thanksgiving but I think I fixed it.

As usual, Admin goofed and rejected the booking I sent before. So I phoned the booking clerk and I sent a memo that I took over by hand so we don't take any more chances and left with Admin too.

I told them when Hodgepodge and Really Me need to set up and when the caf is bringing over the stuff and that Specialties are already working too.

I guess you're just as ticked as I am, this isn't the first time they screwed up with us. Hope we can get it going fast, don't you.

I'll be in class Mon morning when you get back from Oshawa but call me when you can.

---

account when he decided to leave the voice mail? Do you think the voice mail was an effective product in this context? Why or why not?

Memo to Room Booking Office

This time, let's consider the product first. Is a handwritten memo acceptable, or should Jack have word-processed it? (Hint: is it a personal or professional communication? How might the distinction be important in this context?)

Did you notice the spelling mistake in the *To* line? Should Jack have included the year as part of the date? Should he have initialled or signed the memo? Does it make any difference that the *From* line appears above the *To* line? Why might all these things matter?

Here are some other questions you might ask yourself about this memo:

■ Did Jack's message contain all the necessary information? What significant information might be lacking?

- What do you think of the *Subject* line? Would Jack's wording allow the Room Booking Office to find the relevant information easily? How might this issue influence the context?

- Did the memo contain one request or several? Were these requests clearly expressed?

- To whom is the memo addressed? Why did Jack leave a voice mail for a particular person (Kulwinder) but address his memo to "Room Booking Office"? From what you know of Jack so far, do you think he knew whether MU's administration had a section called "Room Booking Office"? Why might this be important?

- Does the first sentence of the last paragraph imply that if the Room Booking Office did not have questions, Jack did not want them to call?

- How might the likely audience respond to the last sentence? Who do you think that audience is? Do you think Jack knew who his audience was likely to be?

Memo to Dorothy

How does the fact that Dorothy is another student (possibly a friend of Jack's) affect the context? Why didn't Jack simply copy Dorothy in his memo to the Room Booking Office? Should he have attached a copy of that memo when he wrote to her? Why or why not?

Here are some other questions to ponder:

- What do you think Dorothy will do with Jack's memo?

- Might the *Date* line be a problem later?

- Words always carry two meanings: the *denotation*, which is the literal meaning; and the *connotation*, which is the emotional content or the impression created. Both meanings have an impact. What is the connotation of Jack's *Subject* line, and what do you think it says about him?

- Do you think Jack's wording says anything about his purpose? (Hint: think about primary and secondary purposes.)

- Is the message clear? Is it specific? Would Dorothy find it useful? Do you think she would have wanted other information? If so, what information?

- Is the language formal or informal? Is it appropriate for this audience, context, message, and purpose? Why or why not?

- Is the product effective? Why or why not?

Revision

Examples of what Jack might have done in his voice mail to Kulwinder Atwal and his memo to the Room Booking Office are shown in Figures 2.7 and 2.8. Note that these versions are not the only correct ones; in fact, an infinite number of possibilities exist.

Figure 2.7: Revised Version of Lee's Voice Mail to Atwal

This is a message for Kulwinder Atwal, the room booking clerk, from Jack Lee, the functions coordinator for the Student Association. It's Wednesday, October 6, 1999, at about 2:00 p.m.

I just tried to reach you but was transferred to your voice mail. I have just seen your rejection notice concerning MUSAEx's request to book Sassoon Hall for the evening of Monday, October 11 for the student Thanksgiving celebration dance.

I apologize for any problem we might have caused when submitting the booking request. I'm afraid that we assumed there would be no problem booking the hall; we've already contracted with two bands, and have had our posters printed showing Sassoon Hall as the venue. Would it still be possible for us to use Sassoon Hall for the dance? If not, would you be able to find an alternative location? I'd really appreciate anything you can do. Please get in touch with me as soon as possible. My local at the Student Association office is 4334. I will be at the office until 5:00 p.m. today and between 8:00 a.m. and 11:00 a.m. tomorrow.

Finally, I should mention that I'm leaving a memo at the main Admin desk. I've been informed that someone else from the Room Booking Office might pick it up in your place if you don't happen to get this voice mail by 5:00 p.m. today.

Thanks very much,

Bye.

2B Reorganization Notice at Radisson Automobiles Inc. (RAI)

Situation

At RAI's head office in Ottawa, Gilles Radisson, the president and CEO, has become concerned about what he sees as increasing decentralization of authority. He feels that RAI's growing network of dealerships has diminished his own control over daily operations and overall company direction.

Recently, Radisson persuaded the board of directors to impose in three months' time an organizational change that will have an impact on all seven RAI dealerships. As of January 1, 2000, each dealership vice-president will report directly to Radisson rather than to the board. Furthermore, each dealership general manager will report not to the respective dealership vice-president, but to the head office company manager, Céline Robillard.

Figure 2.8: Revised Version of Lee's Memo to Room Booking Office

---

MUSAEx Memo

Dominion 243   Mississauga University Student Association Executive   Local 4334

From: *Jack Lee, Functions Coordinator*
To: *Room Booking Office, Administration Building*
cc.   *Dorothy Palliser, President, MUSAEx*
Date: *Wednesday, October 6, 1999*
Subject: *Booking of Sassoon Hall for Monday, October 11, 1999*

I have just seen Kulwinder Atwal's rejection notice concerning MUSAEx's request to book Sassoon Hall for the evening of Monday, October 11 for the student Thanksgiving celebration dance. At approximately 2:00 p.m., I left Ms. Atwal a voice mail asking for assistance, and indicated that I would be remitting this memo as well. On behalf of the MUSAEx, I apologize for any problem with the initial booking request. While conducting our preparations for the student Thanksgiving dance, I'm afraid that we assumed there would be no problem booking the hall; thus, we have already contracted with two bands, and have had our posters printed showing Sassoon Hall as the location. Would it still be possible for us to use Sassoon Hall? If not, would you be able to find an alternative location?

I'd be very grateful for your assistance. If at all possible, please contact me at the MUSAEx office, local 4334 before 5:00 p.m. today or between 8:00 a.m. and 10:30 a.m. tomorrow. Thank you.

The board members were reluctant to endorse this change. They foresaw considerable opposition on the part of dealer vice-presidents and general managers over what might be perceived as a sudden lack of trust in their abilities. Over the last several years, all dealerships have been reporting increased profits and a decline in the number of customer complaints. Local dealership management has thus had good reason to believe that it has been instrumental in RAI's continued success.

The board also argued that three months did not leave sufficient time to work out all the inevitable administrative complications. But Radisson, who remains RAI's principal shareholder, prevailed. Now the dealerships must be notified of the coming reorganization. Radisson has decided to impose his will on the board once again and communicate the news personally. His memo to the dealerships appears in Figure 2.9. His attachments are shown in Figures 2.10 and 2.11.

Radisson Automobiles Radisson

6134 Bank Street
Ottawa ON K2A 2B3
(603) 433-9887
Fax: (603) 435-0098

Head Office / Bureau central
Memorandum

99/09/08

To / À: Dealership Vice-Presidents and General Managers /
                Vice-présidents locaux et gérants généraux locaux

From / De: Gilles Radisson, CEO   *GR*

Re: Reorganization / Réorganisation

cc.   Board of Directors / Conseil exécutif
             C. Robillard

As you know, I believe in being concise and straightforward in all my dealings with both clients and company personnel. Therefore, I am announcing to you now the reorganization of Radisson Automobiles.

As of January 1, 2000, the Current Organization Chart (copy attached) will be superseded by the Revised Organization Chart (copy attached).

The Board of Directors and I recognize that administrative details must still be worked out. Nonetheless, we are confident that the new organization will be to the benefit of the company, a goal we are sure you all share.

Céline Robillard is looking forward to receiving 2000 operational plans from the dealership general managers. I am likewise looking forward to receiving 2000 business plans from the vice-presidents.

I know I can count on your cooperation.

Attachments

Vous savez l'importance que j'attache à la précision et à la concision. Par conséquent, je vous fais état par la présente de la réorganisation des Automobiles Radisson.

Dès le premier janvier, 2000, l'organigramme Organisation révisée (copie ci-jointe) remplaçera l'organigramme Organisation courante (copie également ci-jointe).

Nous sommes conscients, les membres du Conseil exécutif et moi, de la nécessité de finaliser plusieurs détails administratifs. Nous demeurons quand même confiants des bénéfices à la compagnie qu'apporteront ces changements, et certains que vous partagez nos buts à cet égard.

Céline Robillard attend de la part des gérants généraux locaux les plans opérationnels pour 2000; dans la même veine, j'espère recevoir sous peu de la part des vice-présidents leurs plans d'affaires de 2000.

Je vous remercie de votre collaboration.

Documents ci-joints

Figure 2.10: RAI's Current Organization Chart

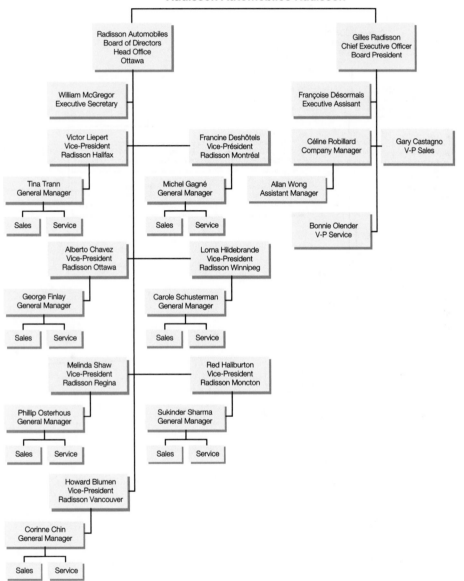

Figure 2.11: RAI's Revised Organization Chart

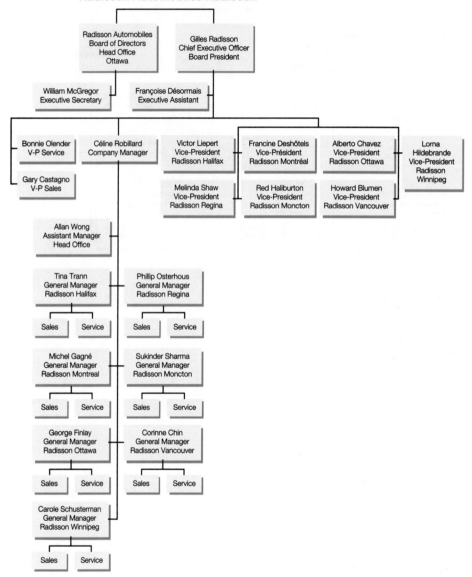

Radisson Automobiles Radisson

Radisson Automobiles
Board of Directors
Head Office
Ottawa

Gilles Radisson
Chief Executive Officer
Board President

William McGregor
Executive Secretary

Françoise Désormais
Executive Assistant

Bonnie Olender
V-P Service

Céline Robillard
Company Manager

Victor Liepert
Vice-President
Radisson Halifax

Francine Deshôtels
Vice-Président
Radisson Montréal

Alberto Chavez
Vice-President
Radisson Ottawa

Lorna
Hildebrande
Vice-President
Radisson
Winnipeg

Gary Castagno
V-P Sales

Melinda Shaw
Vice-President
Radisson Regina

Red Haliburton
Vice-President
Radisson Moncton

Howard Blumen
Vice-President
Radisson Vancouver

Allan Wong
Assistant Manager
Head Office

Tina Trann
General Manager
Radisson Halifax

Phillip Osterhous
General Manager
Radisson Regina

Sales | Service

Sales | Service

Michel Gagné
General Manager
Radisson Montreal

Sukinder Sharma
General Manager
Radisson Moncton

Sales | Service

Sales | Service

George Finlay
General Manager
Radisson Ottawa

Corinne Chin
General Manager
Radisson Vancouver

Sales | Service

Sales | Service

Carole Schusterman
General Manager
Radisson Winnipeg

Sales | Service

In deciding whether or not Gilles Radisson conducted an effective CMAPP analysis before communicating, consider the issues outlined below.

Context

Radisson's position and forceful personality served him well in persuading reluctant board members to endorse his plan. Although we know little about his relationship with the dealership vice-presidents, we can assume that they will not be happy with a reorganization that will have a dramatic impact on two sets of relationships: those between Robillard and the general managers, and those between the general managers and their local vice-presidents.

Another complication is geography. The physical distance between the players means that a minimum of future communications are likely to be face to face.

Product

What is your assessment of Radisson's choice of product? Since the communication is internal (within an organization), a memo rather than a letter is appropriate. On the other hand, what might have been the effect on the relationships if Radisson had first held a conference call and then followed up in writing?

Message

What do you think is the crux of Radisson's message? Can you identify any secondary message? What kind of impression is conveyed by the tone of the memo? (Hint: think about connotation as well as denotation.) What might the message say to the audience about Radisson the man?

Do you think the two attachments help or hinder Radisson's message? Will his audience understand them easily or do you think they will need further explanation? If further explanation is required, what form should it take?

Audience

The memo is addressed to dealership vice-presidents and general managers, with copies going to board members and the company manager. How many different audiences do you think are really involved? Which audience do you think is the primary one? Should they all really receive the same message or messages? What differences in interpretation might there be on the part of these audiences?

Purpose

Does Radisson have more than one purpose? What do you think he is trying to do? What do you think he is actually doing? What do you think the various audiences will identify as his purpose or purposes? Based on their perception of purpose, how do you think they will view the attached organization charts in terms of perceived purpose?

2.1 Define the following terms:
   (a) technical communications
   (b) CMAPP
   (c) transactional model
   (d) feedback
   (e) internal interference
   (f) external interference
   (g) context
   (h) message
   (i) purpose
   (j) product

2.2 Below are two different scenarios. In scenario A, you tell a student at another institution about your financial situation this term. In scenario B, you communicate this information to a loans officer at your bank. For each scenario, provide answers to the CMAPP questions that follow. Invent any necessary details.

Scenario A: Fellow Student

Context
   1. What is your relationship with the student?
   2. Why would the student be interested in your message?
   3. What is the student's own financial situation?

Message
   1. What specific information will the student need or want in order to respond as you would like?
   2. What details should you provide?
   3. Should you exclude any details? If so, what details and why?

Audience
   1. Is the student female or male? How might this make a difference?
   2. What might the student know already?
   3. What would he or she want to know?
   4. What do you know about the student's financial situation?

Purpose
   1. Why are you telling the student about your financial situation?
   2. What kind of reaction do you expect?
   3. What do you want the student to do with the information?

Product

1. What product do you intend to use?

2. Why have you chosen to use that product?

Scenario B: Loans Officer at Your Bank

Context

1. What is your relationship with the loans officer?

2. Why might the loans officer even be interested in your message?

3. What kind of reputation do students have in the banking community?

4. How long have you been dealing with this branch and/or this person?

5. How might your history with the bank affect how your message is received?

Message

1. What specific information and explanations will the loans officer want?

2. What information should you provide?

3. What information might you want to withhold?

4. Should you withhold this information? Why or why not?

Audience

1. What is the sex and age of the loans officer? How might this make a difference?

2. Is the loans officer the only audience?

3. If there is a secondary audience, who is it?

4. What would the loans officer know already?

5. What would the loans officer want or need to know?

6. Is anyone else likely to see or use the information you provide?

Purpose

1. Why are you telling the loans officer about your situation?

2. What do you want him or her to do with the information?

3. Do you have a secondary purpose? If so, what is it?

4. What might the loan officer's purpose be?

5. Is the loans officer's purpose of any relevance to your situation?

Product

1. What product do you intend to use?

2. Why have you chosen to use that product?

2.3 The computer system you purchased from Acme High-Tech Products has given you considerable trouble. Angry, you dash off a letter (Figure 2.12) to Acme's sales manager, R.B. Kim. You do not mail this letter. Instead, you wait until you are calm, then decide to construct a letter that adheres to the principles of good technical communications. The first step is to conduct a CMAPP analysis. For the purposes of this exercise do *not* write the new letter, but simply answer the CMAPP questions that follow.

Figure 2.12: Letter to R. B. Kim

Last month, we purchased a computer from you, sold to us by your Mr. Webley when he came to our home after our phone conversation two days earlier. We spoke with him for a couple of hours, gave him coffee, and eventually decided to buy the PB-2 "User-Friendly Package" that he showed us in the many pages of advertising material he had brought.

When the merchandise arrived two days later, the delivery man, who said he always replaced Mr. Webley on Fridays, really didn't seem to know what he was doing. He kept looking things up in the manuals that came with the package, and had a continual worried look on his face while trying to make little jokes about the complex technology we have in our lives now. Eventually, he seemed to get it all working, and left. It was already 8 pm, some three hours since he'd arrived.

The next morning, I had some spreadsheets to do. As I'd told Mr. Webley before he suggested the PB-2 package, I'd had quite a bit of experience with the old Lotus 1-2-3 at the office. So, we'd bought a copy of Office from Acme, as part of the package, along with a bunch of CDs including Quicken, Quake, Encarta, and Front Page.

Unfortunately, I had one system error after another (I think that's what they were), never did get my work finished, and, to top it off, found the printer—the *Printomatic 554*, also part of the package—wouldn't accept the commands I typed out on the monitor.

No one was at the service number Mr. Webley had left me when I called that afternoon—a Saturday—nor the following day. On Monday, someone answered, but got quite rude when I told my story and demanded that Acme either arrange for <u>real</u> support for its customers or pick up your lousy equipment and give me my damn money back! After that call, I gave up trying to contact anyone and wrote this. On my typewriter, not on your shoddy computer!

I better hear from you in the next couple of days, or you'll be hearing from my lawyer, who's getting a copy of this letter, too.

Context

1. What has prompted you to write a new letter?

2. How would you describe the relationship between you and your audience?

3. What would you be prepared to do if your letter fails to meet its intended objective?

Message

1. What are your main points?

2. If you have any secondary points, what are they?

Audience

1. Who is your audience?

2. If you have a secondary audience, who is it?

3. What do you think your primary audience knows?

4. What do you think that audience needs to know?

5. What do you think that audience wants to know?

Purpose

1. What is your purpose?

2. If you have a secondary purpose, what is it? (Hint: think longer-term.)

Product

1. What product might you have chosen instead of a letter?

2. Why have you chosen to use a letter? (Hint: you might have more than one reason.)

3. What kind of tone will you use?

4. How technical should your letter be?

2.4   Among RAI's products is the Minotaur, a popular luxury car manufactured by Global Vehicles. Having recently discovered a possible manufacturing defect in some Minotaur models, Global composed a notification (Figure 2.13) to deal with the problem. Based on your analysis of the notification, provide answers to the CMAPP questions below.

Figure 2.13 Global Notification

A possible defect relating to the potential failure of a seal in the mounting of the left tie-rod-end assembly may exist in your vehicle. In the event of disconnection, this seal (configured as a supportive component to the front rack assembly) could result in at least partial loss of bilateral vehicle directional control, particularly during unusually significant intentional deceleration. In addition, your vehicle may require adjustment service to the front hub bearing where it comes into contact with the hub carrier beside the right caliper. Should this bearing be improperly aligned, unusually rapid acceleration during excessive directional change might result in a similar loss of bilateral vehicle directional

Figure 2.13 (continued)

control. In certain circumstances, either of these potential failures has the capability of causing unexpectedly severe vehicle handling. You are therefore advised to consider the benefits of contacting your reseller to arrange for relevant adjustment or replacement without personal expenditure on your part.

Context

1. What relationship(s) might exist between Global Vehicles and the audience(s)?
2. How might the relationship(s) change as a result of the notification?
3. What kind of reaction to its notification might Global expect?
4. What impact might the situation have on RAI?

Message

1. Is the information clear and concise? Give examples to justify your response.
2. What do you think the primary audience needs and wants to know?
3. What can you say about the language used in the notification?

Audience

1. Who appears to be the audience for the notification?
2. What other audience or audiences might the notification be aimed at? (Hint: look at the use of language.)

Purpose

1. What is the apparent purpose of the notification?
2. What secondary purpose might be involved?
3. How well do you think Global's current notification fulfills its purpose(s)?

Product

1. What product should Global use?
2. What would make the product effective?
3. Should Global use more than one product? If so, what should it use and why?

2.5   Think of a real-world situation, preferably one having to do with a business or other organization, that requires a response from you. Based on your scenario, construct and answer relevant CMAPP questions.

EXPLORING THE WEB

Here are some Web sites you might wish to investigate.

URL	DESCRIPTION
http://www.dfwnetmall.com/talkbiz/	This page offers helpful suggestions and links to information on various aspects of business communications.
http://www.smartbiz.com/sbs/cats/comm.htm	The Communications page of *Smart Business Supersite* offers a wealth of links to information and advice on business writing, telephone systems, employee communications, e-mail, presentations, mobile offices, faxes, etc.
http://www.clever.net/quinion/words/index.htm	This site, World Wide Words: Michael Quinion's language pages, "is devoted to the English language—its history, quirks, curiosities and evolution."

3 From Data to Information: Outlines and Reference Works

This chapter deals with outlining—using the CMAPP approach to convert data into useful information—and with the reference works that every good technical communicator uses.

Although the outlining process described in the chapter has particular relevance for formal reports and long presentations, its underlying principle applies to all effective communication: in order for your audience to grasp your meaning, your thoughts must be organized and your understanding of what you want to convey must be absolutely clear.

Data versus Information

While the words "data" and "information" are often used interchangeably, there are differences between them. Note, by the way, that *data* is the plural of *datum*. The use of *datum* is becoming rare, and many writers accept the use of *data* with a singular verb ("the data is available"), as well as a plural verb ("the data are all in"). Data are almost always empirical: they can be objectively verified and/or measured. Though data are usually plentiful, their lack of organization makes them difficult to interpret. Information, by contrast, is the useful product that derives from the analysis and manipulation of data. Your audience requires information, not just data.

Process and Structure

Obtaining data is relatively easy. Both primary and secondary sources often yield enormous amounts of it. A much harder task is translating that data into information you can use to produce a CMAPP product such as a report. To accomplish this, many business and technical communicators use a process that involves the following steps: collecting data, organizing data into an outline, and refining and finalizing the outline.

A formal multi-level outline takes the form of a series of headings of different levels. These headings are called level heads. Two level-head numbering systems are shown in Figure 3.1.

Collecting Data

As an example, imagine that you needed to report on your day's activities. Think of the list of activities presented in Figure 3.2 as the *data* you have compiled. But how you translate that data into useful information in the form of a report will depend on the answers to the CMAPP questions you devise.

Figure 3.1: Alphanumeric and Decimal Numbering Systems

Alphanumeric System	Decimal System
I. Level 1 Head	**1. Level 1 Head**
(A) Level 2 Head	1.1 Level 2 Head
(B) Level 2 Head	1.2 Level 2 Head
(1) Level 3 Head	1.2.1 Level 3 Head
(2) Level 3 Head	1.2.2 Level 3 Head
II. Level 1 Head	**2. Level 1 Head**
(A) Level 2 Head	2.1 Level 2 Head
(B) Level 2 Head	2.2 Level 2 Head
(1) Level 3 Head	2.2.1 Level 3 Head
(a) Level 4 Head	2.2.1.1 Level 4 Head
(b) Level 4 Head	2.2.1.2 Level 4 Head
(2) Level 3 Head	2.2.2. Level 3 Head
(C) Level 2 Head	2.3 Level 2 Head
III. Level 1 Head	**3. Level 1 Head**

Organizing Data into an Outline

Assume that your CMAPP analysis reveals that your marketing instructor has asked you for an update on your project. You decide that your product will be a memo, and that you will concentrate on three main topics:

- Marketing project itself
- Other courses that have a bearing
- Related activities

You conclude that the items in Figure 3.2 numbered 9, 10, 12, 16, 17, 18, 19, 20, 21, 22, 24, 26, 30, 31, 32, 33, and 36 might be relevant. The others will not translate into useful information, and so you ignore them. Your next step is to organize under appropriate headings the 17 data elements you have kept, along with the introductory information your instructor will expect to see in the memo. This stage is often complicated by the fact that some data items may appear to fit under more than one topic, so you have to make content decisions as well. Completion of these tasks will result in a first draft of a formal multi-level outline similar to the one shown in Figure 3.3.

Figure 3.2: Day's Activities

1. Woke: 7:00 a.m.
2. I fed my dog Prince
3. Did homework: 1.5 hours
4. Breakfast
5. Lunch was in the cafeteria
6. I ate supper at home as usual
7. New jacket looks great
8. Drove car to campus
9. Attended BusMgmt 305
10. Comm. 302 class
11. Bit late for Acct. 313
12. Marketing 315L: interesting class today!
13. TV: one hour only
14. Went to bed
15. Carlos told me about his new car
16. From Comm. Instructor—info re next assignment
17. Spoke to BusMgmt. instructor about term paper
18. Continued Chapter 3 of Marketing project
19. Read part of latest issue of Maclean's magazine
20. Internet search on Micro-marketing
21. Bought new Marketing textbook
22. Researched Acct. project in library
23. Taped TV program on Discovery Channel
24. Saw results of last Marketing midterm: awful!
25. What the 3 new library books are about
26. Composed part of Comm. assignment on computer
27. Spoke to Jan on phone
28. Asked Dad for raise in allowance: unsuccessful
29. Walked Prince: 1/2 hour
30. Finished Chapter 2 of Marketing project
31. The cover article in Maclean's is going to be useful for Marketing project
32. Discovered that my Accounting term paper also relates to my Marketing project
33. Outline for Marketing term project needed adjusting
34. Got cash from ATM
35. Had coffee with Marge
36. Downloaded search results from Yahoo! Canada

Refining the Outline

Now you have to refine your outline. This stage in the process of translating data into useful information is a painstaking one, particularly if you are working with an outline for a longer, more complex document. Most sophisticated word-processing soft-

Figure 3.3: Initial Multi-Level Outline

I.   *Why I'm Writing a Memo*

    A   Instructor asked for it

II. *Marketing Project Itself*

    A   Finished Chapter 2 of Mktg. project

        1   Continued Chapter 3 of Mktg. project

        2   Outline for Mktg. project needs adjusting

    B   Bought new Mktg. textbook

    C   Mktg. 315: interesting today

        1   Saw results of Mktg. midterm: awful!

    D   Discovered that Acct. term paper relates to my marketing project

III. *Other Courses That Have a Bearing*

    A   Comm. 302 class

    B   Comm. instructor—info re next assignment

    C   Was a bit late for Acct. 313

    D   Attended BusMgmt 305

    E   Composed part of Comm. assignment on computer

IV. *Related Activities*

    A   Spoke to BusMgmt. instructor about term paper

    B   Researched Acct. project in library

    C   What the 3 new library books are about

    D   Did homework: 1.5 hours

        1   Internet search on micro-marketing

        2   Read part of latest issue of Maclean's magazine

            a   The cover article in Maclean's is going to be useful for Mktg. project

    E   Downloaded search results from Yahoo! Canada

V.   *General Conclusion*

    A   Ask instructor to give me feedback

ware has an outlining function. If you know how to use it, your task will be simplified: the software automatically handles renumbering and constantly shows a clean copy. If you decide to develop your outline on paper, you might want to recopy it from time to time so that you can "see through" all the corrections and modifications.

After you have reviewed your initial outline carefully and perhaps made changes (adding or deleting points, changing the position of items, and so forth), you finalize the outline by applying three principles—a process that will require you to examine your outline in detail, and to think carefully and precisely about every line it contains. The three principles that you apply are subordination, division, and parallelism.

Subordination

The principle of subordination is an exercise in logic. It says that every item that appears under a particular level head must logically be a part of the subject matter of that level head. Conversely, the item must not deal with a different issue, and must not be of equivalent or greater importance or scope.

If you look again at Figure 3.3, you will notice that the level 2 head numbered III.B is not really part of the idea of its level 1 head (numbered III.). Probably, III.B should go under the level 1 head numbered IV. You may find other anomalies of this kind, but note that there isn't necessarily any single, right answer. Your CMAPP analysis will allow you to determine what is appropriate in your circumstance. When you find an entry that violates the principle of subordination, you may decide to change the sequence of items, to create another, separate level head, or to change the wording of a level head so that it reflects what you really mean.

Division

The principle of division is, in a sense, an exercise in arithmetic. The principle states that you cannot subdivide the content of any level head into fewer than two parts. For example, if you have a I.A, you must have at least a I.B. Similarly, if you have a VI.A1, you must have at least a VI.A2. If you look at item I.A in Figure 3.3, you will notice that the first level 1 head has been divided into a single level 2 head, contravening the principle of division (and logic, for that matter). Similar problems exist with items II.C1, IV.D2a, and V.A: there is no II.C2, IV.D2b, or V.B.

Once again, how you rectify the problem depends on the results of your CMAPP analysis. You might decide to remove an item, to add an item (taking care not to contravene the principle of subordination), or to make the item itself a higher level head. What you do depends on what you decide you really mean.

Parallelism

The principle of parallelism requires that all level 1 heads exhibit the same grammatical structure, that all level 2 heads exhibit the same grammatical structure, and so forth. Note that level 1 heads may be different from level 2 heads, which may be different from level 3 heads, and so on. If you look at Figure 3.3, you can see that there is no such uniformity of grammatical structure. The level 1 heads numbered I. and III., for example, are subordinate clauses, while the level 1 heads numbered II., IV., and V. are noun phrases. Items III.A and III.B are noun phrases, while III.C, III.D, and III.E are elliptical clauses.

The solution to this problem is to reword items until each of the same-level heads exhibits the same grammatical structure. When applying the principle of parallelism, you may well find that the easiest grammatical structure to work with is a noun or noun phrase. The level 1 heads in Figure 3.3, for example, could become:

I.   Rationale for Memo

II. Marketing Project

III. Related Coursework

IV. Complementary Activities

V.   Conclusion

Figure 3.4 offers a possible completed outline (remember, there is no single, correct version). The principle of parallelism applies not only to outlines, but also to bulleted and numbered lists in a document: each item in a list must have the same grammatical structure.

Figure 3.4: Completed Outline

I. *Rationale for Memo*

II. *Marketing Project* (Marketing 325)

    A Outline (completed)

    B Chapter 2 (completed)

    C Chapter 3 (partially completed)

    D Accounting course term paper (mentioned)

III. *Related Coursework*

    A Marketing 315

        1 Issues related to project

        2 New textbook

    B Accounting 303

    C Business management 305

        1 Course relevance

        2 Conversation with instructor

    D Communications 302

        1 General relevance to Marketing project

        2 Instructor's comments re assignment

Figure 3.4 (continued)

IV. *Complementary Activities*

    A   Library research re Accounting 303

    B   Relevance to Marketing project

    C   Usefulness of three books withdrawn

    D   Homework

        1   Internet search on micro-marketing

        2   Maclean's magazine cover article

        3   Complementary sources

V. *Conclusion*

    A   Summary

    B   Request for feedback

Reference Works

Every technical communicator should make regular use of three reference works: a dictionary, a thesaurus, and a grammar and usage guide.

Dictionaries

A dictionary of a language is not the same as the language itself. Rather, it is a collection of its editors' opinions regarding the usage of the language. Occasionally, the editors are wrong. The 18th-century writer, critic, and lexicographer Samuel Johnson was once asked why he had defined a term incorrectly; his response was, "Ignorance, pure ignorance."

A dictionary wears out, not because people use it too much, but because language changes. New words come into existence (think of *e-mail*, *Internet*, and *URL*), while established words take on new meanings (not too long ago, *gay* meant "lighthearted and carefree" and a *browser* was someone who skimmed a text). New words have been entering the language with increasing frequency—so much so that if your dictionary was last revised more than 10 years ago, it is already out of date.

Dictionaries reflect the language of a particular location. For example, the *Oxford English Dictionary* is an authority on British English, while the *Merriam-Webster Dictionary* is an authority on American English. Three dictionaries that provide a good reflection of contemporary Canadian usage are the *ITP Nelson Canadian Dictionary of the English Language* (1997), the *Gage Canadian Dictionary* (1997), and the *Canadian Oxford Dictionary* (1998).

Thesauri

The word "thesaurus," which derives from the Greek word meaning "treasure," has as its plural either *thesauri* or *thesauruses*. A thesaurus is a book in which words are listed in categories according to their related meanings. Because no two editors see words in the same way, lists of synonyms will vary from thesaurus to thesaurus. Like a dictionary, a thesaurus can become outdated. For example, in James G. Fernald's *Standard Handbook of Synonyms, Antonyms, and Prepositions* (1947), *gay* is listed only as a synonym for *happy*, with the explanation that "we speak of a *gay* party, *gay* laughter."

The function of a thesaurus is to offer options, normally in the form of synonyms and antonyms. Although synonyms have *similar* meanings, they are never exact substitutes; their use permits nuances that allow for finer distinctions of meaning and help maintain the richness of the language. Although some words seem to have exact opposites (*good* versus *bad*, for example), the contrary meanings are not precise (*good* and *bad* are both highly subjective terms). Thus, antonyms allow for further nuances.

Recently published or revised thesauri include *Roget's Desk Thesaurus* (Random House, 1996), *The Merriam-Webster Thesaurus* (Merriam-Webster, 1989), *The Oxford Dictionary and Thesaurus* (Oxford University Press, 1996), D.J. Perry's *College Vocabulary Building,* (South-Western Educational Publishing, 1999), and Eugene Erlich (Editor) and Samuel I. Hayakawa's *Choose the Right Word: A Contemporary Guide to Selecting the Precise Word for Every Situation* (HarperCollins, 1994).

Grammar and Usage Guides

Books offering comprehensive overviews of grammar, style, and usage abound. Some guides are prescriptive/proscriptive ("do this but don't do that"), while others are more descriptive. Most include sections on punctuation, capitalization, numbers, paragraphing, spelling, bias-free language, and documentation of references

Which guide you use matters much less than whether you use one; at times, we all need reminders of standard practice. Recommended guides include J. Finnbogason and A. Valleau's *A Canadian Writer's Guide* (ITP Nelson, 1997), D. Hacker's *A Canadian Writer's Reference* (ITP Nelson, 1996), and M. Fee and J. McAlpine's *Guide to Canadian English Usage* (Oxford University Press, 1997). Two updated classics in the field of grammar and usage are William Strunk, Jr., and E.B. White's *The Elements of Style* (Allyn and Bacon, 1999), and H.W. Fowler and Robert Birchfield's *The New Modern English Usage* (Oxford University Press, 1996).

Electronic References

Most of today's word processors offer the electronic equivalents of a dictionary (spell checker), a thesaurus, and a grammar and usage guide (grammar checker).

Spell Checker

A spell checker is essentially a long list of words. As it checks your document, it compares every word it finds against that list. If it cannot find a match, it alerts you by flagging the offending word. While your spell checker is very effective at finding typos, it pays no attention to problems related to meaning. My own spell checker is quite happy with the sentence "Thee write off Spring is a peace of music thatch eye likes."

Thesaurus

An electronic thesaurus works by offering possible synonyms (and, often, antonyms) for a selected word. It is not uncommon for a word processor to feature a thesaurus that is as comprehensive and useful as a good print version. The one problem with an electronic thesaurus lies in its inconspicuousness. If you don't "call it up," it will be of no assistance; and if you are unaware of distinctions of nuance (which often reflect cultural differences), you are unlikely to use it.

Grammar Checker

Grammar checkers attempt to match what you have written against a complicated series of programmed rules. Most allow you to choose among various sets of rules, perhaps labelled "business writing" or "casual writing." While grammar checkers can help you to avoid some careless errors, and to become more familiar with some common grammatical patterns, they are not without drawbacks. Good writing is complex and subjective. Thus, depending on an electronic grammar checker can be a bit like using a first-year college text on musical composition to judge the work of a seasoned and brilliant composer.

Grammar checkers have a generally poor reputation for accuracy. They tend to ignore nonparallel structure, for example. Conversely, they often find "errors" in material considered highly literate. In reviewing Abraham Lincoln's celebrated Gettysburg Address, my grammar checker suggested using "persons" or "people" in place of "men" in the famous phrase "all men are created equal"; flagged as possibly incorrect each use of the passive; found several sentences too long, to the point of saying it was unable to deal with them properly; recommended not starting the sentences with the word "but"; and suggested that the final lines of the speech did not form a complete sentence.

If you have an electronic grammar checker, by all means use it. Just don't expect it to be a reliable judge of the calibre of your technical communications.

CASE STUDY

GTISU Facilities Leasing Report

Situation

For the last three years, the Grandstone Technical Institute Student Union (GTISU) has leased from the GTI a large student common room and three small adjoining rooms for offices. The lease with GTI includes utilities (electricity and heat); GTISU contracts with the phone company for telephone, fax, and Internet connections.

On August 4, Heather Hong, executive secretary of GTISU, finds in her campus mailbox a formal notice from GTI informing GTISU that it must immediately vacate the facilities it has been renting. Vlad Radescu, the GTISU president, is on vacation in Hawaii, which means that Hong will have to deal with the crisis herself. Upset, she dashes off an e-mail (Figure 3.5) to her friend Sally Johal, a member of the GTISU executive. Then, after drinking a coffee and calming down, she places a call to the Surrey-based firm of Chung Gomes McNamara and explains the situation to Franco Gomes, the GTISU's legal counsel.

Figure 3.5: Hong's E-mail to Johal

```
Hi, Sal!

I guess I'm just venting here. Got a notice from Admin telling
us to vacate right now. And Vlad is off on another of his Hawaii
jaunts, of course! What the hell are they doing? Term starts
again in a few weeks! And now they've given us just a couple of
weeks to get out. Can you believe it? And we've been here for
years and years now, too! The Institute keeps telling us that
they need the space for more classes, and that there was never
any guarantee that we'd get to renew the lease, and that they've
been trying to do something else with the rooms for ages, and
that our reps just wouldn't get together with them — well, like
why should they? Admin's been totally unfair with the rent for
ages, anyway. So what's to talk about? Anyhow, I think I'll try
to get a petition together. We'll keep talking with them, I
suppose, for all the good that'll do. But in the meantime, we
can scout other places, too, just in case we do have to find
somewhere else. And all this just a month before term starts,
too! I'll keep you informed.

Well, hope your summer was better than mine. I guess I'll see
you when you get back into town in a couple of weeks or so. By
the way, how was Vegas? I loved it last year. See you! Oh, and
by the way, it seems that in a pinch we'd be able to rent a
really big room from Apex Holdings just down the block. Pat Chen
... you remember Pat ... has an uncle who's a bigshot there, and
can get it for us pretty cheap. I know ... it is further away.
But it might work!

See ya!
```

Gomes is well aware that the relationship between GTI and the student union has for the last year been rocky at best. Thinking that things have finally come to a head, he asks Hong to prepare a report for him. Hong undertakes the task by gathering data and then working to convert it into information that will be useful to Gomes. The multi-level outline she creates appears in Figure 3.6 (the margin notes in the first column will assist you in analyzing her efforts).

Issues to Think About

1. If you were Gomes, how might you explain the action taken by GTI?
2. To what extent would you expect to see GTI's reasons for the action reflected in the report you've requested from Hong?
3. In what respects does the information in Hong's e-mail to Johal differ from the information in her multi-level outline?
4. How would you explain and/or justify those differences?
5. What questions might Hong have been asking herself as she created her multi-level outline?

EXERCISES

3.1 Describe the differences between data and information.

3.2 Provide an example of a situation in which data are translated into information.

3.3 List some of the benefits of using a multi-level outline in the creation of business and technical communication documents.

3.4 Define and briefly describe the principles of subordination, division, and parallelism.

3.5 In what parts of a business and technical communication document must you apply the principle of parallelism?

3.6 Refer to Hong's multi-level outline (Figure 3.6) in answering the following questions:
     1. Who is Hong's primary audience?
     2. Might a secondary audience emerge at some point? If so, who?
     3. What does the primary audience already know?
     4. What does that audience likely need and/or want to know?
     5. What is Hong's primary purpose here?
     6. What might her secondary purpose be?

3.7 Based on the information you have, are there any omissions in Hong's outline?

3.8 Are there elements of Hong's outline that do not comply with the principles of subordination, division, and parallelism?

3.9 Examine a piece of technical or business writing such as a report or a lengthy brochure. Based on your examination, create the multi-level outline that the author might have used while developing the communication.

Figure 3.6: Hong's Multi-Level Outline

Data > information: allows realistic interpretation.

Introductory information: takes CMAPP into account, allows audience to place situation in context.

Precise details are crux of most technical communications.

Graphic might be useful, but would it enhance? Would it be superfluous?

Balanced approach: Audience will likely need/want arguments of both sides.

Note: Use of *apparent* required for accuracy: information derives from second-hand data.

Options listed because CMAPP analysis reveals what reader will need to know.

Recommendations and deadline specify writer's purpose, and specify action requested and time-frame required.

Logical grouping of items throughout outline helps reader follow argument and see how items might be organized into bulleted or numbered lists in final document.

1. **Situation background**
   a) Agreement between Student Union (SU) and GTI
      i) Implementation date
      ii) Length of agreement
      iii) General terms of lease
      iv) Foreseen SU executive petition
   b) Premises
      i) Location
      ii) Size
      iii) Function
2. **Essentials of disagreement**
   a) SU perspective
      i) Value of SU location to GTI for attracting registrants
      ii) High rent
      iii) GTI's uncompromising approach
   b) Apparent GTI perspective
      i) Several tardy rent payments
      ii) Urgent space requirement for additional classrooms
      iii) Lack of responsible attitude on part of SU representatives
      iv) Lack of time: agreements with contractors
3. **SU's options**
   a) Continued negotiations with GTI
      i) Advantage: possibility of improved lease
      ii) Disadvantage: possibility of wasted time/effort
   b) Relocation to Apex Holdings premises
      i) Advantage: resolution of problem with GTI and good lease terms
      ii) Disadvantage: distance from campus and lower student interest
   c) Abandonment of SU facilities—no real advantage
4. **SU's recommendations**
   a) Attempt at reconciliation/renegotiation with GTI;
   b) If negotiations fail, relocation to Apex Holdings premises
5. **Decision deadline: within 2 weeks**
      Must notify all parties by August 20.

EXPLORING THE WEB

Here are some Web sites you might wish to investigate.

URL	DESCRIPTION
http://www.ipl.org/teen/aplus/	Sponsored by the Internet Public Library, this site is titled "A+ Research and Writing for High School and College Students." Its table of contents offers a wealth of links, including "Preparing to Write—analyzing and organizing your information and forming a thesis statement."
http://www.web.net/cornerstone/cdneng.htm	You can use Cornerstone's Canadian English Page to compare Canadian, American, and British spellings. The page also lists uniquely Canadian words and discusses pronunciation.
http://webster.commnet.edu/HP/pages/darling/grammar.htm	The Capital Community Technical College in Hartford, Connecticut, offers this comprehensive guide to grammar and writing, with links organized by sentence, paragraph, and essay level. The site has a Forms of Communications page that includes links to sample business letters, memos, résumés and cover letters, meeting agendas and minutes, and APA and MLA research papers.
http://techwriting.miningco.com/mbody.htm?PID=2770&COB=home	The About.com Guide to Technical Writing is a comprehensive site with links to information, articles, and guidelines on various aspects of technical writing.
http://andromeda.rutgers.edu/~jlynch/Writing/	The Guide to Grammar and Style page was created by Jack Lynch, Assistant Professor in the English department of the Newark campus of Rutgers University. This well-organized site includes an annotated list of recommended writing guides and links to information on a wide range of grammar, style, and usage matters.

Visual Elements in Written and Oral Communications

For many people, the term "visuals" refers to pictures—graphs, charts, photographs, sketches, and the like. In the field of technical communications, however, the term has a much broader definition, encompassing:

- document visuals, which include typographical and other features affecting the appearance of a document;

- style guides, which are intended to help organizations achieve a consistent style or image in their documents; and

- visuals, which are illustrations of specific ideas within a document or presentation.

Effective technical communications requires the integration of all three elements.

Document Visuals

To make effective use of document visuals, you should be familiar with relevant terminology and have a working knowledge of the various features offered by your computer software. Although you may also use a graphics program (such as PhotoShop), a business presentation program (such as PowerPoint), a desktop publishing program (such as Publisher), or a Web-page authoring program (such as Front Page), you will likely create most of your documents with a word processor (such as Word or WordPerfect). While there are variations among the different software programs currently available, most programs allow you considerable control in manipulating document visual features.

Body Text and Level Heads

The term *body text* refers to the text that makes up your document's paragraphs and bulleted or numbered lists. Body text can be thought of as the main text of your document. Although some writers and publishers prefer a sans-serif font for body text, by far the majority of documents employ a serif font, since most people find it easier to read. More on fonts later in the chapter.

The term *level heads* refers to titles, subtitles, headings, and subheadings of all kinds. The term is useful in that it permits a ready numerical reference. In this chapter, for example, the heading "Document Visuals" is a level 1 head, the subheading "Body Text and Level Heads" is a level 2 head, and the subheading "Margins" is a level 3 head.

Headers and Footers

A *header*, also known as a *running head*, is text that appears at the top of every page. While its content will depend on the nature of the document, the author's name, document title, and page number are standard elements of a header. Headers generally do not appear on the first page of a document. If the document is printed on both sides of the pages, left- and right-hand pages may feature different headers. Having the same elements but appearing at the bottom of every page are *footers*, also known as *running feet*.

White Space

White space refers to the portions of a printed page that are blank. Two examples of white space are margins and line and paragraph spacing.

Margins Some word processors measure all four margins from the top, bottom, left, and right edges of the page. Others measure the bottom margin from the top of the footer and the top margin from the bottom of the header. No matter what software you use, margins should normally be set at no less than 1" on all sides of the page.

Line and Paragraph Spacing *Line spacing* or *line space* refers to the space between each line of text. Your word processor will apply a preset line spacing automatically each time the text wraps to the following line as you type. To create particular effects, however, you can adjust the line spacing.

Paragraph spacing is the space between the last line of one paragraph and the first line of the next. On a typewriter, it was common to hit the return key twice between paragraphs. Most word processors allow you to set paragraph spacing so that it conforms with what you generally find in printed books: greater than a single line space but less than two line spaces. A common practice is to set paragraph spacing at 1.25 to 1.5 times the line space.

Justification

Justification refers to the way in which lines of text relate to the left and right margins of the page. Examples (and descriptions) of left, centre, and right, and full justification appear below.

Left Justification

When you write long-hand on loose-leaf paper, you begin each line at the left margin and conclude it when you run out of room at the end of the line. This is *left justification*, also known as *left flush*. (An exception would be an indented first line of a paragraph, of course.) Since different lines will have slightly different lengths, left justification is also known as *ragged right*. This paragraph, like those of many documents, is left-justified.

Centre Justification

Sometimes lines of text, particularly titles and subtitles, appear equidistant from the left and right margins. This arrangement, not surprisingly, is known as *centre justification* or *centre-justified* text. These lines are centre-justified.

To create certain visual effects, lines of text (often subtitles) may be aligned
with the right margin. This is *right justification,* also known as *right flush* or
right-justified text. Since there is no left alignment, this arrangement of text is
also known as *ragged left.* This paragraph is an example of right-justified
text. Right justification is generally not suitable for body text.

Full Justification In most books (including this one), the text is set so that it aligns
with both the left and right margins. This is known as *full justification* or *fully justified*
text. Many word processors offer full justification as an option. The problem with this
format is that when you use proportional-space fonts (discussed below), different
combinations of letters form words of different lengths that, in turn, require different
line lengths. Ensuring that each line fits precisely between the margins, while ensuring
as well that the apparent space between the words remains constant, is painstaking
work. The shorter the line of text, the greater the problem. Most newspapers use full
justification, setting text in fairly narrow columns. This can produce undesirable
effects such as those apparent in Figure 4.1, which shows this paragraph fully justified
in a four-column format; the "white currents" you see running down the columns are
called *rivers.* In most cases, your word-processed documents will look better if you use
left justification.

Figure 4.1: Full Justification in a Four-Column Format

In most books (including this one), the text is aligned so that it aligns with both the left and right margins. This is known as *full justification* or *fully justified* text. Many word processors offer full justification as an option. The problem with this format is that when you use proportional-space fonts (discussed below), different combinations of letters form words of different lengths that, in turn, require different line lengths. Ensuring that each line fits precisely between the margins, while ensuring as well that the apparent space between the words remains constant, is painstaking work. The shorter the line of text, the greater the problem. Most newspapers use full justification, setting text in fairly narrow columns. This can produce undesirable effects such as those apparent in Figure 4.1, which shows this paragraph in a four-column format; the "white currents" you see running down the columns are called *rivers.* In most cases, your documents will look better if you use left justification.

Fonts

While many typographers and professional printers distinguish between the terms *font* and *typeface*, most word processors do not. In this discussion, I'll use the former term. In the context of technical communications, it is sufficient to think of a font as a particular style of letters, including size and shape. Here are some common font attributes:

- **bold**
- *italic*
- ***bold italic***
- <u>underscored</u>
- UPPERCASE
- SMALL CAPS

There are literally thousands of different fonts, and typographers are creating new ones every day.

Fonts can be either *monospace* or *proportional-space*. Here's an example of a monospace font.

```
Different letters take up different widths. The letter
"i," for example, takes up a fraction of the width of the
letter "n." In monospace fonts, however, the same amount
of horizontal space is accorded to every letter. Such
fonts — an example is Courier, shown in Figure 4.2 — are
necessary for typewriters, since the carriage must move a
set distance to the left, regardless of which type key is
pressed. Thus, in a monospace font, the distance between
the double "i" in "skiing" would be slightly greater than
that between the "s" and the "k." Monospace fonts are
measured in characters per inch (cpi); the higher the
number, of course, the smaller the font. This paragraph is
left justified in Courier New, a monospace font.
```

Most word-processed and published documents use proportional-space fonts. (All but the first sample in Figure 4.2 are proportional-space fonts.) For each of these fonts, width across the line is determined by the respective widths of the letters. For example, an "i" will occupy less width than an "m." However, size is measured not by width but by height, and is usually counted in *points*, of which there are 72 to an inch. Consequently, the length of the same words in different proportional-space fonts may be strikingly different, as exemplified by the samples of Times New Roman and Bookman in Figure 4.2.

Figure 4.2: Font Samples

Courier, 10cpi	The quick brown fox jumps over the lazy dog.
Times New Roman, 10pt.	The quick brown fox jumps over the lazy dog.
Bookman, 10pt.	**The quick brown fox jumps over the lazy dog.**
Arial, 10pt.	The quick brown fox jumps over the lazy dog.
Avant Garde, 10pt.	The quick brown fox jumps over the lazy dog.
Benguiat Frisky, 10pt.	The quick brown fox jumps over the lazy dog.
Old English, 10pt.	The quick brown fox jumps over the lazy dog.
Brush Script, 10pt.	The quick brown fox jumps over the lazy dog.

Fonts fall into three general categories. Times New Roman and Bookman are both *serif* fonts. If you look closely at the samples in Figure 4.2, you will see that the letters have tiny "tails" (the meaning of the word from which *serif* derives) at their extremities. Serifs were reputedly designed by typographers long ago to help the eye move more easily from one letter to the next. In almost all books (including this one), the body text is set in a serif font.

Fonts that do not have "tails" are called *sans-serif* ("without serif"). Examples in Figure 4.2 are the Arial and Avant Garde samples. Sans-serif fonts are commonly used for level heads. Although some technical communications writers do set their body text in a sans-serif font (maintaining that it "looks cleaner"), most typographers feel that sans-serif is harder to read.

The Benguiat Frisky, Old English, and Brush Script samples in Figure 4.2 are examples of *decorative* fonts. These fonts, which may be serif or sans-serif, are designed to create a special visual impression. When used for body text, decorative fonts tend to be difficult to read.

Unless you have a compelling reason to do otherwise, you should use a serif font for the body text of your documents and, in most cases, a sans-serif font for level heads. However, for text projected onto a screen (an overhead acetate or a 35mm slide, for example), most authorities recommend the reverse. Audiences seem to find it easier to read sans-serif text when it is "far away" and "large," as is the case with text projected onto a screen.

Other Attributes

Document visuals may also include features such as the following:

Rules Vertical and horizontal rules are simply straight lines that are intended to help the audience recognize divisions on a page. You may recall the vertical rules between the columns in Figure 4.1. Below this line is a double horizontal rule.

Boxes Text may be enclosed in a blank or a shaded box. For example:

> This centre-justified line appears in a blank box.

> A shaded box (with "shadow") encloses this centre-justified line.

Reverse Text Reverse (also called inverse) text involves placing white letters on a black background. (Other combinations are possible, of course, if you are printing in colour.) While reverse text can be effective in certain circumstances (e.g., in a heading), it should be used sparingly because it is harder to read than the same text set black on white.

> This is a sample of reverse text.

Lists

Technical communications makes frequent use of both bulleted and numbered lists. The two types of lists tend to serve slightly different purposes. Items in a list are often numbered to suggest a particular sequence for a particular reason—order of importance, for example. While bulleted items don't imply sequencing, it would be more difficult to locate the ninth of fifteen items in a bulleted list than in a numbered one.

Which list should you use? As always, your choice should derive from your analysis of context, message, and audience.

Style Guides

Most organizations strive to achieve a consistent image in the documents they produce. Their document style is likely to include specific criteria for all of the document visuals discussed above, as well as for particular formats (e.g., for letters and memos).

The compilation of "rules" for a consistent image is usually known as a *house style*. Although any organization can develop its own house style, well-established styles have been adopted by many institutions and companies. Widely used style guides include the following:

- *APA* If you are producing documents for the social science disciplines (psychology, sociology, etc.), you will probably need to follow the guidelines set out in *The Publication Manual of the American Psychological Association,* commonly referred to as the APA.

- *Canadian Press* Some Canadian organizations refer their personnel to *The Canadian Press Stylebook,* a guide published by The Canadian Press, a national news-gathering service for many of Canada's newspapers and periodicals.

- *Canadian Style* A standard reference work for many business and government organizations is *The Canadian Style: A Guide to Writing and Editing.* A revised and expanded edition of the guide was published in 1997 by Dundurn Press in cooperation with Public Works and Government Services Canada.

- *Chicago* Many North American organizations have modelled their house style on *The Chicago Manual of Style* (University of Chicago Press). For example, the *ITP Nelson House Style Guide,* which is "intended to provide general editing and typographic guidelines for in-house and freelance editors and proofreaders," draws extensively on *Chicago* style.

- *IEEE* Many technical organizations, particularly in the electrical and electronics fields, prefer to use the style guides of the Institute of Electrical and Electronics Engineers: the *IEEE Standards Style Manual* and the *IEEE Computer Systems Manual.*

- *MLA* If you are producing documents for humanities subject areas (literature, fine arts, philosophy, etc.), you will most likely have to follow the style presented in the *MLA Handbook,* published by the Modern Language Association of America. The fifth and most recent edition of the handbook offers guidance in handling documents in electronic form.

Your choice of style guide will depend on your particular circumstances. Diana Hacker's *A Canadian Writer's Reference* (ITP Nelson, 1996) is among the many reference works that include comparisons of APA and MLA styles.

Visuals in Documents and Presentations

Information and Impression

You may recall from Chapter 1 the observation that audiences respond not only to the objective or factual meaning of words (their denotation) but also to their emotional effect (connotation). The same holds true for visuals. When your audience sees your visual, it receives not only "information" from it—the "facts" that you are representing—but also a "visual impression" that evokes a particular response. These two meanings may be quite different. Imagine a photo of someone accused of embezzling funds from a company. The photo provides "information" that allows you to recognize the person's face. Now imagine that the photo had been taken from an unflattering angle, that the lighting had created stark shadows on the person's face, and that the subject had been scowling at the camera operator. The "visual impression" will likely be one of guilt. When dealing with visuals, you have to remain aware of both types of meaning.

Considerations

Here are some points to consider when choosing or constructing your visuals:

- *Relevance* A visual should reflect or advance each of the CMAPP elements: context, message, audience, purpose, and product. Your personal delight with a particular visual will be of no consequence if your audience looks at the same visual and immediately thinks "Why on earth is that here?" In addition to being relevant, your visual should create interest.

- *Simplification and Emphasis* Remember the adage "a picture is worth a thousand words"? Visuals can help increase your audience's understanding of your message by simplifying concepts or data. A visual that confuses an audience is one that has been poorly chosen and/or constructed. Just as a properly chosen visual can be effective in emphasizing a particular point in your message, a visual that lacks focus will tend to distract an audience.

- *Enhancement* The visual should enhance your message, not overwhelm it. Your visuals will not have been a success if your audience walks away from your presentation thinking, "I have no idea who the speaker was or what the topic was, but those sure were great visuals!"

- *Size* Your visual must be large enough for its details to be visible to your entire audience. For example, a car engine diagram that has been photographically reduced to 1" x 1" in your document will be of little utility. Similarly, no one in an audience of 30 developers would benefit if you held up a 5" x 4" photograph of a construction site.

- *Legibility* If its text is not readily legible to your audience, your visual will not contribute to your message; rather, it will generate impatience and frustration. While often a function of size, legibility also depends on clarity of reproduction. A poor-quality photocopy or projected image can severely compromise an otherwise effective visual. So, of course, can a font that is difficult to decipher.

- *Colour* Consider whether colour is necessary. An illustration of the wiring of a home alarm system will probably require the use of colour, while a graph comparing yearly sales figures may not. You have to take into account how you are planning to reproduce your document. In the case of the home alarm system illustration, black-and-white photocopying would defeat the utility of the visual.

Figure 4.3: A Tennis Court

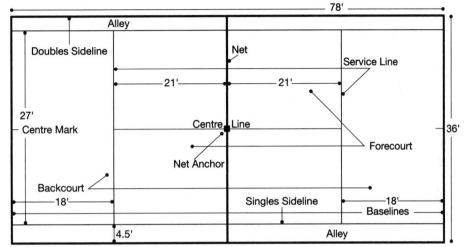

- *Level of detail* Consider the cluttered appearance of the diagram in Figure 4.3. If your purpose were to provide dimension measurements for an audience who wanted to know how to lay out a public tennis court, you could likely have omitted terms such as "Singles Sideline" and "Service Line." Conversely, an audience wanting to learn the rules of the game would not need to see the various measurements. When deciding how much detail to include in your visual, give careful consideration to your audience and your purpose.

- *Scale* If you wanted to discuss transportation problems between Toronto and Vancouver, the map in Figure 4.4 would be an appropriate scale. If, however, you

Figure 4.4: Map of Canada (Small Scale)

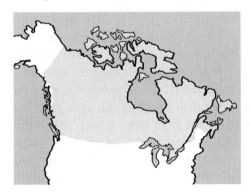

Figure 4.5: Map of Great Lakes (Large Scale)

wanted to discuss transportation links around the Great Lakes, you would need a large-scale map like the one shown in Figure 4.5. Applying a CMAPP analysis to the selection and construction of your visual will help you determine an appropriate scale.

Charts and Tables

Charts (often called graphs) are commonly created from the data generated by a spreadsheet or database program. In both documents and presentations, graphs allow a concise, visual communication of data. Pie charts, vertical bar charts, horizontal bar charts, and line charts are the most common types of charts used in technical communications.

A table consists of data arranged in columns and rows—an arrangement just like that of a spreadsheet. Like data in charts, data in a table may derive from a spreadsheet or database, but may also be compiled directly into its final form. Tables are more likely than charts to display text as well as numbers.

Pie Charts

Whatever the information provided by a pie chart, the visual impression created is that of parts of a whole. Each segment stands for a different category and the data displayed in all of the segments combined add up to 100 percent. The pie chart in Figure 4.6 is an attempt to represent the numbers of registrants in GTI's Business Program over an eight-year period. A pie chart is not an appropriate choice in this case. First, it is unlikely that we want the audience to think of the eight years as parts of a whole. Second, the eight segments, several of similar size, create a visual impression of "some big ones and some small ones"; although percentage labels accompany the segments, precise differences are not visually apparent. Finally, since the purpose of "exploding" a segment is to focus your audience's attention on it, the two exploded segments in Figure 4.6 (1990 and 1992) merely confuse.

Figure 4.6: Ineffective Use of Pie Chart

GTI Business Program Registration: 1990–1997

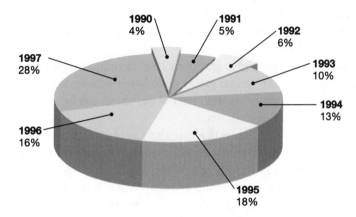

A better use of the pie chart is shown in Figure 4.7. Here the data—the registration percentages for the four program areas that make up GTI's 1997 Co-op Program—lend themselves to representation in a pie chart. The 3-D perspective adds interest and enhances visibility. The use of only four segments avoids the confusing visual impression of Figure 4.6. The single exploded segment leaves no doubt as to which segment the audience should focus on. And finally, the use of a legend allows for less clutter around the pie. Note that the visual's effectiveness depends also on the choice of fills or patterns that allow an audience to easily distinguish one segment from another.

Figure 4.7: Effective Use of Pie Chart

GTI Co-op Programs: 1997 Registration

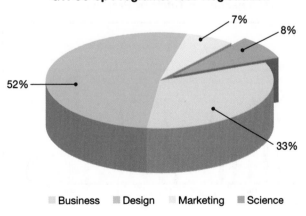

Business   Design   Marketing   Science

Vertical Bar Charts

The visual impression created by a vertical bar chart (also known as a column chart) is that of discrete quantities. The audience expects to see sets of data (often called data categories and data series) ranging along the *x*-axis (the horizontal axis), and quantities increasing up the *y*-axis (the vertical axis). Negative amounts are often shown descending below the *y*-axis.

Vertical bar charts are highly effective in representing comparisons and contrasts. The visual impression they create makes them better vehicles than pie charts for representing precise differences. As well, vertical bar charts can be effective in displaying multiple comparisons and contrasts.

A common misuse of the vertical bar chart is to include too many sets of data. Figure 4.8 exemplifies the clutter and confusion that typically result. The figure, which attempts to compare and contrast eight years of registration figures for seven GTI programs, generates the visual impression of a city skyline. A far more effective use of the vertical bar chart is shown in Figure 4.9. Here the restriction of data to three sets (1990, 1991, and 1992) of two items (Arts and Business) enhances, condenses, and simplifies the message. The legend is far more legible than the one in Figure 4.8. Finally, the horizontal gridlines allow for a more accurate visual impression of the differences in quantities. Be cautious, however: gridlines can lead to clutter.

Horizontal Bar Charts

The horizontal bar chart looks like a vertical bar chart turned 90° clockwise. It, too, is an effective vehicle for presenting one or more comparisons or contrasts (although, as mentioned, your audience's unconscious expectation is to see quantities increasing up the *y*-axis, rather than along the *x*-axis).

Figure 4.8: Ineffective Use of Vertical Bar Chart

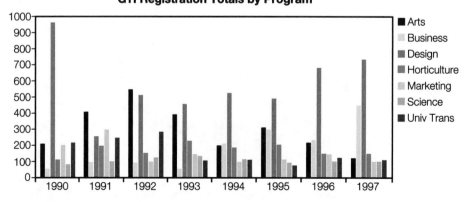

Figure 4.9: Effective Use of Vertical Bar Chart

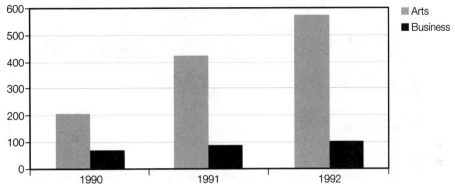

GTI Arts and Business Registration: 1990–1992

A horizontal bar chart's visual impression is conditioned by the overall shape of the chart. By way of example, compare Figures 4.10 and 4.11, which are derived from identical data. The *y*-axis in Figure 4.10 shows the earliest date at the top; Figure 4.11 places it at the bottom. Note how Figure 4.10 creates a visual impression of stability, while Figure 4.11 suggests a situation that is top-heavy (i.e., inherently unbalanced or unstable).

Line Charts

Like vertical and horizontal bar charts, line charts plot data along *x*- and *y*-axes. Accustomed to reading from left to right in English, we expect a line to progress in the same direction. The visual impression of a line chart is normally that of progression over time along the *x*-axis. Thus, a line chart is particularly effective in showing

Figure 4.10: Horizontal Bar Chart with *Y*-axis Showing Earliest Date at Top

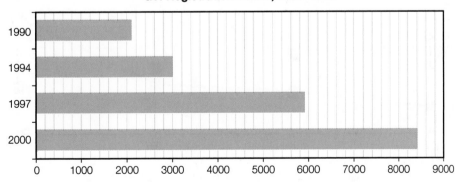

GTI Registration Totals, 2000–1990

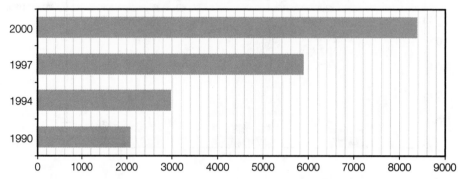

GTI Registration Totals, 1990–2000

chronological change. As Figure 4.12 shows, you can plot more than one data series in a line chart by including more than one line. You can also increase the precision of the visual impression by using markers on the data points. Again, be cautious as you balance precision against clutter.

Note another aspect of Figure 4.12's visual impression. The shape of the lines as they progress from left to right creates an image of partial convergence: registration

Figure 4.12: Line Chart Showing Multiple Lines

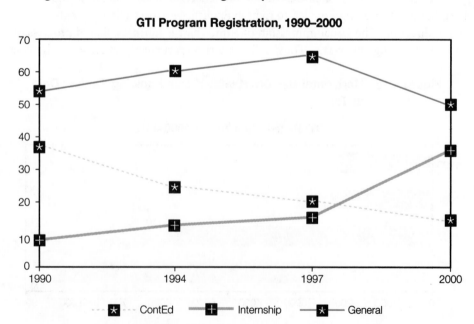

GTI Program Registration, 1990–2000

numbers for the Internship and General programs are growing more and more similar because of the simultaneous increase of the former and decrease of the latter, while Continuing Education appears to grow independently weaker.

Certain aspects of line charts can make them deceptive. Note that the span of years between the x-axis points in Figure 4.12 changes, even though the physical distance separating them does not. Note also that there are registration numbers for each of the indicated years, but not for the intervening ones. An audience might be tempted to extrapolate the registration numbers for the intervening years by using the visual impression—a continuous line showing progression—as a guide. Such extrapolations would be little more than assumptions (and likely inaccurate ones), since we have no data for the intervening years.

Another important aspect of line charts has to do with the scale of the axes and the size of the increments. Consider Figures 4.13 and 4.14. Both charts represent identical GTI Business Program data. The only difference between them is found in their y-axes. The y-axis in Figure 4.13 begins at 0, ends at 1000, and progresses in increments of 100; by contrast, the y-axis in Figure 4.14 begins at 50, ends at 500, and shows increments of 50. Simply as a result of the different y-axis scales and increments, the former chart suggests steady growth, while the latter chart conveys an impression of rapid change.

Does taking advantage of this phenomenon mean that you are deceiving your audience? Recall our discussion of ethics in Chapter 1. If you deliberately mislead your audience, you are probably being unethical. If, on the other hand, you are merely making effective use of visuals to present your message in conformity with your purpose—and if that purpose is not deception—you are probably on solid ethical ground. In any event, when you construct line charts or interpret those of others, remember the distinction between meaning and visual impression.

Figure 4.13: Line Chart Suggesting Steady Growth

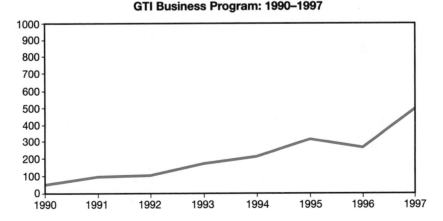

GTI Business Program: 1990–1997

Figure 4.14: Line Chart Suggesting Rapid Change

GTI Business Program: 1990–1997

Tables

A surfeit of rows and columns of data in a table can produce what we might call "visual information overload." The table shown in Figure 4.15 is relatively uncomplicated, giving a visual impression of interrelated, if not readily understandable, numbers. Faced with a table in a document, a motivated audience could carefully examine every cell, discerning relationships, trends, and so forth. But if you use a table as a projected visual, your audience can do little with it but follow your lead.

Figure 4.15: Table Showing RAI Sales and Repair Data

Sales to Service Event Ratio: 1990–2000

	Autos Sold / Leased	Repair / Service Events
1990	1676	15424
1991	1745	15377
1992	1756	14326
1993	1748	14114
1994	1751	13598
1995	1763	13112
1996	1798	12123
1997	1895	11112
1998	2024	10199
1999	2135	10168
2000	2368	9945

In discussing the numbers in Figure 4.15, for example, you could leave two very different impressions. On the one hand, you could say:

In 1990, almost 1700 sold or leased vehicles accounted for the unacceptably high figure of over 15,000 repair or service incidents. In 2000, a full decade later, the sales-to-service ratio showed moderate improvement, but the almost 10,000 repair or service events for the 2000-plus vehicles sold or leased was still unacceptably high.

On the other hand, you could say:

In 1990, we were forced to deal with approximately 10 repair and service incidents for each vehicle we sold or leased. Within 10 short years, we effected a dramatic improvement. In 2000, there were only about 4 repair and service incidents for every vehicle leased or sold.

Thus, you could use the same table to leave a negative impression of ongoing difficulty or a positive impression of successful change. Use the results of your CMAPP analysis to guide your treatment of tables, but (again) don't ignore the ethical questions.

Clip Art

Clip art is electronic artwork—sketches, drawings, line art, and pictures—that you can import and use as visuals for documents or presentation materials. Thousands of colour or black-and-white clip art images are available through software packages and clip art Web sites. Figures 4.16 and 4.17 are examples of public domain clip art available on the Internet.

Figure 4.16: Public Domain Clip Art: Cartoon

Figure 4.17: Public Domain Clip Art: Image of an Overhead Projector

A note of caution. A growing number of electronic formats exist; not all are compatible with every computer application, and not all clip art can be effectively printed or projected. Further, you should consider the ethical—and legal—issue of copyright.

While you may generally use public domain clip art (such as the cartoon in Figure 4.16 and the overhead projector in Figure 4.17) without seeking copyright permission, much clip art is proprietary. Software licences are often ambiguous about what you may do with the clip art included with applications.

CASE STUDY

AEL Engineering Report

Situation

In January 1999, MU's Department of Physical Plant, responsible for all university buildings, was notified by the university's principal real-estate insurance company, Upper Canada Life and Property, of a problem in Vanier Place, a 35-year-old building used primarily as a warehouse. The Upper Canada Life and Property inspector, who had observed fissures in the concrete panels around the truck loading bays, indicated that a policy renewal would not be forthcoming until the necessary repairs were completed.

MU contracted with Accelerated Enterprises Ltd. to investigate the damage and submit an engineering report. The assignment went to Deborah Greathall, an AEL senior associate specializing in civil engineering. Greathall, who works out of the firm's Edmonton office, spent the month of March 1999 in the Toronto area.

During examination of Vanier Place, she discovered that the truck loading bays, installed in 1989, had been carved from what had been an exterior wall. Unfortunately, the construction had not taken into account the long-term impact of large trucks backing up into the loading bays. The ongoing shocks, Greathall concluded, had eventually led to cracking in the concrete panels that made up the west wall of the building.

Greathall considered various options for repairing the wall. (The situation was complicated by the fact that segments of the panels were below exterior grade. As well, the university had no alternative loading bays that it could use during reconstruction.) She eventually decided on a course of action. She submitted her preliminary engineering report, introduced by a cover letter, to Dr. Joan Welstromm, chair of MU's Civil Engineering Department, who had been appointed by Dr. Helena Paderewski, MU's president, to be the university's liaison. Greathall sent a copy of the report to Frank Nabata, the AEL senior partner in Winnipeg who had arranged for her to take the MU contract.

Greathall's cover letter and preliminary report appear in Figures 4.18 and 4.19 respectively.

Figure 4.18: Greathall's Cover Letter

 **Accelerated Enterprises Ltd.**

342 Dundas Street West
Toronto Ontario M3B 5T5
Tel: (416) 222-9989 Fax: (416) 222-9900

Deborah Greathall, Senior Associate

March 30, 1999

Dr. Joan Welstromm
Chair, Civil Engineering
Mississauga University
5827 Dixie Road
Mississauga ON
L2J 2J2

Dear Dr. Welstromm:

Having completed my examination of the west side of *Vanier Place*, I am pleased to present my preliminary report regarding proposed repairs.

Once you have had the opportunity to examine my findings, please contact *AEL* to advise us of how and when you would like to proceed.

Once you have had the opportunity to examine my findings, please advise AEL of your wishes. Since I must shortly return to **Edmonton**, Dr. Noam Avigdor, AEL's senior associate in Toronto, will be happy to assist you. Should you so wish, he could also recommend competent construction contractors. You may reach him at the numbers shown above, or at his direct line:

> **Dr. Noam Avigdor**
> **Senior Associate, AEL Toronto**
> **222-9989**

Yours sincerely,

Deborah Greathall

Deborah Greathall (Ms.)
Senior Associate, Civil Engineering

p.s. AEL will submit its invoice under separate cover.

cc: Frank Nabata (AEL Winnipeg)

Figure 4.19: Preliminary Engineering Report

Accelerated Enterprises Ltd.

342 Dundas Street West Toronto Ontario M3B 5T5
416.222.9989 Fax: 416.222.9900

Preliminary Engineering Report

March 30, 1999

Specifications and procedures to rehabilitate lift-up panels at the industrial building called Vanier Place, on the campus of Mississauga University, at 5827 Dixie Road, Mississauga.

The building was constructed on a pre-loaded site of approx. 4 acres in 2 phases

1. the first in 1972 and
2. the second in 1977.

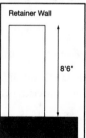

At issue are the twelve $5\frac{1}{2}$"-thick reinforced concrete lift-up panels that make up the west wall. <u>Each is 32' high and approx. 16' wide.</u>

The lower half of 9 of the lift-up panels, all dating from the 1977 construction phase, show signs of cracking and deterioration. The damage likely derives from trucks backing into the panels when

1. manoeuvring to load or unload, and/or
2. from stresses during construction while the panels were being lifted by a crane into position onto their footing (probably before the reinforced concrete had fully matured).

These panels are marked on the attached sketches; note that in the original construction drawings that I consulted, they likewise appear within building lines 2–5.

Strengthening

It was decided to strengthen damaged panels by attaching them to newly formed 6" reinforced concrete retainer walls of approx. 8'6" height as measured from the top of the panel footing. As panel footings are competent and wide enough, they will also serve as a footing for the retainer walls. However, the above holds good only for the five panels marked A through E, and one panel marked F. The panel marked G is very similar but the height of the retainer wall is governed by an exhaust duct opening.

Figure 4.19 (continued)

Note

Please note that panel F is, in effect, combined with panel B: a hollow steel rectangular column, 4'' wide by 6⅜'' thick, is attached to the footing by means of a ½''-thick steel plate bolted to the footing and welded to the column (¼'' weld); this column is also attached to the south side of the existing reinforced concrete loading platform of panel B. It is intended to carry the weight of a horizontal retainer concrete beam attached to panel B above the door opening.

As panel C also contains an opening door with a cantilevered loading platform, its strengthening is in part achieved by another reinforced concrete beam, 6'' thick, attached to the panel and resting on concrete retainer walls at both ends.

No retainer wall is attached to panel B or panel C below the loading platforms. Instead, two 8'' reinforced concrete walls at right angles to the panels are being provided for both, and connected to the panels.

Retainer Walls

The retainer walls are to be reinforced with 20-mm bars vertically at **2'** o/c and horizontally with 10-mm bars at **1'** o/c. The retainer beams above the doors are reinforced along their entire length with a 20-mm bar placed at the top and at the bottom. The reinforcement in the retainer walls is confined to its centre by 10-mm L-shaped anchors. These anchors are placed at 2'' each way into the panel. The anchor's legs are 6'' long, one ensconced in a **12-mm** diameter hole drilled 3'' deep into the panel, with the other free leg parallel to the panel wall. The retainer beams are attached to the panels by the same type of anchors

Procedures Requested
1) Footing of panels of all 9 panels (approx. total length: 144'') to be revealed.
2) Footing areas of panels "B" and "C" to be extended to the outline shown on the sketch.
3) All panels to be sandblasted to required height with "Black Pearl" coal slag to expose a visible profile and the aggregate of the concrete.
4) Holes of **12-mm** diameter, 3'' deep, to be drilled at required spacing (**12''** e/w into panels) as required by retainer walls or beams.
5) All sandblasted areas to be power-washed.
6) Anchors to be placed into the drill holes after filling them with epoxy.
7) Panels to be soaked with water for a minimum of 24 hours and then let dry back to a "saturated surface dry" state, immediately prior to placement of concrete.
8) Dry-to-wet epoxy paint to be used for bonding top 15'' of space for retaining beams and walls/panel location just before concreting.
9) Vibrator to be used to place concrete against panels within form work.

- 2 -

Figure 4.19 (continued)

10) Visible cracks in the panels (up to top of retainer beam height and outside of retainer walls or beams) to be cleaned out, washed, and then filled with epoxy paint.
11) All parts to be painted to the full height of the retainer beams with elastomeric paint to match existing light colour.
12) Grade to be reinstated and asphalt to be renewed in the operation area.

Concrete Performance Requirement

1. Conform to CSA A231 type 10 normal Portland cement
2. Supplementary: class F Fly ash
3. Exposure class F2
4. Minimum compressive strength: 28 M Pa
5. Maximum concrete aggregate: 14 mm
6. Slump at point of discharge: 160 plus/minus 20
7. Air content 6 plus/minus 1
8. Minimum water ratio to cement: 0.55
9. Admixtures: normal dosage

Conclusion

This concludes my preliminary report.

Deborah Greathall

Deborah Greathall, Prof. Eng.

p.s. Sketches not quite ready; will be sent by courier within a day or two.

- 3 -

Issues to Think About

Let's assume that Greathall is a competent engineer, that she is conscientious about her work, and that she wants to make a good impression on both Welstromm and Nabata.

Cover Letter

1. What kind of font is used for the letterhead?
2. Is the letterhead effective in conveying an impression of the firm's solidity and professionalism?
3. Is the body text font an effective choice? What makes it appropriate or inappropriate?
4. What kind of document visual is used to present Avigdor's name?
5. Would you have used that document visual? Give reasons for your answer.
6. What can you say about Greathall's use of other document visuals?

Preliminary Report

1. How does the letterhead differ from that in the cover letter (Figure 4.18)? Should the two letterheads be the same or different? Explain your answer in terms of the CMAPP dynamic.
2. What kind of font has Greathall used for the report's body text? Explain why you think the choice is a good or bad one.
3. What type of justification is used for the body text? What are the advantages/disadvantages of the choice given the context and the message?
4. Do you approve of the use of the two-column format in the "Note"? Give reasons for your answer.
5. Do the rules and the box serve a useful purpose? Why or why not?
6. What do you think of Greathall's use of bold and underline? Cite examples from the report in your answer.
7. The sketches referred to in the report are not, in fact, attached. How might this oversight affect Greathall's audience?
8. Evaluate the two visuals embedded in the report in terms of the following:
   (a) relevance of message
   (b) relevance to audience
   (c) size
   (d) level of detail
   (e) scale
   (f) calibre

9. Evaluate Greathall's use of level heads in the report.

Revision

Revised versions of Greathall's cover letter and preliminary report appear in Figures 4.20 and 4.21. In examining these documents, consider specific improvements that have been made with respect to clarity, organization, and consistency. You should assume that the sketches *are* attached to the revised report.

EXERCISES

4.1 Define the following terms:
   (a) body text
   (b) level head
   (c) white space
   (d) header
   (e) footer

4.2 Describe the differences between monospace and proportional-space fonts.

4.3 Describe the main characteristics of serif, sans-serif, and decorative fonts.

4.4 Suggest the most common use in standard technical communications documents for each of the three font categories.

4.5 How might you qualify your answer to question 4.4 if "the most common use" was in reference to text projected onto a screen?

4.6 What are the different purposes served by bulleted lists and numbered lists?

4.7 Identify the types of document issues commonly addressed in style guides.

4.8 Name two or more style guides that are widely used in North America.

4.9 Briefly explain the terms "information" and "impression" as they relate to the message carried by visuals.

4.10 Briefly explain why three or more of the following are important points to consider when choosing or constructing visuals.
   (a) relevance
   (b) simplification
   (c) enhancement
   (d) size
   (e) legibility
   (f) colour

4.11 Find an example of a visual that includes too much detail. Give reasons for your selection.

4.12 Find an example of a visual whose scale is too large. Give reasons for your selection.

Figure 4.20: Revised Cover Letter

 **Accelerated Enterprises Ltd.**

342 Dundas Street West
Toronto Ontario M3B 5T5
Tel: (416) 222-9989 Fax: (416) 222-9900

March 30, 1999

Dr. Joan Welstromm
Chair, Civil Engineering
Mississauga University
5827 Dixie Road
Mississauga ON
L2J 2J2

Dear Dr. Welstromm:

Having completed my examination of the west side of Vanier Place, I am pleased to present my preliminary report regarding proposed repairs.

Once you have had the opportunity to examine my findings, please advise AEL of your wishes. I must shortly return to Edmonton, but Dr. Noam Avigdor, AEL's senior associate in Toronto, will be happy to assist you. You may reach him at the number shown above.

Yours sincerely,

Deborah Greathall

Deborah Greathall (Ms.)
Senior Associate, Civil Engineering

p.s. AEL will submit its invoice under separate cover.

cc: Frank Nabata (AEL Winnipeg)

Figure 4.21: Revised Preliminary Engineering Report

 **AEL Accelerated**
Enterprises Ltd.

342 Dundas Street West
Toronto Ontario M3B 5T5
Tel: (416) 222-9989 Fax: (416) 222-9900

March 30, 1999

Preliminary Engineering Report: 5827 Dixie Road, Mississauga ON

Re: Specifications and procedures to rehabilitate lift-up panels at the industrial building called Vanier Place, on the campus of Mississauga University, at 5827 Dixie Road, Mississauga.

Background

The building was constructed on a pre-loaded site of approx. 4 acres in 2 phases, the first in 1972 and the second in 1977. At issue are the twelve 5 $\frac{1}{2}$"-thick reinforced concrete lift-up panels that make up the west wall. Each is 32' high and approx. 16' wide.

The lower half of 9 of the lift-up panels, all dating from the 1977 construction phase, show signs of cracking and deterioration. The damage likely derives from trucks backing into the panels when manoeuvring to load or unload, and/or from stresses during construction while the panels were being lifted by a crane into position onto their footing (probably before the reinforced concrete had fully matured). These panels are marked on the attached sketches; note that in the original construction drawings that I consulted, they likewise appear within building lines 2–5.

Strengthening

It was decided to strengthen the damaged panels by attaching them to newly formed 6 " reinforced concrete retainer walls of approx. 8'6" height as measured from the top of the panel footing. As panel footings are competent and wide enough, they will also serve as a footing for the retainer walls. However, the above holds good only for the five panels marked A through E, and one panel marked F. The panel marked G is very similar but the height of the retainer wall is governed by an exhaust-duct opening.

Note

Please note that panel F is, in effect, combined with panel B: a hollow steel rectangular column, 4" wide and 6 $\frac{3}{8}$" thick, is attached to the footing by means of a $\frac{1}{2}$"-thick steel plate bolted to the footing and welded to the column ($\frac{1}{4}$" weld); this column is also attached to the south side of the existing reinforced concrete loading platform of panel B. It is intended to carry the weight of a horizontal retainer concrete beam attached to panel B above the door opening.

.../2

Figure 4.21 (continued)

- 2 -

As panel C also contains an opening door with a cantilevered loading platform, its strengthening is in part achieved by another reinforced concrete beam, 6" thick, attached to the panel and resting on concrete retainer walls at both ends.

No retainer wall is attached to panel B or panel C below the loading platforms. Instead, two 8" reinforced concrete walls at right angles to the panels are being provided for both, and connected to the panels.

Retainer Walls
The retainer walls are to be reinforced with 20-mm bars vertically at 2" o/c and horizontally with 10-mm bars at 1" o/c. The retainer beams above the doors are reinforced along their entire length with a 20-mm bar placed at the top and at the bottom. The reinforcement in the retainer walls is confined to its centre by 10-mm L-shaped anchors. These anchors are placed at 2" each way into the panel. The anchor's legs are 6" long, one ensconced in a 12-mm diameter hole drilled 3" deep into the panel, with the other free leg parallel to the panel wall. The retainer beams are attached to the panels by the same type of anchors.

Recommended Procedures
1) Footing of all 9 panels (approx. total length: 144") to be revealed.
2) Footing areas of panels "B" and "C" to be extended to the outline shown on the sketch.
3) All panels to be sandblasted to required height with "Black Pearl" coal slag to expose a visible profile and the aggregate of the concrete.
4) Holes of 12-mm diameter, 3" deep, to be drilled at required spacing (2" e/w into panels) as required by retainer walls or beams.
5) All sandblasted areas to be power-washed.
6) Anchors to be placed into the drill holes after filling them with epoxy.
7) Panels to be soaked with water for a minimum of 24 hours and then let dry back to a "saturated surface dry" state immediately prior to placement of concrete.
8) Dry-to-wet epoxy paint to be used for bonding top 15" of space for retaining beams and walls/panel location just before concreting.
9) Vibrator to be used to place concrete against panels within form work.
10) Visible cracks in the panels (up to top of retainer beam height and outside of retainer walls or beams) to be cleaned out, washed, and then filled with epoxy paint.
11) All parts to be painted to the full height of the retainer beams with elastomeric paint to match existing light colour.
12) Grade to be reinstated and asphalt to be renewed in the operation area.

.../3

Figure 4.21 (continued)

- 3 -

Concrete Performance Requirement
- Conform to CSA A231 type 10 normal Portland cement
- Supplementary: class F Flyash
- Exposure class F2
- Minimum compressive strength: 28 M Pa
- Maximum concrete aggregate: 14 mm
- Slump at point of discharge: 160 plus/minus 20
- Air content 6 plus/minus 1
- Minimum water ratio to cement: 0.55
- Admixtures: normal dosage

This concludes my preliminary report.

Deborah Greathall

Deborah Greathall, Prof. Eng.

Attachment: Preliminary engineering sketches (5)

4.13 Figure 4.22 shows data obtained from Global Motors concerning the firm's national sales since 1980. Think of two different ways of presenting that data visually. For each of your suggestions, produce a brief CMAPP analysis. Then produce a draft of the visual you would use for each analysis.

Figure 4.22: Global Motor Sales

In 1980, 9% of Global Motors' vehicle sales across Canada came from its innovative *Traveller* line of sport utility vehicles. The *Trend* line of sport sedans accounted for 19% of sales, while the *Security* line of passenger vehicles accounted for the remaining 72%. In 1986, the *Traveller* line accounted for 14%, the *Trend* line for 23%, and the *Security* line for 63%. In 1990, the figures were 20% for *Traveller*, 21% for *Trend,* and 59% for *Security*. In 1995, the figures were 27% (*Traveller*), 25% (*Trend*), and 48% (*Security*). In 1998, 42% of sales were *Travellers*, 39% were *Trends*, and only 19% were *Securitys*. Global predicts that by 2002, fully 55% of its sales will be attributable to *Traveller* models, 30% to *Trend* vehicles, and 15% to the *Security* line.

Global sold 7,000 vehicles in 1980, 11,400 in 1986, and 22,900 in 1990. In 1995, sales totalled 35,400, rising to 48,400 in 1998. A total of 57,000 vehicle sales is predicted for 2002.

4.14 Obtain a copy of a business document that contains graphics. Supporting your points with examples, assess its use of document visuals and visuals.

EXPLORING THE WEB

Here are some Web sites you might wish to investigate.

URL	DESCRIPTION
http://sierra.savvysearch.com/search?q=Style+Manuals&op=p&cat=12	This SavvySearch results page provides many links to style guides and other writing reference sites.
http://www.standards.ieee.org/guides/style/index.html#contents	This is the online version of the 1996 *IEEE Standards Style Manual* published by the Institute of Electrical and Electronics Engineers.
http://www.lias.psu.edu/refstyle.html	This Penn State University Libraries page provides links to writing resources and a variety of Internet style manuals, including APA and MLA.

http://bailiwick.lib.uiowa.edu/journalism/cite.html	Compiled by Karla Tonella of the University of Iowa, this page provides links to citation style guides, including MLA.
http://www.canpress.ca	The home page of Canadian Press provides information on its various services and publications, including *The Canadian Press Stylebook*.
1. http://www.artswire.org/kenroar/links/clipart.html 2. http://www.webplaces.com/html/clipart.htm 3. http://webclipart.tqn.com/msub28.htm 4. http://www.columbia.k12.mo.us/rbhs/clipart.htm	These four sites provide links to sites offering a variety of public domain and proprietary clip art and other images.

Complementary Attributes of the CMAPP Model

The CMAPP model involves a dynamic analysis of context, message, audience, purpose, and product. Before you begin to create your communication, you pose appropriate questions regarding all the CMAPP components. Although every situation will dictate its own distinct set of questions, your analysis of message and product should include a consideration of five complementary CMAPP attributes: 5WH, KISS, ABC, CFF, and CAP. Each of these attributes is either an abbreviation or an acronym.

What is the difference between an abbreviation and an acronym? The *ITP Nelson Canadian Dictionary* (1997) defines the former as "a shortened form of a word or phrase." Thus, *Sept., Encl.,* and *attach.* are the abbreviations of *September, enclosure* and *attachment,* respectively. Traditionally, abbreviations were characterized by the use of periods, as in *Mr., Ms.,* and *Mrs.* In recent years, it has become acceptable to omit the period in many abbreviations, with *Mr, Ms,* and *Mrs* becoming common. Other examples include CBC (Canadian Broadcasting Corporation), CRTC (Canadian Radio-television and Telecommunications Commission), EI (Employment Insurance), RRSP (Registered Retirement Savings Plan), and HIV (Human Immunodeficiency Virus).

The *ITP Nelson Canadian Dictionary* defines acronym as "a word formed from the initial letters or parts of a word, such as *PIN* for *Personal Identification Number.*" Thus, you might say that while all acronyms are abbreviations, not all abbreviations are acronyms. To be considered an acronym, the abbreviation has to be pronounced as a word. While some acronyms retain their characteristic capital letters, others more commonly appear in lower case. Examples include AIDS (Acquired Immune Deficiency Syndrome), ASCII (American Standard Code for Information Interchange), modem (modulate and demodulate), NATO (North Atlantic Treaty Organization), radar (radio detection and ranging), and scuba (self-contained underwater breathing apparatus).

Now let's turn our attention to each of the five complementary CMAPP attributes.

5WH

Much technical communications is concerned with what can be observed, quantified, or verified—that is, with facts. The abbreviation 5WH refers to the five questions that are often associated with objective journalism: who, what, when, where, why, and how. Since these questions seek facts, asking them as part of your CMAPP analysis will help you decide what is pertinent for your message.

But just what do we mean by the word "fact"? If asked in what year American astronauts first walked on the moon, you might reply (correctly) 1969. If asked how you know that the moonwalk actually occurred, you might say that you saw footage of the event on TV, that you read about it in a history book, that you once saw a moon rock in a museum, or that you learned about the 1969 moon mission in school. However, you probably also know that much of what you see on TV is not real, that history books are not immune from bias, that you are taking the museum's word for it that the moon rock is the genuine article, and that not everything you learn in school is true.

On reflection, most of us accept that we do not have our own evidence that the 1969 moonwalk really happened; rather, we *choose to believe* that the event is a "fact." Recall, also, that for several centuries, Western scholars accepted as fact the theory that the earth was flat and that the sun revolved around it. What changed was not the solar system, but our belief—the fact.

Now consider this definition in the *ITP Nelson Canadian Dictionary*:

> **Fact.** *n.***1.** Information presented as objectively real. **2.** A real occurrence; an event: *the facts of the accident*. **3.a.** Something having real, demonstrable existence. **b.** The quality of being real or actual.

Note particularly the first definition. It would seem to imply that we might call something a "fact" merely because someone *claims* that it is real. So, when you are asking yourself the 5WH questions—searching for the "facts" to include in your message—consider whether your "facts" should themselves be questioned. Finally, ask yourself how your choice of vocabulary is likely to affect your audience. Have you tried to express your "facts" in words that carry strong denotation but low connotation? Have you considered what kinds of impressions your words may create, and whether you are practising good communication ethics?

KISS

The acronym KISS translates as, "keep it simple, stupid." While its wisdom may apply to many things, view it as good advice for technical communications. Here are some points to consider:

- Don't overcomplicate your CMAPP analysis. Look at each component, but avoid second-guessing yourself or allowing the answers to your CMAPP questions to become a first draft of the Great Canadian Novel. In all your business and technical communications, try to find the least complicated response to the "problem" that your communication is addressing, and try to find the simplest way of conveying that response.

- Avoid the temptation of having your document display evidence of every option that your new word processor offers, or every piece of clip art you just acquired. The KISS principle very much applies to the issues discussed in Chapter 4 regarding the use of visual elements in both documents and presentations.

- Don't make the mistake of assuming that your message will seem more educated, formal, or sophisticated if you use complicated sentences and uncommon vocabulary. Normally, the opposite is true: effectiveness usually increases when you keep your message as simple as possible. Of course, the degree to which you use specialized vocabulary in your message will depend on the audience and the context.

ABC

The abbreviation ABC refers to three aspects of your message and your product: accuracy, brevity, and clarity.

Accuracy

When composing your message, ask yourself:

- Have I chosen the right facts for this situation? In other words, are all my facts pertinent to my context, my audience, and my purpose?
- Are all my data correct? (Have I checked?)

Remember that your audience "needs" your information; as you learned in Chapter 1, technical communications is audience-driven. But your audience does *not* need data that will muddy the issue. Recall as well that your message represents you to your audience, and thus your reputation hangs on it. Imagine the consequences if your audience were to find an error in your information: your message would lose credibility, as would you, the "messenger." Once lost, your credibility would be very hard to regain.

Brevity

A practical definition of brevity might be, "Say what you need to say, and then stop." If you include in your document or presentation material that is not relevant to your context, message, audience, and purpose, your audience may be confused, irritated, and/or bored—and all your efforts will have been wasted.

Clarity

Clarity is a function of the words and grammatical structures you use, of the organization of your information, of the logic and cohesion of your arguments, and of the way you present your message to your audience. When examining your message and your product, therefore, ask yourself: Is everything as clear as I can make it? Can I safely assume that my message will be as understandable to my audience as it is to me?

The abbreviation CFF refers to content, form, and format. The article entitled "The Total Package" (see Box 5.1), which appeared some ten years ago in a publication aimed at small and home-based businesses, discusses each of these components in terms of what the author characterizes as the "total package" formed by your message and your product. The points made in this article are at least as valid now as they were in 1990. And they apply just as strongly to a student writing an essay as they do to the business audience the author was addressing.

Box 5.1: The "Total Package"

Everyone these days seems to want us to buy a "package deal." Whether it's a stereo (a "sound system"), a computer (an "integrated system"), or clothing (a "lifestyle"), it has become more and more difficult to purchase a single item. According to my own rather limited research, I'm always being asked to walk away with a combination of some kind.

To be honest, most of us want to sell a "package deal," as well. For some of us, it may be merchandise; for others, it's services. To compete, however, we have to be ready, willing, and able to offer a whole rather than a part. Coordinating the various pieces can be time-consuming and, occasionally, frustrating. But it is the way of the commercial world we live in, and it does have its undeniable value.

Making sure the package is complete and that all the tab A's will fit into the appropriate slot B's often requires additional expertise, which we sometimes have to learn from scratch. Since, for most of us, time is more than just money, that necessity can easily become a burden we'd rather not shoulder.

Each and every piece of writing you send out represents you to the people who pay your bills. Just as you'd never sell them a package of goods that don't fit together properly, you shouldn't send them a document that doesn't, either. You should look at everything you write as being a set of integrated components: the content, the form, and the format.

Content

This is something only you can decide on. But you should ask yourself a question each and every time: am I writing the right thing to the right person at the right time? Unless your answer to each of these questions is an unqualified "yes," think again about what you want to do and why you're doing it.

That may sound like a profound statement of the obvious. However, most of us have a tendency to just sit down and start writing. A lot of planning (not a little—a lot) can make just as much of a long-term difference. Ask anyone who's later had to defend in court what he or she wrote in a hurry.

Form

The language you use when confronting your teenage son who has just crunched the fender on your new car is not the same as the language you use in a contract proposal. Similarly, constructing a logical argument isn't all-important when you're having a backyard beer with your neighbour—but it is when you're making a presentation to a potential client.

Form—the language you use—should vary according to the situation. This is important each time you use your company stationery. You have to make sure that the language you've chosen is right for your context, and that you've put things into an order that is both easy to follow and very convincing. Otherwise, your reader may react just the way your son did.

Format

A letter's just a letter, right? Not so. It's unlikely you'd be impressed if your lawyer or your biggest supplier sent you an invoice scrawled illegibly on an old piece of foolscap, forgot to date it, or left out your company name or address.

Your readers aren't going to be impressed with your company if you don't choose an accepted business letter format, either. There are a number of such standard formats. (The most common is called "block.") Which you choose is not at all as important as using the same one accurately and consistently. And it would be well worth your while to make that decision yourself, rather than leaving it to an assistant. After all, you're the one who should be most concerned with the image you're creating.

One of the consequences of the technology that surrounds us is that people's expectations have risen. We used to be fairly blind to things like poorly spaced text on a page, evidence of corrected letters or words, inconsistent or poor-quality print, and even the occasional typo. We knew how long it took to do it over, and so we were usually sympathetic.

We're more discriminating now. We notice that crossed-out address and the new one typed beside it. We can tell what type of printer you've used, and we make judgments about the quality of your stationery. That may not be fair, and it may not really have much to do with the quality of what you're selling. But it is reality. And if you ignore it, your bottom line will eventually suffer.

To sum up ... Whatever your message and your audience, put together the best total package you can afford. Don't assume that people won't notice or that, if they do notice, they won't care. They'll do both.

CAP

The acronym CAP refers to the adjectives concise, accessible, and precise. These elements relate to the way you construct your message and your product, and all play a role in ensuring that your "total package" is effective.

Concise

The meaning of "concise" can be summed up in the sentence, "If you can say something in 6 words, don't use 26." Assume that your audience is busy, and will want to gain the necessary information as quickly as possible.

Consider the following two notifications, each advising regular committee members of an upcoming meeting:

1. All of the various individuals who regularly present themselves in attendance at the normal meeting of the committee usually referred to as the SCPI (the Standing Committee on Personnel Issues) are invited to the upcoming regular meeting of the Committee, to be held from 3:00 p.m. to 5:00 p.m., on Wednesday, March 15, 2000, in the customary meeting place, Room 215.

2. The next SCPI meeting will be held March 15, 2000, from 3:00 p.m. to 5:00 p.m., in Room 215.

Which would you prefer to read during a hectic day at the office?

Accessible

Accessibility refers to the way the document has been structured so as to permit the audience to extract important information quickly and easily. As discussed in Chapter 1, you must assume that your audience may not have either the time or the inclination to read every word of your document. Rather, he or she will probably want—at least at first—to scan, noting the significant ideas and gaining a sense of the document's organization.

You make information accessible through clarity of language and presentation. Consider the documents in Figures 5.1 and 5.2. Both present information about Gilles Radisson, the CEO of Radisson Automobiles Inc. However, the information in Figure 5.1 is presented in the form of a standard paragraph or traditional prose format, while the information in Figure 5.2 appears in a format that a technical communications audience would consider more accessible. Note how the arrangement of headings and lists in the latter figure takes the place of the more traditional topic, supporting, and concluding sentences in Figure 5.1. Notice, too, how the organization and the presentation of the information in Figure 5.2 allow you to grasp the essential facts at a glance.

Figure 5.1: Traditional Prose Format

Gilles Radisson is the 56-year-old president and chief executive officer (CEO) of Radisson Automobiles Inc.

In the early 1960s, Gilles left Ottawa and hitchhiked to British Columbia. With much energy but little enthusiasm, he completed an automotive mechanics diploma at Grandstone Technical Institute in Langley, a small city east of Vancouver. Having suddenly identified a goal, Gilles spent a tiring three days and three nights driving back to Central Canada with a friend. He soon registered at Mississauga University. While completing his studies over the next four years, he worked part-time and lived frugally. Upon receiving his Master of Business Administration degree, he accepted his father's gift of a first-class plane ticket and returned to his home in Ottawa to work with Maurice in the family car business.

Gilles began as a lowly mechanic's assistant but soon obtained his mechanic's ticket. Shortly thereafter, his father promoted him to the sales floor, where he proved himself an eager and able salesman. Some time later, Maurice had Gilles take over a junior position in the company's administrative office, so that he could become familiar with the business's financial operations. In 1979, Maurice decided to retire and persuaded the board of directors to appoint Gilles president and CEO. Since then, Gilles has devoted himself to Radisson Automobiles Inc., overseeing the creation of dealerships in Montreal, Halifax, Moncton, Winnipeg, Regina, and Vancouver.

Despite the rapid and successful expansion of what he continued to view as "his company," Gilles insisted on maintaining his head office in the Ottawa neighbourhood in which his father had set up the first dealership. The office address is 6134 Bank Street, Ottawa, Ontario K2A 2B3. Head office staff can be contacted at (613) 433-9887 (phone) or (613) 435-0098 (fax). Though in the past he did so commonly, Gilles now rarely offers a client or an employee his home telephone number of (613) 733-7374. More and more, this self-made millionaire enjoys the time he spends away from what he views as the constant struggle of the marketplace.

Figure 5.2: Technical Communications Format

Gilles Radisson:	**President and CEO, Radisson Automobiles Inc. (RAI)**
Age:	56
Home phone:	(613) 733-7374
Education:	Automotive mechanics diploma (1964), Grandstone Technical Institute, Langley, BC
	MBA (1968), Mississauga University, Mississauga, ON

Figure 5.2 (continued)

RAI positions:	Mechanic's Assistant (1968–70)
	Certified Mechanic (1970–72)
	Junior Sales Associate (1972)
	Sales Associate (1972–74)
	Administrator (1974–76)
	Partner (1976–79)
	President/CEO (1979–present)
RAI Head Office:	6134 Bank Street, Ottawa, ON K2A 2B3
	Phone: (613) 433-9887
	Fax: (613) 435-0098
RAI dealerships:	Ottawa, Montreal, Halifax, Moncton, Winnipeg, Regina, Vancouver

Precise

Most technical communications require precise language. Note how Figure 5.2 uses specific dates, while Figure 5.1 relies on such abstractions as "in the early 1960s" and "some time later." As always, you must tailor your language to your audience, context, and purpose.

Following are examples of imprecise versus precise language.

Imprecise (nontechnical)	Precise (technical)
The earth is *round*.	The earth is *spherical*. (*Round* is two-dimensional.)
The staircase is *spiral*.	The staircase is *helical*. (*Spiral* is two-dimensional.)
The package is *like a small box*.	The package is *an 8" cube*. (*Like a small box* is abstract and vague.)
We *recently* ordered *a lot of apples*.	*On April 3, 1999*, we ordered *200 kg* of *Golden Delicious* apples. (*Recently* and *a lot of apples* are imprecise.)

You will often have to balance the need for precision against the need for brevity and concision. Consider the SCPI meeting notice discussed earlier in this chapter. Through your CMAPP analysis, you have to judge exactly how much information your audience actually needs. If you were entering a reminder in your Daytimer (in which case you would be your own audience), you might require nothing more than:

SCPI: 00/03/15 3–5 215

A reminder to the clearly defined audience of SCPI members would probably be a bit more expansive:

Next SCPI meeting:

March 15, 2000

3:00 p.m. to 5:00 p.m.

Building D, room 215

RSVP local 4538

If you were sending a notification to someone who was not a member of the SCPI, you would probably include such details as the street address of building D. You would likely provide the complete phone number, rather than just the local extension of 4538. Finally, you might include a list of SCPI members and an agenda.

In each successive notification described above, the message would be precise but increasingly less brief and concise.

CASE STUDY

Mississauga University Registration

Situation

A few years ago, Mississauga University (MU) instituted an automated telephone registration system referred to by the university as T-Reg, though often called TerrorReg by the students who have to use it.

Once they obtain approved standing, students receive specific dates and times during which they must use the system to register for the following semester's courses. For security purposes, students are required to use their student number along with a six-digit personal information number (PIN) that they have chosen for themselves. As well, they must know the six-digit semester code (SC), the course identification number (CIN), and the section number (SN) for every course for which they wish to register. The system accepts credit card payments.

On May 17, 2000, Lester Mont, a 20-year old MU student, receives approval to register for his second year of Management Science, which is to commence in September 2000. Telephone registration starts at 8:00 a.m. on Monday, June 5, 2000. Unfortunately, Lester's summer job as a Help Desk Assistant at Canberra Industries in London, Ontario, obliges him to undertake a training course that day. He won't have time or opportunity to make the lengthy and often frustrating calls that have characterized MU's T-Reg.

At the beginning of June, Lester asks his father, who lives in Thornhill, Ontario, to register for him. Mr. Mont agrees but points out that he is unfamiliar with what Lester calls TerrorReg and, in fact, with the university. Lester assures his father that the procedure is quite simple, and that he will soon fax all the necessary information. In the late afternoon of Saturday, June 3, Lester faxes to his father the following materials:

■ a handwritten note that includes an explanation of how to use the T-Reg system (Figure 5.3);

Figure 5.3: Lester's Faxed Note

Saturday, June 3

Hey, Dad!

Sorry it took me so long to get this off to you. Things got hectic. Thanks very much for registering for me. It'll be a snap. Particularly since I'm only taking 4 regular courses this coming term. I made arrangements last term when I took an extra one so I'd have an easier time this Sept when I'm going to be really busy anyway, what with the part-time job and all. I'm also hoping to have the time to get back out to the big city to see you and Mom and Brenda, by the way. That'll be fun. Maybe we can get out to the Island again, like we did when we were kids.

Anyway, here's the info you need to do TerrorReg for me. You can see that it's pretty simple. You'll find the SC, CIN, and SN on the info I've sent, too. All you do is dial the number and then follow the prompts, just like you do for your own voice mail at the office. So just think that you're like one of those automatons I'm supposed to be learning to program here at Canberra. By the way, the job is just great. I'm learning all kinds of really neat stuff. I can't wait till I see you guys later on to tell you about it. The kind of stuff they're building out here is really awesome! In case you get stuck, I've sent a diagram of how TerrorReg actually works. And I've sent you a clipping from the MU calendar. By the way, you're going to need a bunch of numbers. My St# is 4226980878, and my PIN is 833848. Do you mind putting all this on your own Mastercard and I'll pay you back later in the summer. So you'd better have the card handy when you're phoning.

I'm going to need either one of the two accounting courses, and either one of the marketing courses, plus the two computer sci courses. If you can, I'd prefer to get my classes over with earlier rather than later, but sometimes it's hard to get the sections you want. Oh, please try to get me Goldberg and Cornelian, they're both really good.

I'll give you a call when I get back. Had to go to London over the weekend but I'll be back at work dark and early on Monday for that training session that keeps me from registering myself. So I guess I'll phone you after supper on Mon. Don't forget that you have to phone in my reg at 9 on Mon. If you leave it until later, a lot of the sections will likely be filled up and I won't get what I want. The whole thing should take you about half an hour I figure.

Thanks again, Dad! Love you guys!

Les

- a diagram, taken from MU's Fall 2000 calendar, of the T-Reg system (Figure 5.4);
- an extract from the course timetable (Figure 5.5).

Figure 5.4: Diagram of MU T-Reg System

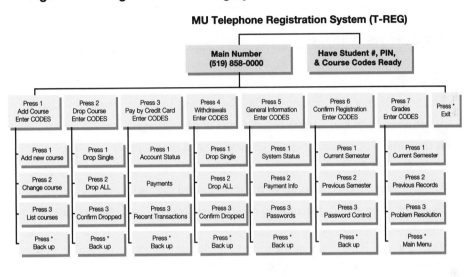

Figure 5.5: Extract from MU Course Timetable

ACTG2100 Principles of Accounting 2
A339940	001	M W	08:30 10:00 F2100	Shen, A.
A339941	002	M W	11:30 13:00 F2239	Sayers, R.
A339942	003	T H	10:00 11:30 F2100	Parl, R.
A339950	004	W F	15:30 17:00 R2240	Singh, B.

ACTG2200 Statistical Analysis 2
A489901	001	T H	10:00 11:30 F2100	Goldberg, P.
A489903	002	M W	10:00 11:30 F2230	Parl, C.
A489905	003	W F	08:30 10:00 R2240	Singh, E.

CMPP2500 Comparative Languages
| C11100 | 001 | T H | 10:00 11:30 P1000 | Harby, I. |
| C11103 | 002 | W F | 15:30 17:00 P1005 | Weischart, F. |

MKTG2112 Marketing Trends
M22001	001	W F	11:30 13:00 A1100	Gatmar, E.
M22003	002	T H	08:30 10:00 A1115	Dijani, F.
M22005	003	T F	10:00 11:30 A1115	Hollings, A.
M22007	004	T F	14:00 15:30 A1100	Porseau, R.

Figure 5.5 (continued)

MKTG2118 Research Methodology

M32222	001	M W	08:30 10:00 A2110		Dijani, F.
M32233	002	T F	08:30 10:00 A2100		Colworth, W.
M32244	003	W F	14:00 15:30 A1100		Atwal, A.

Issues to Think About

Lester's Note

Think about Lester's note in terms of the CMAPP attributes covered in this chapter.

1. What do you think of Lester's organization of his message?
2. Is the content of Lester's message in keeping with his purpose?
3. Is the form of the message appropriate given the audience?
4. Is the format effective in terms of the message and the audience?
5. Does the note reflect the aspects of accuracy, brevity, and clarity? Justify your answer.
6. Does the note reflect each of the three CAP elements (concise, accessible, precise)? Support your answer with examples.
7. What improvements would you make to the note?

T-Reg Diagram

1. To what extent do you think the diagram will benefit Lester's father?
2. Will the form and format of the diagram make the message easier for Lester's father to understand and use?
3. How well does the diagram match the information Lester provided about it in his note?

Course Timetable

You'll recall that you often have to strike a balance between precision and brevity, and that to do so you have to think about your context, your audience, and your purpose. As you answer the following questions, put yourself in Mr. Mont's position. Keep in mind the fact that he had informed his son that he was unfamiliar with MU.

1. How is Mr. Mont likely to react to the high level of accuracy, brevity, and concision expressed in the timetable information?
2. What elements might present the greatest difficulty for Mr. Mont? For example, to what extent will he understand what each of the columns represents?
3. What do you think Mr. Mont, as Lester's audience, needs and wants to know?

5.1   Give brief definitions of the following complementary CMAPP attributes:
      (a) 5WH
      (b) KISS
      (c) accessible
      (d) accuracy
      (e) brevity
      (f) clarity
      (g) concise
      (h) content
      (i) form
      (j) format
      (k) precise

5.2   Assume that you have decided to purchase a new computer system. Inventing all the
      details you may require (e.g., about the system and the vendor), create one message
      for each of the following audience/context combinations:
      (a) You are leaving yourself a note about purchase details so that you can later
           update your expense log (whether on paper or through a computer application
           such as Quicken or Money).
      (b) You are writing or e-mailing a friend, indicating your delight (and slight appre-
           hension) about the learning curve you will probably face.
      (c) You are informing a computer-literate instructor who has intimated that your
           computer-generated assignments could be more professional.

5.3   Using what you have learned about technical communications so far, create revised
      versions of each of the documents prepared by Lester in the case study.

5.4   Obtain a technical communications document from a private- or public-sector
      source. (You may use something you have received, such as a letter or a manual.)
      Illustrating your points with examples from the document, briefly assess its effective-
      ness in terms of the following:
      (a) 5WH
      (b) KISS
      (c) accessibility
      (d) accuracy
      (e) brevity
      (f) clarity
      (g) concision
      (h) content
      (i) form
      (j) format
      (k) precision

EXPLORING THE WEB

Here are some Web sites you might wish to investigate.

URL	DESCRIPTION
http://www.junketstudies.com/rulesofw/	The 11 Rules of Writing site offers useful guidelines for writing more effective prose, including "Omit unnecessary words" (rule 11). Examples of each rule and links to related sites are provided.
http://www.andromeda.rutgers.edu/~jlynch/Writing/links.html	Jack Lynch's Resources for Writers and Writing Instructors page offers a wealth of links to information on effective communications.
http://www.acronymfinder.com	The *Acronym Finder* is a searchable database that you can use to look up more than 131,000 acronyms/abbreviations and their meanings.
http://www.twnn.com/Wrs/Wrs2index.htm	The Acronyms and Abbreviations page links to more than a dozen sites dealing with acronyms and abbreviations.

Communication Strategies (1): News, Technical Description, and Simple Instructions

6

Based on their CMAPP analysis, technical communicators tend to follow certain strategies when creating their messages. In this chapter, we will examine the following common strategies:

1. News
   (a) Good news (also called *direct*)
   (b) Bad news (also called *indirect*)
   (c) Neutral news (also called *modified direct*)

2. Technical Description

3. Simple Instructions

Since choosing a strategy is, in effect, following a pattern (a template, in a sense), are you not simply "filling in the blanks" rather than creating original communication? Computer information systems development often follows a set sequence: investigation, analysis, design, development, testing, and implementation. While you might see that, too, as a template, it is a strategy that permits a consistent approach to a multitude of widely varied situations. Similarly, a particular communication strategy can be appropriate for limitless variations of context, message, audience, purpose, and product. And because it is a kind of road map to help reach a goal, you will normally select your strategy based in large part on your purpose.

News

Conveying Good News

The term "good news" applies to much more than the concept "Congratulations! You've just won the 649!" Rather, it encompasses a broad variety of ideas, including:

- You have been appointed to the position.
- You have been accepted into the apprenticeship program.
- Your shipment will arrive on time;
- The repairs are covered by your warranty.
- Your materials have arrived in our warehouse.
- We are reinstating your membership.

In effect, good news is any information that your audience is likely to be pleased to receive. To convey it, and regardless of the particular CMAPP product involved, you will normally construct your message to fit the *good news* or *direct* strategy.

This strategy comprises three parts:

1. *State the good news.* Present the news directly, simply, and clearly. In doing so, you will communicate that part of your message that responds to what your audience wants to know.

2. *Explain the situation.* In this segment of the good news strategy, you explain the main points and significant details of your message. When preparing the "meat" of your message, remember to take into account the complementary attributes of the CMAPP model—particularly 5WH—discussed in Chapter 5.

3. *Conclude on a positive note.* Although the second phase essentially completes your message, the conventions of the direct strategy dictate that you finish with a brief, positive comment of some kind. Your conclusion might be something as simple as "Thank you for choosing AEL"; it might be a reiteration of the good news itself, as in "Again, I would like to congratulate you on your appointment"; or it might be an expression of continued interest, as in "We look forward to serving you again in the future."

In the letter body shown in Figure 6.1, Angelos Methoulios, the coordinator of GTI's Internship Program, used the direct strategy to notify Karima Bhanji of her acceptance into the program. Notice that the first paragraph—one sentence only—conveys the good news; the second paragraph provides the explanation; and the final paragraph offers the positive conclusion. As always, the specifics of your own message will be dictated by your context, your audience, and your purpose.

Figure 6.1: Direct Strategy

I am pleased to inform you of your acceptance into the MIS Internship Program, which commences in September 2000.

According to your application, dated April 12, 2000, you meet all the entrance requirements for the program. Within the next week, therefore, I shall be sending you the Internship Program Registration Kit. It will inform you of the registration procedures you should undertake between July 5 and July 9 of this year. It will also answer general questions you might have about the program. Should you require further information, please do not hesitate to contact my office at 881-4412 during regular business hours.

In the meantime, please accept my personal congratulations on your acceptance into a program that has proven itself highly successful over the years. I look forward to working with you next term.

Conveying Bad News

You are likely to use the *bad news* or *indirect* strategy whenever you believe that your audience will *not* be pleased to receive your message. An extreme case of bad news would be "You're fired." Less dramatic examples might include:

- We will not be contacting you for an interview.

- The new parts for your equipment have still not arrived.

- The photocopier I bought from you still does not work properly.

- We are unable to ship the goods at this time.

- Your account is overdrawn.

- The text you requested is no longer in print.

Sometimes, as in the third example, your bad news would in fact be a *claim letter*—a statement of a problem with a product or service, coupled with a request for appropriate redress. The bad news conveyed in the fourth example might be followed up with an offer, on the part of the communicator, of some sort of compromise or recompense.

More complex than the good news strategy (and thus often resulting in a longer product), the bad news strategy is composed of five parts:

1. *Describe the context.* Use your first paragraph to explain the overall situation.

2. *Provide details.* Expand on your introductory paragraph by offering the main points and significant details that will prepare your audience for what follows.

3. *Deliver the bad news—tactfully.* Indicate the real purpose of your communication, but try to do so diplomatically. This will involve using language that is not as clear or direct as it could be. Communicators of bad news often use passive-voice constructions, since they permit a more oblique expression. If your language is too circuitous, however, your audience, who would presumably prefer good news to bad news, may misinterpret.

4. *Provide supplementary details.* This fourth phase is optional. Depending on the circumstances, you may wish to include additional information that will have the effect of further softening the blow.

5. *Offer conciliation and/or encouragement.* You will normally have a secondary purpose in this type of communication—namely, to maintain a working relationship with your audience. Consequently, you will offer some kind of "consolation prize" (e.g., a discount on repair charges or on goods shipped late, an offer of substitution, or an alternative course of action). At times, the consolation will be less tangible—an expression of your commitment to service, for example, or a confirmation of your continued interest.

In the letter body shown in Figure 6.2, Methoulios is communicating rejection rather than acceptance. Many technical communicators dislike such use of the indirect strategy, in large part because its oblique presentation of information deviates from the CMAPP attributes of brevity, concision, and precision. Nonetheless, use of this strategy is so widespread that a departure from its conventions may cause your audience to see your message as brusque or even rude.

Figure 6.2: Indirect Strategy

Thank you for your application, dated April 12, 2000, for the September 2000 Internship Program.

You will recall that the Internship Program Criteria Bulletin specifies a minimum of 4.11 for the overall GPA for the year previous to the Internship intake, and a mark of at least 80% in the relevant core introductory course, in your case INFO 101. Our records show that although you received a grade of 84% in INFO 101 last term, your mark of 66% in INFO 104 brought your overall GPA down to 3.87.

The Bulletin also specifies that a student's application must be accompanied by at least three letters of reference, two of which must be from GTI faculty. Only one of your referees, Ms. Pat Hayakawa, is on our faculty. Your two other referees, Dr. Janice Fleming and Mr. Edward Skoplar, appear to offer personal references only.

In light of the above, therefore, I am not currently able to further your application for the September 2000 intake in the MIS component of our Internship Program.

I do note that most of your marks were entirely satisfactory, and that Ms. Hayakawa's recommendation was highly favourable. Unfortunately, the number of applications we receive far exceeds the number of Internship Program places available; thus, we have found that we must apply the selection criteria quite rigorously.

Your record at GTI suggests that you are enthusiastic about a career in MIS, and that you show some promise in the field. Consequently, I would urge you to make all efforts to raise your GPA this coming term, and to seek appropriate references for the January 2001 intake. Grandstone's MIS Internship Program would welcome your reapplication.

Neutral News

A great many of the messages that form part of real-world communications convey neither good news nor bad news. They are, in effect, simply information. For example:

- Here is the catalogue you requested.
- The meeting will take place on March 15.
- The report details the following points.
- Fourteen members attended the seminar.
- The price is $125.

These types of messages follow a strategy that we will call the *neutral news* or *modified direct* strategy. Like the direct strategy, the modified direct strategy has three parts:

1. *Introduce the content and intent.* Briefly indicate what the communication is about, thereby situating your audience within the context.

2. *Explain the situation.* Provide whatever main points and significant details are required. Keep in mind the complementary CMAPP attributes of 5WH, brevity, concision, and precision.

3. *Conclude with an action request or summation.* Indicate clearly what you want your audience to do next. If you are looking for no real action on the part of your audience, provide a *brief* summation.

Angelos Methoulios's follow-up to his good news letter to Karima Bhanji appears in Figure 6.3. Note the brevity of the content. The delivery of neutral news in technical communications brings to mind the trademark line of Sergeant Joe Friday, hero of the 1950s television show *Dragnet*, "Just the facts, ma'am."

Figure 6.3: Modified Direct Strategy

Please find enclosed the registration kit for the MIS Internship Program commencing in 2000.

As you read through the entire kit, note in particular that (a) by June 16, you must arrange for your precommencement interview, which must take place on campus between July 5 and July 9; and (b) by July 16, you must have completed the automated course registration process (T-Reg).

In the kit, you will find detailed information regarding registration procedures, course and work-study requirements, and recommended extracurricular volunteer activities.

As soon as possible, please call my office at 881-4412 during regular business hours to set a date and time for your interview. I look forward to meeting with you.

Technical Description

A common task for a technical communicator is to describe something. The object might be as simple as a particular type of paper clip, described precisely for a patent application or a new manufacturer, or as complex as the avionics system of a newly designed military jet. Describing how something works rather than what it is like is termed *process description*. Examples of process description might include how a project plan is approved, how a cyclotron works, or how pricing is calculated.

You will apply the strategy for technical description to a variety of CMAPP products. In letters and memos, for example, you will frequently have to describe an issue; in reports, you may have to describe an object or a process. The structure of the description itself will vary according to the nature of what is being described. To describe items that can be perceived as linear (e.g., the general layout of a rec room you are building, or the stops along a proposed bus route), you would in most cases apply a simple technical description strategy.

Simple Technical Description

The strategy for simple technical description involves the following steps and considerations:

1. *Introduce the item.* Provide a brief general description that includes the name of the item and its main use(s).

2. *Specify all relevant details.* Describe the characteristics of the item in detail. Include all relevant details such as length, width, height, depth, weight, density, colour, texture, and shape. Choose vocabulary that is concrete rather than abstract, denotative rather than connotative, and precise rather than vague. For example:

Say	Instead of
Spherical (for three dimensions)	Circular (for two dimensions)
Cubical (for three dimensions)	Square (for two dimensions)
Pyramidal (for three dimensions)	Triangular (for two dimensions)
Helical (for three dimensions)	Spiral (for two dimensions)
The bus travels north on Main Street	The bus goes up Main Street
The sign is 750 metres straight ahead	The sign is a fair distance ahead
The marker lies at 49° 12'15" North	The marker is just north of the border
Anjou pears are available at $2.84/kg.	You can get some pears at a good price
The temperature reaches 150°C	It gets very hot

In consideration of your CMAPP analysis, you should choose an organization pattern that your audience will find logical and understandable. If you were describing a golf course, you might choose a *spatial* organization pattern (each of the holes in order). In describing weather or climate, you might choose a *chronological* pattern of month by month, or a *geographical* pattern of city by city. In describing a ballpoint pen, you might choose a *topical* organization (component by component).

If appropriate, include one or more visuals. (Be sure to apply what you learned in Chapter 4 about choosing or constructing effective visuals.) As well, pay particular attention to your use of document visuals; if your audience cannot readily follow and understand your description, your communication will not have achieved its purpose.

3. *Conclude.* A brief concluding statement may be used to sum up some aspect of the item.

The description of the letter opener in Figure 6.4 is an example of simple technical description. Note that the concluding statement in this description has to do with the item's purpose.

Figure 6.4: Simple Technical Description

A Letter Opener

A letter opener is a common household or office tool designed to be inserted under the unglued portion of the diagonal edge of a sealed envelope and then used to slice open the top edge of the envelope without damaging any documents inside. Letter openers are commonly made of wood, metal, plastic, or a combination of materials. Their utility is often enhanced by decorative characteristics.

The decorative letter opener shown exhibits the following characteristics:

Shape:	Slightly convex, bevelled, double-sided, double-edged sword blade surmounted by a curved-horned mountain goat whose four feet are planted on the base of the sword hilt.
	Mountain goat's features cast in relief on both front (shown in figure) and rear. For a letter opener, blade point and edges are sharp.
Composition:	Solid brass throughout.
Texture:	Sword blade smooth, burnished; noticeable bevel along longitudinal axis of sword blade. Mountain goat's hide and horns emphasized by unpolished serrations.
Maximum height:	17 cm from point of blade to top edge of horns.
Height of sword blade:	10.5 cm from point to top of hilt.
Maximum width:	4 cm horizontally from tip of goat's tail to outer edge of its horn.
Width of sword blade:	0.9 cm
Depth of sword hilt:	(thickest point of letter opener) 0.35 cm
Weight:	45 g
Appearance:	The style of the blade of the letter opener is reminiscent of medieval European sword blades, although lacking a suitably wide crossbar on the hilt. The relief sculpture of the mountain goat is slightly stylized, but readily recognizable and anatomically correct. Overall aspect is that of an antique style.

In conclusion, the blade of the letter opener is effective for its purpose. The mountain goat sculpture, however, presents an uncomfortable and unwieldy handle in the hand of an adult. Thus, this letter opener is designed as much for decorative appeal as for utility.

Complex Description

Some descriptions cannot be seen as linear because they involve several interdependent components. Examples might include the design of a new blood test, an automobile transmission, or the problem of acid rain. In developing your description, you will have to decide which ordering of the various components will best suit your audience, context, and purpose. Following the general guidelines for simple description, you can follow this strategy:

1. Introduce the item.
2. Describe the overall relationship among the components.
3. Describe in turn each component and any subcomponents.
    (a) Component A
    (b) Component B
        (i) Subcomponent B1
        (ii) Subcomponent B2
    (c) etc.
4. Review the interrelationships.
5. Conclude.

Computerized Hyperlinks

If you are engaged in computer- or Web-based technical description, you can employ a nonlinear approach by taking advantage of hyperlinks. These familiar features of Web pages give users immediate access to key areas throughout the site. The addition of graphics, sound, animation, and/or video can further enhance the effectiveness of such description. Figure 6.5 shows the links that might be included in a description of an item containing only three components, one of which includes four subcomponents.

Simple Instructions

In your professional and your private life, you will undoubtedly have to write simple instructions from time to time. Examples would include instructions a fellow employee is to follow while you are on vacation, guidelines for the tenants of a building you own, or directions to your home for an out-of-town guest. Since instructions by definition refer to processes, they might be considered a special class of process description. Their purpose, however, is different. In standard process description, you want your audience to see or understand how something works; in instructions, you want your audience to be able to do something. This distinctive purpose, of course, affects the specific message.

Figure 6.5: Hyperlinked Description

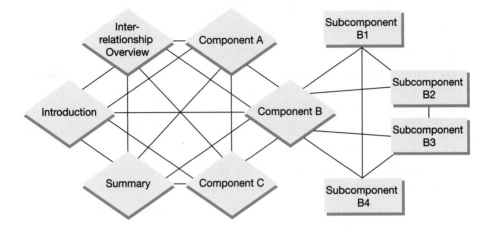

Note the differences between these two examples:

At this stage, it is crucial that the power light be green. Gear A now activates gear B. Immediately thereafter, cam C, turning on shaft D, lifts rod E 3.5 cm, causing it to make contact with plate F.

CAUTION: Ensure that the power light shows green before undertaking the following steps. If it is not green, do not proceed; call the supervisor at once.

1. Allow gear A to activate gear B.
2. Turn shaft D clockwise, until cam C lifts rod E 3.5 cm, so that it makes contact with plate F.

The first example is appropriate for process description, the second for instructions. Notice that:

1. We recognize an instruction (which is similar to a command or an order) by the use of the imperative mood.
2. Instructional steps are easier to follow when they are numbered.
3. A warning must be readily visible (remember "accessibility"), must appear before the step to which it applies, and must be clearly distinguished from the instructions themselves.

Strategy

The strategy for instructions is fundamentally the same as that for technical description.

1. Introduce the topic and provide any necessary preamble.
2. Specify all relevant details—the instruction steps themselves.
3. Conclude.

As you plan and create the instructions, ask yourself the following questions:

1. Do I understand the process? (It is unlikely your audience will if you don't.)

2. Who is my specific audience?

3. What level of technicality is appropriate?

4. How do I plan to reproduce these instructions? Think about such things as the legibility of photocopies, and the use of colour. For example, a diagram of electrical wiring may depend on colour distinction.

5. How are the instructions to be distributed? Are they to be posted on a wall, included with a purchased item, attached to a memo?

6. How should my audience deal with any confidential information such as code numbers?

7. Have I indicated how long it should take to complete the instructions?

8. Have I given a complete list of required equipment and/or materials? (Your audience will not appreciate discovering at step 8 that a specific tool is needed.)

9. Am I beginning at the appropriate spot or should I begin earlier or later in the process? For example, will my audience already know how to reach what I indicate as the first step? (Your CMAPP analysis will help you answer this question.)

10. Do I need visuals? Consider number, position, size, legibility, scale, and level of detail.

11. Is my numbering system clear and consistent?

12. Is the order of the steps the most logical?

13. Is it the safest sequence?

14. Are warnings or cautions properly placed, highly visible, and clearly worded?

15. Have I indicated how subcomponents relate to major elements, and have I expressed them in a logical and workable order?

16. Have I indicated when and how the audience can interrupt the process if necessary? (Consider such circumstances as bathroom breaks and quitting time.)

17. Have I distinguished between instructions and notes or other information? (Remember to use the imperative mood for instructions, and to make effective use of document visuals.)

18. Should I provide hints to help my audience recognize whether particular steps have been successfully completed?

19. Is my language as precise and specific as possible?

20. Have I tested the instructions myself?

21. Can I have the instructions tested by someone who does not yet know how to perform the tasks involved?

6A Acceptance Letter from GTI

Situation

Karima Bhanji is a 20-year-old student from the Ottawa suburb of Orleans. She had moved to the West Coast and registered at Grandstone Technical Institute because she wanted to take its highly regarded two-year Management Information Systems (MIS) Diploma Program with Internship option. Students who do well in their first year often gain a semester of real-world work experience with participating firms. After graduation, some of these students have been able to obtain full-time employment with the companies in which they served as interns.

Midway through her first year of the MIS program, Karima had applied for admission to GTI's Internship Program. On May 23, she receives the letter shown in Figure 6.6. She is distressed to discover that:

■ The letter had been sent to her permanent address in Ontario rather than to her temporary address in Surrey, British Columbia.

■ Her parents had redirected the letter, but postal delays had taken their toll.

■ She has thus missed the deadline for confirming her acceptance of admission to the Internship Program.

Issues to Think About

1. What communication strategy has Methoulios used in his letter to Karima? Give reasons for your answer.

2. Has Methoulios provided the right amount of information? Justify your answer.

3. How would you have changed the letter?

4. What would you suggest Karima do now?

5. What specific CMAPP product(s) would you recommend she use? Why?

6B Rejection Letter from RAI

Situation

Jerry Quelton grew up in Montreal but moved to Scarborough, Ontario, in 1979. By 1995, he was in his late forties and the divorced father of two grown children who were both living abroad. With more free time on his hands, Jerry began to make regular visits to Montreal, reestablishing old friendships. Eventually, he decided to leave his well-paying job selling luxury cars at Slipstream Motors in downtown Toronto and to seek work in his old home town.

Figure 6.6: GTI Acceptance Letter

Internship Office
9999–2011th Street
Langley BC V1V 0M0
(604) 444-4412
Fax: (604) 444-6754

May 2, 2000

Ms. Karima Bhanji
1152 St. Ambrose Crescent
Orleans ON K2V 2B7

Dear Ms. Bhanji:

Congratulations on your successful application to Grandstone's Internship Program.

I have examined your transcripts and studied the recommendation report submitted on your behalf by your instructor, Pat Hayakawa. In the light of these documents, I have registered you in the MIS Group of the Internship Program.

Enclosed are profiles of the local firms among whom we hope to find a two- to three-month work placement for you in the second semester of your second year. Please examine the company profiles and think about how one or more of them might benefit from the skills and personal qualities you feel you possess. Note that you will have to put your request for placement with particular companies in writing when you submit your Internship Placement Preference form in early June.

Note also that you must phone or fax me within the next two weeks to confirm your acceptance; otherwise, we may have to allocate your place to another student.

I look forward to working with you during your Internship Program, and offer my best wishes for your success.

Yours sincerely,

Angelos Methoulios

Angelos Methoulios
Encl.

c. Mariana Lembo, Assistant Registrar

It was around this time that Jerry's boss at Slipstream, Reg Planck, offered the name of a former acquaintance, Francine Deshôtels, now vice-president of Automobiles Radisson de Montréal. Jerry wrote to Deshôtels to ask for a job. About three weeks later, he received the letter shown in Figure 6.7.

Issues to Think About

1. Which communications strategy has Deshôtels used in this letter? How can you tell?

2. The letter contains no specific references to the fact that Jerry actually applied for a job—or that Deshôtels has rejected him. What specific words or phrases in the letter would lead Jerry to conclude that his application was rejected?

3. Do you think Deshôtels thought about CMAPP when she was writing? Do you think she had a secondary purpose as well? How does the tone of her letter affect the context?

4. From what you already know about RAI's hierarchy, explain the "copy" indicator in terms of the CMAPP analysis that Deshôtels might have conducted.

EXERCISES

6.1 Give brief definitions of good news, bad news, and neutral news.

6.2 Give the alternative name for each of the strategies named in question 6.1.

6.3 Specify the components of the good news strategy.

6.4 Specify the components of the bad news strategy.

6.5 Specify the components of the neutral news strategy.

6.6 Briefly explain why some technical communicators dislike the bad news strategy.

6.7 Reexamine the acceptance letter from GTI to Karima Bhanji in Figure 6.6. Suppose that Methoulios had wanted to accept Karima's application, but that there had been problems with her transcript. What strategy might he have applied? Construct an outline of the possible contents of this alternative letter.

6.8 Give a brief definition of simple technical description.

6.9 Specify the components of the strategy for simple technical description.

6.10 Provide three or more examples showing the distinction between vague and precise terminology.

6.11 Identify a process connected with your job (if you are working) or with your educational institution. (Examples might include how orders are filled, how standardized tests are conducted, how the staffing process works, or how you register for a particular

Figure 6.7: Rejection Letter from RAI

Radisson Automobiles Radisson

Automobiles Radisson de Montréal
855 boulevard René-Lévesque ouest Montréal PQ H3B 9A0
Tél: (514) 858-1818 Fax: (514) 858-1833 E-mail: radiss.mtl@cars.com

2 February, 2000

Mr. Jerry Quelton
#1345–1219 Lawrence Ave. E.
Scarborough ON M5X 2A3

Dear Mr. Quelton:

I want to thank you for taking the trouble to write to me last month, and to apologize for my delay in responding.

I have taken the liberty of sharing your letter of January 3, 2000, with Michel Gagné, our general manager, and with Maurice Duclos, our sales manager. We were all impressed with your success at Slipstream, and with the considerable expertise you have acquired in 15 years of selling high-quality automobiles.

You were perhaps unaware of the fact that the great majority of our new car sales are in the mid-range: our biggest sellers have traditionally been two Global products, the Minotaur and the Whirlwind. In recent years, we have reduced the already small number of more expensive vehicles that we offer our mainly middle-class customers.

Consequently, I must regretfully note that Automobiles Radisson de Montréal cannot be particularly optimistic at this time. Should conditions here change, I shall of course think of you again.

In the meantime, thank you again for your letter, and for the greetings from my old friend Reg Planck.

Yours sincerely,

Francine Deshôtels

Francine Deshôtels
Vice-présidente

cc: G. Radisson

program.) Using visuals if appropriate, create a technical description detailing that process.

6.12 Specify the components of the strategy for simple instructions.

6.13 How does an instruction (or a command) differ from a description?

6.14 Locate a set of instructions used where you work or go to school. Using the list of 21 questions on page 104, assess the effectiveness of the instructions.

EXPLORING THE WEB

Here are some Web sites you might wish to investigate.

URL	DESCRIPTION
http://www.io.com/~hcexres/tcm1603/acchtml/acctoc.html	This page is the table of contents for *The Online Technical Writing Course Guide*, a text "used by students in online technical-communication courses worldwide." The online textbook includes the sections "Applications of Technical Writing," "Document Design," and "Processes and Guidelines in Technical Writing."
http://www.io.com/~hcexres/tcm1603/acchtml/instrux.html	This page in *The Online Technical Writing Course Guide* provides comprehensive, practical advice on writing instructions.
http://www.stc.org/region8/sdc/www/01cezar.htm	Offered by the San Diego chapter of the Society for Technical Communication, this page features an article titled "Revisiting the Foundations: Technical Communication and Rhetoric." The article, by Cezar Ornatowski, offers a concise explanation of how traditional rhetoric is applicable to contemporary technical writing.
http://www.howstuffworks.com	Created by author and former computer science teacher Marshall Brain, this interesting and unusual site presents a wide variety of process descriptions (often enhanced by graphics and animation), with topics ranging from electric motors and steam engines to microprocessors and the effects of caffeine.

7 Communication Strategies (2): Persuasion

This chapter examines two common CMAPP strategies for persuasive communication: (1) persuasion that targets the intellect (logical argumentation), and (2) persuasion that targets the emotions (AIDA).

Persuasive Strategies

Persuasive strategies are vital to a variety of contexts, from advertising and marketing to analytical reports and meetings. While some persuasive strategies depend on logic and argumentation and others more on emotional appeals, all such strategies are based on establishing a connection with an audience and providing something that the audience will relate to and respond to.

Intellect versus Emotion

Many years ago, I attended a talk given to an audience of professionals—mainly electrical and electronics engineers. The speaker was trying to convince them of the value of what was then a new and unproven technology—fibre-optic cable in the telecommunications industry. His basic approach was to provide a host of facts, examples, and statistics to bolster his message of the advantages of fibre-optic cable. The technical expertise of his audience was his rationale for persuading them by appealing to their intellect. This strategy attempts to convince through logic, supporting assertions through reason and/or examples. Consequently, it relies heavily on the denotative value of its words, and on the precise structure of its arguments.

Now consider most television advertising. Instead of being presented with a wealth of information, you are invited to sense, to feel, to experience (in some unreal way), and to believe. The message uses words of high connotative value and features dramatic images. Few facts intrude—after all, is one brand of sugar-coated cereal significantly different from another? Even in cases of real differences—between a small Chevrolet and a small Porsche, for example—the message relies primarily on intangibles: the "feel of the road," the "excitement of the drive," and so forth. Such persuasion is commonly expressed through slogans such as "whiter than white," "nine out of ten doctors" (whoever they might be), "tried, tested, and true," and "built for the human race." All these slogans would collapse if subjected to logical analysis. Of course, this type of persuasion is not meant to be parsed or analyzed; it targets your emotions, not your intellect.

Targeting the Intellect: Logical Argumentation

The essence of an appeal to the intellect is the logical progression from the assertion of a claim to its proof. This process follows one of two paths: deductive strategy or inductive strategy.

110

Deductive Strategy If your CMAPP analysis determines that your audience already knows the issue under consideration and/or is likely to react favourably to your message, you should probably use the *deductive* strategy, which comprises three parts:

1. *Make your assertion.* Provide clear statements. Remember accuracy, brevity, concision, and precision.

2. *Justify your assertion.* Your justification must consist of a series of cohesive points, organized chronologically, topically, or spatially. Each point should be the logical consequence of those that have come before. (Think of your argument in terms of the construction of a building, with a solid foundation required for each successive story.)

3. *Conclude.* Briefly summarize your argument. Then refer your audience to the necessary conclusion—your initial assertion. (You have thus come full circle: from your claim, through corroboration, and back to your claim.)

Note that the length and complexity of the second component will depend on your context and your message, while your level of technicality will derive from your audience analysis.

Inductive Strategy   If your audience lacks the background necessary to follow your reasoning easily and/or is likely to be averse to receiving your message, you should likely use the *inductive* strategy, which comprises the following parts:

1. *Introduce the issue.* Briefly describe the issue under consideration, situating it in a way that will be relevant to your audience.

2. *Provide your arguments.* Make your points just as you would if using the deductive strategy: each point must stem logically from what has come before.

3. *Draw your conclusion.* Briefly summarize your arguments, and then state your assertion as their logical conclusion.

Figures 7.1 and 7.2 are two versions of a persuasive memo that Melinda Shaw, Radisson Automobiles' Regina Vice-President, might send to Gilles Radisson, the firm's Chief Executive Officer. Having received Radisson's memo regarding the reorganization (see Case Study 2B on page 26), Shaw would like to persuade him to at least postpone the reorganization until discussions can be held with the vice-presidents. The first version uses the deductive strategy. It reflects Shaw's recognition of Radisson's understanding of the issue, and presumes that he will be amenable to feedback from his senior executives. The second uses the inductive strategy. Its premise is that Radisson may be unaware of all the implications of his decision and/or may view Shaw's remarks as inappropriate criticism from a subordinate. Note that the different strategies presume different contexts and thus generate apparently different products, whose basic message, however, remains the same.

Syllogism In making your arguments, you can take advantage of a standard component of logical argumentation known as the syllogism. A syllogism comprises a

Figure 7.1: Persuasive Memo—Deductive Strategy

Radisson Automobiles Radisson

2102–11th Avenue
Regina SK S2N 0H7
(306) 433-9900
Fax: (306) 432-6534

Regina Dealership

Memorandum

99/09/24

To: Gilles Radisson

From: Melinda Shaw   *mS*

Re: Reorganization

cc.

I have read your memo of September 8, 1999, to vice-presidents and general managers, regarding RAI's reorganization for January 1, 2000. I would like to suggest you consider postponing implementation.

Over the years, vice-presidents have developed good working relationships with the Board of Directors. While I personally feel that reporting to a single individual—you—rather than to a group will make my job easier, I am concerned that abruptly severing our long-standing ties with the Board may lead to the interruption of important projects across the country. Further, I suspect that many vice-presidents will be resentful of the "surprise" nature of the announcement.

We vice-presidents have come to rely on our general managers, who seem to trust and respect us in return. The success of these relationships is in large part due to their having ready access to us in their respective jurisdictions. I am certain they will be dismayed to unexpectedly find themselves accountable to Céline Robillard in Ottawa, a great distance away for most of them. I think that many are liable to infer that the company suddenly lacks faith in their competence and loyalty.

Successfully implementing the reorganization will, I fear, require far more than the "administrative details" to which your memo refers. The new structure will impose fundamental changes in the way we manage our dealerships. Consequently, I would ask you to reconsider your January 1, 2000, deadline, so that the vice-presidents could meet with you for full discussion.

I would be grateful if you would communicate your decision within the next two weeks.

Figure 7.2: Persuasive Memo—Inductive Strategy

2102–11th Avenue
Regina SK S2N 0H7
(306) 433-9900
Fax: (306) 432-6534

Regina Dealership

Memorandum

99/09/24

To: Gilles Radisson

From: Melinda Shaw   *m♀*

Re: Reorganization

cc.

I have read your memo of September 8, 1999, to vice-presidents and general managers, regarding RAI's reorganization for January 1, 2000.

Successfully implementing the reorganization may well require far more than the "administrative details" to which your memo refers. The new structure will impose fundamental changes in the way we manage our dealerships.

Over the years, vice-presidents have developed good working relationships with the Board of Directors. While I personally feel that reporting to a single individual—you—rather than to a group will make my job easier, I am concerned that abruptly severing our long-standing ties with the Board may lead to the interruption of important projects across the country. Further, I suspect that many vice-presidents will be resentful of the "surprise" nature of the announcement.

We vice-presidents have come to rely on our general managers, who seem to trust and respect us in return. The success of these relationships is in large part due to their having ready access to us in their respective jurisdictions. I am certain they will be dismayed to unexpectedly find themselves accountable to Céline Robillard in Ottawa, a great distance away for most of them. As well, I think that many are liable to infer that the company suddenly lacks faith in their competence and loyalty.

Consequently, I would ask you to reconsider your January 1, 2000, deadline, and to arrange for all vice-presidents to meet soon so as to allow full discussion.

I would be grateful if you would communicate your decision within the next two weeks.

major premise (an overall truth), a *minor premise* (something specific that derives from the major premise), and a *conclusion* (something that results from the application of the major premise to the minor premise). For example:

Major Premise:	All published college textbooks are printed on paper.
Minor Premise:	This book is a published college textbook.
Conclusion:	This book is printed on paper.

A syllogism is invalid when the major premise is a specific truth from which the minor premise does not derive, as in the following example:

Major Premise:	The Edmonton telephone directory is thicker than an issue of *Maclean's* magazine.
Minor Premise:	This textbook is thicker than last week's issue of *Maclean's*.
Conclusion:	This textbook is an Edmonton telephone directory.

A related flaw occurs when there are faulty connections between two or more of the three elements, as in the following examples:

Major Premise:	All dogs have four legs.
Minor Premise:	My cat has four legs.
Conclusion:	My cat is a dog.

Major Premise:	Robotics technology can now undertake many dangerous manufacturing tasks formerly performed by workers.
Minor Premise:	After his injury, my father could no longer work on the blast-furnace floor.
Conclusion:	My father's job was cut because of the introduction of robotics technology.

Logical Fallacies   Logical argumentation can be undermined by other weaknesses as well, including what are referred to as logical fallacies. One such fallacy is known as *faulty consequence,* or *post hoc ergo propter hoc* (a Latin phrase meaning "after this, therefore because of this"). The basis of this fallacy is the assumption that something seen to happen after something else is necessarily its consequence. For example, I could give reliable evidence that for several days last year, CBC Radio's national news began just after I watched the sunset from my window. If I were to try to make the case that the CBC national news was triggered by the arrival of sunset in my area, I would be committing the error of faulty consequence.

Another logical fallacy is known as *hasty generalization*—postulating a general truth that is based on insufficient evidence. You would be guilty of this logical fallacy if you told your audience of two separate occasions on which an ATM dispensed less cash than the amount shown on the receipt, and then asserted that ATMs are therefore unreliable. Another example would be citing the tragic results of a head-on collision and then claiming that the city's roads are unsafe for public use.

Undisprovable theory is the logical fallacy of claiming that something is true simply because it cannot be proved false. For example, the statement "The designers of the Egyptian pyramids were inspired by telepathic communication from aliens" might sound absurd to you, but you cannot logically *disprove* it. Equally undisprovable is the claim that since the turnover to January 1, 2000 did not produce computer catastrophe, Canadian business and government should not have spent the fortune they did on Y2K readiness.

Another logical fallacy is *false dichotomy*—the presentation of an issue as being either white or black, when in fact it could be any of a multitude of shades of grey. A true dichotomy (not a logical fallacy) could be exemplified by the statement "The light switch is on or off" (it cannot be both on and off at the same time). An example of false dichotomy would be the claim that if someone is not tall, he or she is short. There are two problems with this claim: first, the terms "tall" and "short" are imprecise and highly subjective; and second, a significant proportion of the world's population is neither tall nor short. Another common example is the statement "If you're not for us, you're against us." Obviously, one can take any number of stands that are neither truly "for" nor truly "against" something. A similar example would be the claim "A vote for her opponent is a vote against democracy."

If you were to try to persuade your audience that pornography is evil because it is inherently pornographic, you would be guilty of *tautology* (making an assertion based on a redundancy). The problem, of course, is that you have not really explained what pornography means. Another example would be claiming that your product is better simply because it is superior to your opponent's.

Logical fallacies can appear convincing, particularly to an audience of nonexperts. As an ethical communicator, however, you should guard against them. (And as a consumer, you should be alert to their use by others.) Remember that logical argumentation demands that your premise and your arguments not just *appear* sound, but *be* sound.

Targeting the Emotions: AIDA

Particularly apt for persuasion that targets the emotions is a strategy called AIDA, an acronym that stands for attention, interest, desire, and action. Although you can examine the elements independently, they tend to function as a kind of continuum, with each element leading into the next.

Attention   Your audience is constantly being bombarded with persuasive material, whether on television, radio, billboards, or the Web. Thus, if you want your message to be noticed, it must catch your audience's attention. In print documents, you can make use of the following techniques:

- Colour—coloured paper stock, coloured type or graphics, sharply contrasting colours

- Shape—nonstandard envelope and/or stationery, contrasting shapes on the page

- Font—decorative or otherwise unusual typeface or font size

- Visual—eye-catching graphic or unusual document visuals

- Wording—words such as "free," "new," and "improved" are standards (look at the products on any supermarket shelf); words or phrases such as "Congratulations!" and "Are you a winner?" can also be effective (note that connotation plays a larger role than denotation).

As well, cultural preferences and cultural referents (discussed in Chapter 1) are likely to play a role in what catches your audience's attention.

Interest   After obtaining your audience's attention, you must find a way of sustaining that attention by generating interest. You might ask, for example, "How would you like to see the world from your very own yacht?" You generate interest in this sense by eliciting from your audience a feeling of curiosity about what your message is about. Once again, connotation is important; you are not trying to inform your audience, but to elicit an emotional response from them. As is the case with the *attention* element, your audience's cultural background will in part determine the effectiveness of this step. Always ask yourself the appropriate CMAPP questions.

Desire   Now that your audience is willing to examine what you have to communicate, you need to convince them that they *must* have whatever it is you are offering. Advertisers traditionally create desire by suggesting that using their product or service will make us richer, stronger, healthier, happier, more beautiful or handsome, more sophisticated, and so forth. We see this kind of message embodied in the television ads featuring young people whose happiness is dependent on a particular brand of beer. The aim of such ads is not to provide concrete information, but to target emotions.

Advertising slogans such as "Coke. It's the real thing!," "Be part of the Pepsi generation!," "Mazda: it just feels right!," and "Just do it!" mean nothing in rational terms. In emotional terms, however, they are memorable, and they work. In these and other slogans, connotation speaks more loudly than denotation, evocative abstractions replace specific detail, and precision yields to vague promise. Experience has shown these tactics to be highly effective; as consumers, we are not all susceptible to the *same* emotional stimuli, but we are susceptible.

Action   Once you have persuaded your audience to desire your product or service, you must tell them how to satisfy that desire. You need a clear call to action, which could range from the somewhat pushy "Operators are standing by. Call now!" to the more restrained "We hope to hear from you soon." Unless you specify an action, your persuasive message may be lost.

Consolidation   Some companies that have achieved widespread product recognition are able to consolidate all four elements of the AIDA strategy into a single, implicit message. Consider the representation of the Coca-Cola ad in Figure 7.3, for example. When you look at this simple representation, you are likely to imbue it with the product's well-recognized colours. A billboard containing only these words encapsulates attention, interest, desire, and action: you notice the ad (from prior recognition), it stimulates your interest (perhaps to see if it's any different from others), it creates desire (unless you happen to be a fan of a rival product), and implies action (almost everyone in North America knows how and where to buy a Coke).

Figure 7.3: Representation of a Coca-Cola Ad

The representation of the McDonald's ad (shown in Figure 7.4) accomplishes the same task. The single word successfully encapsulates all four AIDA components, largely because of the company's well-established brand recognition. A billboard featuring the word "pizza" attracts your attention (you may see specific colours in your mind's eye), stimulates your interest (the unusual shape of the individual characters), generates desire (unless you dislike pizza or McDonald's), and suggests action (do you know anyone who doesn't know where to find a McDonald's?).

Figure 7.4: Representation of a McDonald's Ad

Pi33a

A Note on Ethics

That AIDA can be a highly persuasive strategy is reflected in the fact that North American companies spend billions of dollars each year creating persuasive messages.

But is this type of persuasion ethical in the sense discussed in Chapter 1? Is it a deliberate attempt to deceive and therefore unethical? Advertisers might argue that it cannot truly be deceitful to suggest that a successful life depends on a floor that is "cleaner than clean" (whatever that means) because any thinking adult would be able to recognize the absurdity of the claim. In implementing AIDA, aren't advertisers merely asking a reasonable person to suspend disbelief long enough to enjoy a moment of whimsy?

These are difficult questions without easy answers. What cannot be disputed is that learning how the AIDA strategy is applied makes us less susceptible to being unconsciously influenced by it, and that in itself is worthwhile.

CASE STUDY

Persuasive Messages from MUSAEx

Situation

At a series of meetings of the Mississauga University Student Association Executive, the executive president, Dorothy Palliser, has argued in favour of a special Student Association "technology" levy of $25 per term. This money would be used to purchase MUSA-owned computers, peripherals, and software for student use on MUSA premises. The hardware would be linked both to MU's student-accessible network (currently available only through computers in the MU Library) and to the World Wide Web.

Despite strong opposition to her proposal, Palliser has managed to convince the executive to put the issue to a student vote. MUSAEx has also set aside a small amount for "campaign fees" to be used by both sides in the debate. Part of Palliser's strategy is to send a form letter to every student. Seeking advice, she contacts Aimée Bouthillier, MU's senior development officer, and asks for assistance. Bouthillier agrees to help. A week later, she provides two versions of text for a form letter, along with a note that says, in part, "Since you know your audience better than I do, Dorothy, you'll have to decide between these." The two texts that Bouthillier created are shown in Figures 7.5 and 7.6.

Issues to Think About

1. Why do you think Bouthillier created two different versions? How would you explain her motivation in terms of context, audience, purpose, form (particularly the level of technicality), and format?

2. Examine each of the versions in terms of message. What differences can you identify?

3. How do the two versions differ with respect to level of technicality?

4. Does either version target intellect? If so, would you say the argumentation is deductive or inductive? Give reasons for your answer.

5. Does either version target emotions? If so, what specific features suggest this? (Think about the AIDA strategy and its emphasis on connotation, abstractions, etc.)

Figure 7.5: Form Letter, Version A

Dear <Studentfirstname>,

As a mature university student, you will already have recognized the increasingly important role played by technology. From the efficient production of professional-quality class materials such as essays and projects, to the research opportunities available through the World Wide Web, computer literacy and ready computer access have become a *sine qua non* for academic success.

If you have home access to today's generation of hardware and software, you are undoubtedly aware of your advantage, and concerned about those among your fellow students who lack such access. Although university computers are available— on a first-come, first-served basis—in a few campus locations, access to the university network and to the World Wide Web is available only through the computers found on the second floor of the library. Many of you have been frustrated by the strong competition for use of those computers, or have had your grades lowered because of poor-quality printers.

As a member of both the university community and the community at large, you are keenly aware of the increasing costs of higher education. Your fees have risen more than 23% over the last two years. Over the same period, the Student Association has managed to mitigate the impact of higher fees by imposing an 8% cap on increases to your Student Association allocation.

The fact that you have enrolled at Mississauga University demonstrates that you are committed to the long-term benefits of a postsecondary education, that you are willing to work hard to achieve those benefits, and that you appreciate their cost. Access to computers and the Web has become an indispensable feature of quality education. A modest $25 increase in the Student Association levy is a small price to pay for increased access for MU students.

When called upon to exercise your franchise, let reason and compassion prevail over parsimony: vote in favour of the MUSA technology allocation.

WHO CARES?

I think you do, <Studentfirstname>, because it's shameful!

Costs have soared, but you still need your education! Student fees keep sky-rocketing, even though the Student Association tries to put some kind of lid on the cauldron by holding the line on MUSA allocation. And what's the result? You still can't get to do the work you need to do when you need to do it.

You can't succeed unless your work looks good. But what if you don't have the latest hardware and software at home? You can use the campus computer rooms, but how often can you actually get in? How often can you get the computers to work? How often do the printers actually have ink or toner?

And what if you have to connect to MU's network, or if you absolutely have to do research on the Web? Well, the library lets you sit at one of its dozen stations—for less time than it takes to download just about any page or file you really need!

So, what's the solution, <Studentfirstname>? MUSAEx wants to have the computers that students really need. And we want them here, in our own MUSA rooms, hooked up to the MU network, wired to the Web, and available 24 hours a day to any registered MU student.

<Studentfirstname>, I know you care. Help us show MU that we all do! Make sure that we **all** have the technology we need. When the ballot boxes come out, vote for the $25 ticket that'll buy everyone access to a computer!

6. Both versions include the indication of a mail-merge code, <Studentfirstname>.

   (a) How do the two versions differ in their use of this item?

   (b) In what ways do you think the uses are effective or ineffective?

EXERCISES

7.1 Explain the difference between targeting the intellect and targeting the emotions.

7.2 Explain when you might use the following:
   (a) deductive strategy
   (b) inductive strategy

7.3 Identify and briefly describe the three components of a syllogism.

7.4 Provide an example of each of the following:
   (a) valid syllogism
   (b) invalid syllogism

7.5 Identify and briefly explain two or more types of logical fallacies, using an example to illustrate each.

7.6 Identify and briefly explain the four components of the AIDA strategy.

7.7 Choose a magazine advertisement or a television commercial, and assess its use of each of the four AIDA components. Then discuss your chosen example of AIDA persuasion in terms of ethics.

EXPLORING THE WEB

Here are some Web sites you might wish to investigate.

URL	DESCRIPTION
http://spider.hcob.wmich.edu/bis/faculty/bowman/persuade.html	Understanding Persuasion, created by Joel P. Bowman of Western Michigan University, offers an excellent description and explanation of approaches to persuasion in the context of North American business.
http://www.hu.mtu.edu/~dsulliva/rn/	The Rhetoric Notes home page of Dale Sullivan of Michigan Technological University (MTU) offers links to information drawn largely from work by MTU graduate students, on the use of rhetoric and logical argumentation.
http://www.hu.mtu.edu/~dsulliva/rn/cn/reason.htm	Basic Helps for Practical Reasoning, also by Dale Sullivan, offers concise explanations of various types of logical argumentation.

http://owl.english.purdue.edu/Files/123.html	Argumentation/Persuasion: Logic in Argumentative Writing (part of a collection of instructional materials used in the Purdue University Online Writing Lab) provides clear explanations of the constituents of logical arguments, the means by which they can be constructed, and the fallacies that often plague them. The page also offers links to additional resources.
http://staff.gc.maricopa.edu/~mdinchak/eng101/arglearn.htm	Learn about Argumentation offers concise explanations of different approaches to logical argumentation, as well as related links.
http://www.intrepidsoftware.com/fallacy/welcome.htm	Developed by Stephen Downes, a Canadian academic and consultant who describes himself as an "information architect," this is the home page of Stephen's Guide to Logical Fallacies.
http://newsline.byu.edu/communications/faculty/whiting/comms310/toulmin.html	This article on what is known as the Toulmin model of reasoning is the work of Gordon Whiting, a member of the Communications Faculty of Brigham Young University in Utah.

Common Products (1): Letters, Memos, Faxes, and E-mail

In this chapter, we look at letters, memos, faxes, and e-mail. These common CMAPP products share two principal characteristics: (a) they rarely exceed a few pages in length; and (b) they tend to follow an established format.

While people have been sending each other letters for hundreds of years, and memorandums have been used in the business environment for close to a century, faxes have become ubiquitous only in the last decade or so. The use of e-mail, spurred by cheap and convenient access to the Internet, has exploded only in the last five years.

We might define the above-mentioned CMAPP products as follows.

- *Letter* A letter is a hard-copy written communication that is directed from outside an organization to an audience within that organization. Although letters normally contain only text, they can include visuals as well.

- *Memo* The word "memo" is an abbreviation of "memorandum," a Latin word meaning "something to be remembered." A memo is written communication that is used internally within an organization. Hard-copy versions are commonplace, although electronic transfer of memos is gaining popularity. Memos tend to consist of only text, but like letters can include visuals.

- *Fax* The word "fax" is an abbreviation of "facsimile," meaning exact copy or replica. A fax is written communication that is often created and received as hard copy, but transmitted electronically (most commonly across telephone lines). Faxes may contain only text, text and visuals, or only visuals.

- *E-mail* E-mail (short for "electronic mail") is written communication that is created, transmitted, and received electronically. While an e-mail message normally includes only text, it's possible to attach to it a copy of almost any computer file, and some e-mail applications permit the inclusion of visuals.

Letters

Imagine it is 1850, 17 years before Confederation. Gilles Radisson's great-grandfather, Marcel, sells high-quality carts and carriages. His company (RAI's predecessor), Les Carrosses Radisson/Radisson Quality Coaches, does business (in both French and English) with a select clientele all over the nine-year-old Province of Canada.

Marcel would have had only one way of communicating with Marcus Dougherty, the president of Toronto Township College (the predecessor of Mississauga University). Sitting in his candlelit Quebec City office, Marcel would have taken his best quill pen and (perhaps on his best linen paper) written a letter. Having closed with a phrase such as, "I remain, Sir, your humble and obedient servant, Marcel Ignatius

Radisson," he would have entrusted the document to the postal service, hoping that Dougherty would receive it within the next week or so.

Both society and technology have changed dramatically since then. At the same time, there has been a movement toward standardization in many areas. For example, in the early part of this century, not every car manufacturer placed the clutch pedal on the far left and the gas pedal to the right of the brake pedal. Over time, however, uniformity of design became the rule. The same tendency has been reflected in the development of standard formats and conventions for business letters.

The effectiveness of your correspondence will in part be in inverse proportion to the extent that your audience is consciously aware of those formats and conventions. When they are in some way violated, your audience is likely to notice the violation and to react negatively to the entire message. For example, if you were to receive a letter in which the sender's letterhead and your name and address appeared at the end of the letter rather than on the first page, you would be distracted, perhaps to the point of suspecting something was wrong with the letter's content as well. Similarly, if you received a letter that concluded with the phrase "I remain your humble and obedient servant," you would be bemused and possibly suspect an attitude of sarcasm on the part of the sender.

Block and Modified Block

Two standard business letter formats are the *block format* and the *modified block format*, shown in Figures 8.1 and 8.2 respectively. (Note that in both letters the body text is devoted to an explanation of the format.) The conventions for both formats are discussed below.

Letterhead   The individual's or organization's letterhead, or return address, appears on the first page of the letter. (Note that this page does not normally include a page number, while succeeding pages are numbered but include no letterhead.) When designing a letterhead, you should keep in mind the document visual guidelines discussed in Chapter 4.

Date   The format of the date should be unambiguous. While there is no doubt about what *January 3, 2000* means, *3/2/00* could be interpreted as either February 3 or March 2. While the date January 3, 2000 would be clear if written as *00/01/03* (year, month, day), it is standard practice in business letters to write the date in full.

Inside Address   The inside address specifies the letter's primary audience. Here is the standard formula for an inside address:

Honorific + First Name or Initial + Last Name

Title

Company

Figure 8.1: Block Format

9999–2011th Street
Langley BC V1V 0M0
(604) 881-4412

Grandstone
Technical Institute

April 3, 2000

Ms. Françoise Désormais
Executive Assistant
Radisson Automobiles Inc.
6134 Bank Street
Ottawa ON K2A 2B3

Dear Ms. Désormais:

This letter illustrates the **block format**.

You will notice that there is no punctuation at the end of any of the lines of the inside address—all of which are left flush—and that the two-letter abbreviation for the province (Canada Post's current standard) does not contain periods. As well, the salutation is followed by a colon.

You should note the following common conventions.

Body text paragraph spacing (¶) is normally 1 ¼–1 ½ times line spacing. At least three line spaces separate the date from the inside address, and the inside address from the salutation; only two line spaces separate the salutation from the first paragraph of the text. Each line of the inside address is separated by a line space, not a ¶ space.

The complimentary close is one ¶ below the last text line, and three to six ¶s separate the complimentary close from the signature line. Any enclosure notation will be one ¶ below the signature line, and any (carbon) copy indicator will fall one ¶ below that. Within body text, separate paragraphs by one ¶ only; use only a single space (space bar) after punctuation.

Unless your house style requires otherwise, use left (not full) justification.

Yours truly,

P.R. Hayakawa

(Ms.) Pat Hayakawa, Instructor, MIS
Encl.

c. Boris Milkovsky

Figure 8.2: Modified Block Format

5827 Dixie Road
Mississauga ON L2J 2J2
(905) 998-9989

April 3, 2000

Mr. Flavio Santini
Senior Consultant
Accelerated Enterprises Ltd.
352 St. Mary Avenue
Winnipeg MB R2R 1M8

Dear Mr. Santini:

This letter uses the **modified block style**. Please note the following conventions.

In this form, the date begins at the horizontal centre of the page. The format for the inside address and the body text is the same as that used in the block format.

The complimentary close and signature block, like the date, begin at the centre of the page.

Attachment and (carbon) copy indicators are set flush left, as in the block style. Use left justification unless your house style requires you to do otherwise.

Yours sincerely,

Roger Concorde

Roger Concorde
Registrar

Attachment
c.c. Nancy McDiarmid

Street Address

City + Province + Postal Code

Honorific refers to a title such as Mr., Ms., or Dr. Note that some writers put the postal code on a separate line.

Salutation   The salutation should take the following form:

Dear + Honorific + Last Name:

Note the use of a colon at the end of the salutation line.

In the absence of an honorific (as is often the case in direct-mail salutations), the salutation would be:

Dear + First Name or Initial + Last Name:

Some audiences might regard that salutation as too impersonal because it lacks an honorific. A more informal variation would be:

Dear + First Name:

You should consider your audience carefully before deciding on a first-name salutation: some might regard it as informal to the point of being presumptuous.

Complimentary Close   Here are the most common complimentary closes found in Canadian business letters today:

Yours truly,

Yours very truly,

Yours sincerely,

Sincerely,

Note the use of the comma at the end of each close.

Signature Block   The signature block contains two elements: the *signature* itself and, immediately below it, the *signature line*, in which the sender's full name is typed. The name is sometimes followed, either on the same line or the subsequent line, by the sender's professional title (see Figures 8.1 and 8.2 for examples).

The Simplified Format

Many technical communications professionals who want to adhere to the preceding conventions run into difficulty when confronted by the fact that we do not (as yet) have a standard honorific that does not show gender. The article in Box 8.1, which first appeared in a Vancouver business publication almost a decade ago, addresses the problem.

Box 8.1 Honouring Thy Signee

A long time ago, English solved a social problem that many languages still have. It did away with the distinction between formal and informal second-person pronouns.

If you were a friend of Will Shakespeare, you would have been used to using "thou," "thee," "thy," and "thine." As well as indicating that you were addressing only one person, the words denoted definite social familiarity. You said "thou" to a child, to your spouse (though perhaps not to your mother-in-law), to a close friend, or to a "social inferior." But you always said "you" to a superior. (Just to make things more complicated, the "informal" pronoun was also used to address the deity.) Occasionally, it was difficult to decide what to call whom ... and many an insult resulted.

Things seem a lot simpler now. But we do have the problem of what to call women in business correspondence. When you address a letter to "Mr. John Smith," the "honorific" indicates gender and number: "Mr." refers to a man and is singular. But every time you write "Dear Mrs. Brown" or "Dear Miss Jones," you are also stipulating civil status. And in a business letter, a woman's civil status is— unless she feels otherwise—no one's business but her own.

The last decade or so has witnessed the introduction of a new creation—"Ms." Although some people don't like it, I find it a highly useful and appropriate addition to the language. Although the sound of "Ms." may not please a lot of traditional ears, the word itself succinctly transmits a necessary message.

Just as everyone should have the right to choose a form of address, it's also good business etiquette to let people know what you prefer. Let's suppose I received a letter signed "J.R. Smith." If I don't know who "J.R. Smith" is, what should I put in the salutation in my reply?

If I use "Mr.," "Mrs.," or "Miss" (or simply "Dear Sir" or "Dear Madam"), I'm making an assumption I might later regret. "Dear Sir or Madam" always seems a trifle clumsy, while "To Whom It May Concern" makes me think of a new service charge or a warning against toxic gas. And although "Dear Mr./Mrs./Miss/Ms. Smith" does cover all the bases, it might not impress a potential client.

Old J.R. could have saved me a lot of frustration by letting me know in the signature line how he/she likes to be addressed.

It's a courtesy I try to extend to others. Although my actual signature—which is quite illegible—has only my initials, I use my given name in the typed signature line. Up to now, almost everyone has assumed "David" means I would prefer "Dear Sir" or "Dear Mr. ——."

But what if your first name is Pat or Les (or Charlie, for that matter)? If you have found some variety in the honorifics people use when they write you, you might want to express your preference a little more clearly.

How—or whether—you do so is entirely up to you. If you're male, chances are you won't need to worry. Most men—and women—still assume an unidentified business correspondent is male and write accordingly. (That's not right, but I'm afraid it's still largely true.)

If you're female, you could ignore the issue and smile at "Dear Sir." You could include your second name in full (if you have one, and if it is considered gender specific in our society). Or you could put the honorific you prefer in parentheses before or after your name.

As our population becomes an increasingly multicultural one, this "problem" will grow more acute. While we can (usually) guess the gender of names we're familiar with, the number of names that many of us don't easily recognize as masculine or feminine is growing. Both courtesy and efficiency dictate that we make allowances—either in what we write or in the way that we write it.

Some years ago, the burgeoning direct-mail industry in the United States needed to deal with the gender-specific honorific problem. The companies that compiled and maintained the mailing lists often did not know their audiences' preferred honorifics, but it was to their commercial advantage to offend as few people as possible. Consequently, the industry helped popularize a very practical solution: a different style of business letter called the *simplified format* (also known as the simple format). The letter shown in Figure 8.3 is an illustration of the simplified format. (Again, the letter's body text explains the format.)

The main disadvantage of the simplified format is that some audiences respond negatively to it. Perhaps because of the format's origins in the advertising industry, many audiences equate its use with someone wanting to sell them something. Again, consider the impact of CMAPP: what you know about your audience should condition your product.

Memos

A few years after establishing Accelerated Enterprises in Winnipeg, Sarah Cohen and Frank Nabata rented a small office on Portage Avenue. When Frank had a message he wanted to leave for Sarah's comments, he would take a sheet of foolscap, put the date at the top, write *Sarah*, scribble his message, add his name, and leave the page in Sarah's in-box. After reading the message, Sarah would append her comments, initial or sign the message, and leave it in Frank's in-box.

The transmission of memos today can be considerably more complicated, particularly in large organizations. For example, one federal government department in which I worked in the late 1980s employed two different memo forms, handwritten

Figure 8.3: Simplified Format

Newfoundland Office
101 Signal Hill Road
St. John's NF   A1B 9A7
709 843-1147 Fax 709 833-7788

April 3, 2000

T. Trann
General Manager, Radisson Automobiles Inc.
1970 Brunswick Street
Halifax NS B3J 3K6

SIMPLIFIED FORMAT

This letter illustrates the simplified format. Its use is more common in the United States than in Canada, where it is often viewed as an advertising style.

The inside address does not have any required components (honorific, initial, etc.). You simply include whatever relevant information you have.

There is no salutation. Instead, there is a subject heading, always in full caps, normally set off by three line spaces above and below. No punctuation appears at the end of the subject heading.

This format often uses full rather than left justification.

Note that there is no complimentary close. The signature block area begins 1–2 ¶s below the last line of body text. Note that the signature line is normally in full caps.

Reference initials or an indication of an attachment or enclosure would begin one ¶ below the signature line.

Leila Berakett
LEILA BERAKETT
SENIOR ASSOCIATE

and typed. Exchanged between audiences at the same hierarchical level, the hand-written memo had a form that was divided into *originator's* and *respondent's* segments, and had two carbonless copies attached. You wrote your message, kept copy 2, and sent off the other sheets. The recipient wrote a reply, kept copy 1, and returned the original. The typed memo was used for a senior management audience. The form for this memo was not divided, and had only one copy attached. You carefully typed your memo (on a typewriter—this was before PCs and shared printers), kept the copy, and sent off the original. If the department's "big guns" deigned to respond, you would receive their original.

Although complication of that order may not be common, there are a number of conventions you should follow when using memorandums (note the alternative plural, *memoranda*):

1. Remember that memos are used *within* an organization. If you are writing to an audience that is not part of your organization, use a letter.

2. The word *Memo* or *Memorandum* should appear at or near the top of the form, often accompanied by the organization's name.

3. The memo will show the date. (Some memo forms preface the date with the word "Date," an element many technical communicators find redundant.)

4. There will be a line headed *To* on which you stipulate the audience or audiences. Many memo forms also have a line headed *cc.* or just *c.* on which you can indicate any copies (in effect, you may be identifying secondary audiences).

5. There will be a line headed *From* on which to identify the originator.

6. There will be a line headed *Subject* or *Re* (Latin for "with regard to") that should indicate in concise terms the topic of the memo. Note that most memos will address one topic only. Note also that the information in the *Subject* line is not the same as that given in the introductory sentence of the memo. The former specifies the *issue* that the memo addresses; the latter introduces the situation, often by sum-marizing it.

7. Memos are more likely than letters or reports to include bulleted and/or numbered lists.

8. The memo will be initialled or signed, often beside the typed name of the origi-nator. Memos do *not* contain an inside address, a salutation, a complimentary close, or a signature block.

Memos are designed to convey information quickly. In creating a memo, therefore, you should adhere to the principles of brevity and concision. You should also regard a memo, as you would a letter, as a CMAPP product to which CMAPP strategies and analysis should be applied. The somewhat tongue-in-cheek memo shown in Figure 8.4 provides further information about this CMAPP product.

Figure 8.4: Memorandum

Formidable Forms, Inc.
Internal Memorandum

April 3, 2000

To:	A. Lert
	Manager, Memo Division, Regional Office
c.	G. Whiz, Comptroller
From:	Peter Carborundum *PC*
	Supervisor, Effectiveness Branch, Headquarters
Re:	Company Memoranda

For some time now, we have been considering the development and production of in-house memo forms. You will recall that:

- the meetings were interminable;
- the points were irrelevant; and
- the results were inconclusive.

Consequently, I have decided to take all this bull by the horns and barge full steam ahead (please excuse the mixed metaphor). Following are some guidelines.

The word *Memo* or *Memorandum* will appear prominently.

A standard memo form contains provisions for indicating *date, to, from,* and the *subject.*

The message usually deals with one issue only, and the style is often point form.

There is no inside address, salutation, complimentary close, or signature block. Nonetheless, you must initial a memo (unless your house style requires a full signature) to indicate that you have examined it before sending it out. You will normally do so beside your name on the *From* line or at the bottom of the text.

Unless your company house style requires otherwise, you should use left justification for the body text.

Electronic Communications

When desktop computers started becoming a mainstay of offices and homes a number of years ago, pundits breathlessly predicted the imminent death of the print medium. (Your use of this textbook refutes that prophecy.) Other so-called experts confidently foresaw the emergence of the paperless office. In fact, studies have shown that the volume of paper consumed by business worldwide has increased enormously since the entrenchment of computers in the workplace. At the same time, more and more technical communication is being carried out electronically. This apparent contradiction may be partially explained by the fact that many computer users prefer to edit and revise printed drafts, and to print out copies of almost everything.

The two main forms of person-to-person electronic communication are faxes and e-mail. Another form of electronic communication, the Web page, is rarely used to communicate with a single individual. As you surf the Net, however, you might consider the CMAPP aspects of the pages you access. In particular, think about whether the designers of those pages have successfully incorporated the complementary CMAPP attributes covered in Chapter 5. I suspect you will find that all too often, Web pages sport more sizzle than steak.

Faxes

Fax machines started to become commonplace in the mid-1980s. If AEL's Deborah Greathall had at that time needed to send a copy of a contract from the Edmonton office to her colleague Leila Berakett in St. John's, she would have dialled Leila's fax number and transmitted the pages, perhaps accompanying them with a short, handwritten note. Were Deborah to fax the contract to Leila *today,* she would attach a cover page such as the one shown in Figure 8.5. Most organizations now require that their employees use standard cover pages, following conventions similar to the ones they follow when creating memorandums. Most current fax software is accompanied by a battery of modifiable cover-sheet templates, with designs ranging from the sedate to the outlandish.

Fax conventions include the frequent use of bulleted or numbered lists and the clear indication of

- product (e.g., *Fax Transmission*)
- date of transmission
- company name
- primary audience, including phone and fax numbers
- sender, including phone and fax numbers
- number of pages being transmitted
- topic of the fax

Elaborate fax cover pages, like the memos on which they appear to be modelled, are likely here to stay. Therefore, use the most professional-looking product that your organization offers.

A Note on Ethics   Many fax machines include a broadcast function that enables you to have the same fax sent to a list of numbers automatically. Some purveyors of junk faxes maintain that the business generated from unrestrained broadcast more than

Figure 8.5: Fax Cover Page

Internal Fax Transmission

AEL Accelerated
Enterprises Ltd.

Edmonton Office (Main Fax #: 403-254-5900)

Date:	May 8, 2000
To:	Leila Berakett
Office:	St. John's
At Fax Number:	833-7788
c.c.	
From:	Deborah Greathall *DG*
Phone:	263-3117
Fax:	254-5922

Number of pages (including this cover page): 5

If you do not receive all pages, please telephone (403) 263-3117

Subject:	Harbourview Contract

Leila,

Attached is a copy of the four (4) pages of the signed Harbourview contract.

Please fax me your comments ASAP.

makes up for the inevitable cohort of angry or offended recipients. In the wake of protest and concern, some provinces have regulated the use of broadcast-fax advertising.

Regardless of whatever legal restrictions may exist, tying up your audience's fax machine with unrequested (and probably unwanted) messages is hard to justify in terms of communication ethics. Furthermore, many fax machines are found in home-based businesses. The arrival of a junk fax in this setting will seem doubly offensive to recipients who regard it as intrusion into their personal lives.

E-mail

To the millions of Canadians who now have Internet access, e-mail has become an essential technical communications product. More and more, it is supplanting letters (facetiously referred to as "snail-mail") and memos as the preferred vehicle for rapid written communication. Not only can you now expect all but instantaneous delivery of your message, regardless of where on the planet your audience may be, but you can readily attach other electronic files to your message (documents, graphics, sound, video clips, etc.).

The Privacy Issue   Canadian legislators, like their counterparts in many other countries, are just beginning to recognize that existing communications law is not up to the task of dealing with the rapidly changing world of the information highway. They are still grappling, for example, with the legal and ethical issues surrounding the question of whether (and to what degree) employees' e-mail should be protected as private communication, as letters are once in the hands of Canada Post. Many people believe that e-mail should be subject to the scrutiny of the employers who provide the means to create and send it, and who may reasonably expect that e-mail generated in the office will be work-related and therefore open to review by management.

Netiquette   E-mail is still in what we might call its administrative infancy, just as faxes were a couple of decades ago. Nevertheless, a few conventions that apply to e-mail have emerged. For example, some corporations now insist that employees include a signature file in every message. A signature file is the e-mail equivalent of a letter's signature block. A company may stipulate that the signature file contain the firm's name and the employee's e-mail address, full name, and office phone number.

More entrenched are conventions that are often referred to as *netiquette*. The rules of netiquette are still quite loose. Rather than being issued by a central authority, they constitute the preferences of a multitude of unconnected (and often uncooperative) users. Here are some netiquette conventions:

- Do not use capital letters for emphasis; they are the e-mail equivalent of shouting.
- To emphasize a word or phrase, *enclose it within asterisks*.
- Remember that for your audience what you see is what you get. Subtleties like irony generally don't travel well.
- Do not overuse "emoticons" such as :-) or :-(. Emoticons are combinations of punctuation marks that when viewed at a 90° angle produce "smiles," "frowns," or other "commentary."
- Keep your messages as brief as possible; many people receive scores of e-mails every day.
- Before sending a reply, delete the parts of the original message that are no longer critical; otherwise, an exchange of several responses can produce a gigantic—and mostly useless—message.
- If you are sending a file as an attachment, consider whether your audience has the software to permit proper opening, viewing, or editing of that file.
- If you want to attach a file, take into consideration your audience's download time; a lengthy download delays the receipt of other messages.

- Remember to check an attachment for viruses before you send it; sending an infected file can have devastating consequences.

- If you are part of a network, do not overuse the option of sending messages (or replies) to every single member of that network. Remember the CMAPP injunction to carefully consider your audience.

- Do *not* *spam*; that is, do not send out unsolicited junk e-mail to hundreds or thousands of recipients, regardless of the ease with which you can do so. Like junk mail and junk faxes, junk e-mail is usually resented.

- Don't send messages based on impulse or emotion (especially anger). Take a moment to reflect (e.g., about possible consequences) before you click on *Send*. Also, make sure that you have thought about CMAPP and about the strategy that you are using.

CASE STUDIES

8A   Mississauga University: Interdepartmental Memorandum

Situation

In July 1999, Kaz Lowchuk, a promising civil engineering student, received a letter from MU's Admissions Office informing him that he would not be allowed to complete his registration for his third year because he had failed two of his compulsory second-year courses, Architectural Design 223 and Drafting Principles 200. Stunned, Kaz went to the Admissions Office and pointed out to the admissions officer that his marks before the final exams in those courses had been 78% and 82% respectively. He stressed that he was certain he had done well on the exams, and that his other course marks were all very good.

The admissions officer checked the computer record and informed Kaz that the two engineering professors had submitted his marks as required. According to the system, Kaz's marks for AD223 and DP200 were 38% and 48% respectively. The admissions officer told Kaz that both professors were on vacation, but that he could launch a formal appeal of grades, although the process normally took six weeks.

Not wanting to lose admission to his third year because of what he was sure was an error, Kaz set up an appointment with Joan Welstromm, chair of the Civil Engineering Department. To prepare for the meeting, Welstromm examined Kaz's records and managed to contact the professors at their homes. At the meeting, she was able to reassure Kaz that he would be permitted to register.

After Kaz left, Welstromm composed the memo that is shown in Figure 8.6.

Figure 8.6: Welstromm's Memorandum

Interdepartmental Memorandum
Office of the Chair, Civil Engineering

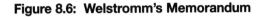

Mississauga
University

Date:	July 12, 1999
To:	Roger Concorde, Registrar
From:	Joan Welstromm, Chair *JW*
cc.	John Vanetti, Hans Scart
Subject:	Kaz Lowchuk

It is <u>unfortunate</u> that another lapse on the part of your staff has once again created a situation that has caused a student worry and work and presented senior administrators with a problem they must resolve *despite their heavy workload.*

Your _Admissions Office_ denied **Kaz Lowchuk** (Student Number **100888938**) admission to his <u>3rd</u> year of **Engineering** because of *their own error* in recording his grades. Their best advice to him was to "appeal"—a process that would have put him well beyond the <u>registration deadline</u> for this **September.**

I telephoned the two professors involved, **Vanetti** and **Scart,** interrupting their vacations, and received assurances from them that **Kaz** had, in fact, continued to do very well indeed in the courses in question. Their records—which, by astounding luck, they both had at home—confirm that **Vanetti** had entered a mark of **83%** and Scart a mark of **84%.** I am sure I need not further detail the sequence of *careless* events that led to **Kaz** being refused admission by your office.

I have assured Kaz that his registration will proceed without further delay. An immediate memo from you confirming this would be appreciated.

Issues to Think About

1. Why you think that Welstromm used a memo for this communication?

2. What other product might she have used instead? Why?

3. To what extent does the memo reflect the conventions outlined in this chapter? In particular, what would you say about Welstromm's use of
   (a) language (what does it say about her?)
   (b) document visuals (what improvements would you make?)

4. After conducting a CMAPP analysis of the memo, answer the following questions:
   (a) What kind of relationships with her audience does Welstromm appear to presume?
   (b) How well do you think she has gauged the context here?
   (c) What effect do you think her content will have on the context?
   (d) Will her purpose be clear to her audience? (Give reasons for your answer.)
   (e) What secondary purpose does her memo suggest?

Revision

A revised version of Welstromm's memo is presented in Figure 8.7. Consider it the version she would have sent had she waited until anger no longer clouded her normally strong appreciation of good CMAPP usage.

8B Student Association Cooperation: Fax from MU to GTI

Situation

In October 1999, the Mississauga University Student Association (MUSA) held a Thanksgiving party at which two popular bands, Hodgepodge and Really Me, appeared. On behalf of the MUSA executive, Jack Lee, the functions coordinator, had signed contracts with both bands.

Following the event, Hodgepodge's leader, Tommy Eldridge, complained that the sound system had broken down twice during the band's performance, and that as a consequence, the set had run about an hour later than originally scheduled. Eldridge demanded that MUSA pay the band an extra $100 to cover the overtime. Jack conceded that Hodgepodge had stayed later than intended, but he countered that the band had breached the contract on the following grounds:

- The band's lead singer, Buzzy, had been absent, and his replacement, a relative unknown, was in Jack's view not up to par.

- Despite repeated requests from the audience, Hodgepodge had not performed the band's signature number, "Night Is Nowhere."

Following a heated argument with Jack, Hodgepodge packed up and left. A week later, Dorothy Palliser, the president of MUSA, received an angry letter from Eldridge, in which he not only threatened a lawsuit, but warned that MUSA would be blacklisted and would never be able to hire a professional band again.

A month later—and with no further word from Hodgepodge—Dorothy was talking on the phone with an old friend, Tayreez Mushani, a student in the Electronics Program at Grandstone Technical Institute in British Columbia. Tayreez happened to mention that the GTI Student Union was planning a big pre-Christmas bash, and that

Figure 8.7: Welstromm's Revised Memorandum

Interdepartmental Memorandum
Office of the Chair, Civil Engineering

Mississauga University

Date:	July 12, 1999
To:	Roger Concorde, Registrar
From:	Joan Welstromm, Chair *JW*
cc.	John Vanetti, Hans Scart, Kaz Lowchuk
Subject:	Final grades for Kaz Lowchuk, Student #100888938: AD223 and DP200

The above-named student was recently advised by the Admissions Office that his final grades in AD223 and DP200 were 38% and 48% respectively, and that if he disagreed with them his only recourse would be to appeal. Since the appeal process is time-consuming, he would likely have missed the registration deadline for his third year of Engineering.

I contacted Professor Vanetti (for AD223) and Scart (for DP200). Having checked their records, they maintain that they submitted grades for Kaz Lowchuk of 83% and 84% respectively. It would appear the numbers were inadvertently transposed during the data-entry process. Professors Vanetti and Scart will shortly be faxing the relevant grade sheets to your office.

Please consider this memo my official request, on behalf of professors Vanetti and Scart, that you (1) correct Kaz Lowchuk's grades without delay so that he may complete his registration before the deadline of August 16, 1999; and (2) send me a copy of the grade correction form by return campus mail.

If you have any questions, please contact me at local 4887 or by internal e-mail at welstrommj.

Thank you for your prompt attention to this matter.

her boyfriend was thrilled that Hodgepodge was one of the bands that would be performing. Taken aback, Dorothy told Tayreez about MUSA's experience with Hodgepodge. They decided that Dorothy should warn the GTI Student Union of potential problems.

The following day, after obtaining from Tayreez the name and number of GTI's Student Union president, Dorothy composes and sends the fax shown in Figure 8.8. Along with this message she faxes a copy of the contract with Hodgepodge and Jack's handwritten notes detailing his argument with Eldridge.

Figure 8.8: Palliser's Fax to GTISU

Fax Transmission

Dominion 243   Mississauga University Student Association Executive   Local 4334
Phone: 519 998-4334 Fax: 519 998-1421 Email: musaex@wnet.com

To: *Vlad Radescu*
         President, GTI Student Union

Fax: *604 444-0505*

From: *Dorothy Palliser*
         President, MU Student Association

Subject: *Warning re band Hodgepodge*

Number of pages in total: 7

You don't know me, but I'm the President of the MU Student Association. A friend of mine, Jayreez Mushani, just told me you're planning to hire Hodgepodge to play at GTI, and I wanted to warn you about doing that.

     We hired them a while ago, and it was a really bad scene. They didn't really give us what they were supposed to, and they wanted more money, and now they're threatening to sue us.

     I'm attaching some things I think will help you know what you're probably up against, including a copy of our contract with them, and some notes I got from our functions coordinator, Jack Lee, who dealt with them personally.

     I think it's really important for student associations to talk to each other and help each other. So, when you've looked through this stuff, you can get in touch with me if you want more details.

     Good luck!

Attached: 6 pages

1. What is your reaction to the mixed product (a handwritten message on a printed fax cover sheet)? Why might MUSA be using it? What are its advantages or disadvantages?

2. Should Dorothy have used a different product or perhaps more than one? If so, what product(s) and why?

3. Do you notice anything missing in the fax's header section (the printed segment that precedes the message itself)? How might that omission later affect the message and the context?

4. How would you describe Dorothy's perception of the context here? To what extent do you think she undertook a CMAPP analysis? What might she have done to get more information before proceeding?

5. If you were Radescu, how do you think you would react to the fax? What impact would your actions have on the ongoing context of this scenario?

6. To what extent does Dorothy's fax follow the conventions discussed in this chapter?

7. What strategy has Dorothy used in her message? Do you think she used it effectively? Why or why not?

8. In terms of technical communications ethics, do you think Dorothy should have sent a copy of the fax to anyone else?

9. Should Dorothy have faxed copies of the MUSA-Hodgepodge contract and Jack's notes? Why or why not?

Revision

If Dorothy had taken the time to conduct a CMAPP analysis, her fax might have resembled the one shown in Figure 8.9. Note the following differences between the original and revised versions:

- The revised fax has been word-processed, making it easier to read and more professional in appearance.

- Information is more precise and accessible.

- The approach is more even-handed.

- The language is less connotative and more denotative.

- Copies of the contract and Jack's notes are not attached.

Figure 8.9: Palliser's Revised Fax to GTISU

Fax Transmission

Dominion 243   Mississauga University Student Association Executive   Local 4334
Phone: 519 998-4334 Fax: 519 998-1421 Email: musaex@wnet.com

Date: November 26, 1999
To: Vlad Radescu
              President, GTI Student Union
c.   Tayreez Mushani
              Jack Lee
Fax: 604 444-0505
From: Dorothy Palliser
              President, MU Student Association
Subject: Hiring of the band Hodgepodge
Number of pages in total: 1

Tayreez Mushani, a GTI Electronics Program student and a personal friend, recently mentioned to me that the GTI Student Union is planning to contract with Hodgepodge to perform at your pre-Christmas party. I felt that I should apprise you of the MU Student Association's dealings with that band.

Last October, our functions coordinator, Jack Lee, contracted with Really Me and Hodgepodge to perform at our Thanksgiving dance. During the performance, our sound system broke down twice and consequently the event ran about an hour late. Despite the mishap, the performance by Really Me was highly professional, and we would recommend them without reservation.

Our experience with Hodgepodge was less positive. When its leader, Tommy Eldridge, demanded an additional $100 because of the overtime, Jack Lee pointed out the following:

- Buzzy, the band's lead singer (and the main reason we had hired Hodgepodge in the first place) was replaced by Harley Monk, a new member of the band.
- Monk's performance provoked a number of complaints from the audience both during and after the show.
- Despite repeated requests from the audience, Hodgepodge refused to perform "Night Is Nowhere," the band's signature song.

A week after the event, I received a letter from Eldridge informing me that he intended to sue the MU Student Association for breach of contract, and that he would attempt to blacklist us so that we would be unable to hire professional bands in the future. I notified our lawyer, but to date we have heard nothing further about the threatened lawsuit.

Our experience with Hodgepodge leads me to suggest you might wish to exercise caution in your dealings with the band. If you wish to discuss this matter further, please don't hesitate to contact me.

8C E-mail: Personal Communication at RAI

Situation

About a year ago, RAI's board of directors had approved the creation of a Radisson intranet—a private electronic network connecting all Radisson dealerships and including an e-mail gateway to the Internet. Once up and running, the system allowed Radisson employees to send messages to each other and make use of Internet-based e-mail as well. Salespeople who gave clients and potential customers their Radisson e-mail addresses found that the additional communications option increased sales.

For the last 11 years, Walter Stephenson has been selling cars for Radisson Automobiles in Halifax. Walter is popular with his colleagues and his customers. With repeat sales that are consistently among the highest in Radisson's seven dealerships, he has been named salesperson of the month more often than any of his colleagues.

When Victor Liepert, the Halifax dealership vice-president, received Gilles Radisson's curt memo announcing the impending reorganization (see Figure 2.9 on page 28), he decided to share it immediately with his staff. Among the most offended were the people who had been with the firm for a long time, including Walter Stephenson. The more he thought about it, the angrier he got. As far as Walter was concerned, the reorganization was a typically highhanded power grab by people in head office who hadn't the faintest idea what things were like in local dealerships, and had probably never sold a car in their lives. (In fact, Gilles Radisson had hands-on experience in every aspect of the firm's operations.)

One late December evening, Walter, still angry about the imminent changes, sent the e-mail message that appears in Figure 8.10. On New Year's Day, 2000, Walter was at home. He decided to log on to the Radisson intranet to see if any customers had sent him messages. What he found was a message, shown in Figure 8.11, from Céline Robillard, the head office company manager.

Walter is dumbfounded. The message makes him angrier than he has been in ages, confirming in his mind his suspicions about Head Office personnel. The tone of the message and its timing also leave him slightly apprehensive about going in to work after the New Year's Day holiday.

Issues to Think About

1. Answer the following questions concerning Stephenson's use of e-mail as a product.
   (a) Is his message clear?
   (b) How many people might make up his intended audience?
   (c) What do you think his primary purpose was?
   (d) Do you think he had a secondary purpose? Is so, what might it be?
   (e) What kind of response might he have been expecting from his audience?
   (f) Does his message comply with the general rules of netiquette?

Figure 8.10: Stephenson's E-mail

```
Date:      December 23, 1999, 20:25:22 CST
To:        dwang@infra.com
           fharmnn@nosuch.ca
           harmon2@nosuch.ca
From:      "Walter Stephenson"<wstephenson.radiss.reg@cars.com>
cc.        listserv@auto.int.new.ca
           listserv@beanies.com
NEWSGROUPS:   alt.business.harangues.personal
              alt.complaints.management.people
Subject: Dilbert's cohorts strike again!
MESSAGE
```

Thought you might like to know what's still happening in the world of big business ... However, KEEP THIS CONFIDENTIAL!!! cause I don't want to get kicked in the you-know-what yet again by the bosses.;-/

Heard of Radisson Autos, right? I've been there almost a dozen years now and thought I'd seen everything. Guess not. Seems that that cartoon character Dilbert, the one who shows up all the idiocy in business, has been walking around Radisson at Head Office. Big shot in Central Canada ... aren't those Ottawa hotshots all alike? ... just told us that they're reorganizing the whole damn company. Our boss at least had the guts and decency to tell us all. HEAD OFFICE DIDN'T EVEN BOTHER!:-(

Is this going to help sales? NOPE! Is this going to help morale (which was OK anyway)? NOT A CHANCE! Is this going to get the unions in a snit? WHAT DO YOU THINK, EH? Are we going to take it lying down? Probably. JOBS ARE HARD TO FIND AND THEY KNOW IT, TOO!

Yeah, I'm mad. At least writing this gets it off my chest. Now I guess I have to hope none of the management types subscribe to the lists or newsgroups I do.:-| Unlikely. They're probably too busy trying to find new ways to screw us working slobs.

Have a nice day from "Supercar"!

```
----------------------------------
W. Stephenson
Radisson Automobiles Inc.
Halifax NS
wstephenson.radiss.reg@cars.com
```

Figure 8.11: Robillard's E-mail to Stephenson

```
Return-path: <radiss@cars.com>
Date: December 29, 1999, 20:25:22 CST
Sender: owner- <radiss.cars.com>
From: "Céline Robillard" <robillard.radiss.ho@cars.com>
To:    "Walter Stephenson" <wstephenson.radiss.reg@cars.com>
cc:    "Victor Liepert" <vliepert.radiss.reg@cars.com>
       "Tina Trann" <ttrann.radiss.reg@cars.com>
       "Gilles Radisson" <gradisson.radiss.ho@cars.com>
SUBJECT: Your misuse of company intranet e-mail and
consequences of your action
```

```
On December 23, 1999, wstephenson.radiss.reg@cars.com wrote:
>To: dwang@infra.com, fharmnn@nosuch.ca, harmon2@nosuch.ca
>From: "Walter Stephenson" <wstephenson.radiss.reg@cars.com>
>cc. listserv@auto.int.new.ca, listserv@beanies.com
>NEWSGROUPS:      alt.business.harangues.personal
>                 alt.complaints.management.people
>Subject: Dilbert's cohorts strike again!

>MESSAGE
>Thought you might like to know what's still happening in the
>world of big business ... However, KEEP THIS CONFIDENTIAL!!!
>cause I don't want to get kicked in the you-know-what yet
>again by the bosses ;-/
>Heard of Radisson Autos, right? I've been there almost a
>dozen years now and thought I'd seen everything. Guess not.
>Seems that that cartoon character Dilbert, the one who shows
>up all the idiocy in business, has been walking around
>Radisson at Head Office. Big shot in Central Canada ...
>aren't those Ottawa hotshots all alike? ... just told us that
>they're reorganizing the whole damn company. Our boss at
>least had the guts and the decency to tell us all. HEAD OFFICE
>DIDN'T EVEN BOTHER! :-(
>Is this going to help sales? NOPE! Is this going to help
>morale (which was OK anyway)? NOT A CHANCE! Is this going to
>get the unions in a snit? WHAT DO YOU THINK, EH? Are we going
>to take it lying down? Probably. JOBS ARE HARD TO FIND AND
>THEY KNOW IT, TOO!
>Yeah, I'm mad. At least writing this gets it off my chest.
>Now I guess I have to hope none of the management types
>subscribe to the lists or newsgroups I do. :-| Unlikely.
```

Figure 8.11 (continued)

>They're probably too busy trying to find new ways to screw
>us working slobs.
>Have a nice day from "Supercar"!

MESSAGE
You are no doubt aware that
- the Radisson intranet is company property;
- all e-mail originating through that intranet must be work-
related;
- all such e-mail *is and remains the property of* Radisson
Automobiles Inc.
You may *not*, however, recall that Head Office conducts spot
checks on all intranet internal, incoming, and outgoing e-
mail, so as to ensure its efficient and economical use, and
to verify that the hardware and software are functioning as
expected.
As it happens, your message of Dec 23 was one of those chosen
for scrutiny. In the opinion of the Board of Directors, you
have:
- misused Radisson property for your own benefit;
- brought shame on the Radisson good name;
- without foundation accused the Company of improper,
unethical, and perhaps illegal activities;
I have been in communication with your Vice-President, Victor
Liepert, and with Tina Trann, your General Manager. Please
report to Ms. Trann at 9:00 am on Tuesday, Jan 4/00. She will
inform you of the action we have decided to take.
Note that I am sending copies of this message to Mr. Liepert,
Ms. Trann, and Mr. Gilles Radisson, president and Chief
Executive Officer of Radisson Automobiles Inc.

Céline Robillard
Company Manager
Radisson Automobiles Inc.
radiss.ho@cars.com

2. Is Stephenson's use of company e-mail to criticize the company ethical? Why or why not?

3. What do you think Robillard's primary purpose was?

4. Do you think she had a secondary purpose? If so, what might it be?

5. What changes in the context do you think these messages have generated? (Hint: think of various relationships within the company.)

6. How do you think the messages will affect the context of Stephenson's meeting with Trann on January 4?

7. What do you think of the ethics of RAI's monitoring of e-mail?

EXERCISES

8.1 Give brief definitions of the following components of business letters:
   (a) inside address
   (b) salutation
   (c) complimentary close
   (d) signature block

8.2 Name two or more common business letter formats and provide a description of each.

8.3 Describe the principal differences between letters and memos.

8.4 Review Welstromm's original memo in Case Study 8A (page 137). Putting yourself in Roger Concorde's position:
   (a) construct a brief CMAPP analysis in planning a reply to Welstromm;
   (b) create a product that reflects your analysis.

8.5 Outline conventions for each of the following:
   (a) letter
   (b) memo
   (c) fax
   (d) e-mail

8.6 Obtain a copy of the house style guide used by your company or educational institution and refer to the guidelines for:
   (a) letter format and conventions
   (b) memo format and conventions
   (c) fax cover pages

   Assess the material in terms of:
   (a) consistency of image
   (b) KISS
   (c) accessibility
   (d) potential audience reaction

   If your company or educational institution does not have a house style guide, you may refer instead to one of the style manuals cited in Chapter 4.

8.7 Find out your organization/institution's policy with regard to employee e-mail privacy. Express and defend your opinion of its ethics.

8.8 Do you think that an educational institution that provides e-mail accounts for both faculty and students should apply the same e-mail privacy policy to both groups? (For example, should faculty be considered "employees" and students "clients"?) Give reasons for your answer.

EXPLORING THE WEB

Here are some Web sites you might wish to investigate.

URL	DESCRIPTION
http://www.canada.justice.gc.ca/en/ps/atip/index.html	Available through the Department of Justice Canada Web site, the Access to Information and Privacy page offers links to information on privacy-related laws and policies, including Treasury Board policy on the monitoring of electronic networks.
http://rhet.agri.umn.edu/Rhetoric/misc/dfrank/index.html	Created and maintained by Douglas Frank, the E-Mail Privacy Page provides a host of links to information on the issue of electronic communication and privacy.
http://www.albion.com/netiquette/index.html	The Netiquette Home Page provides links to information about netiquette, including the online edition of *Netiquette* by Virginia Shea. Part III of *Netiquette* deals with the subject of business netiquette.
http://www.hotwired.com/hardwired/wiredstyle/	Inspired by the book *Wired Style: Principles of English Usage in the Digital Age* (HardWired, 1996), the Wired Style Web site features material not found in the book and threaded discussions on English usage in electronic communications.

Common Products (2): Proposals

Fundamentally, a proposal is a CMAPP product designed to offer a solution to a problem. Because solving a problem invariably costs time, money, and energy, your proposal must persuade your audience (by targeting the intellect, as discussed in Chapter 7) that your solution warrants those expenditures. At the same time, your proposal must clearly and precisely explain the solution and its costs and benefits. Thus, a proposal usually combines persuasion with technical description (see Chapter 6). Proposals can take a variety of forms, including memos and letters.

Classification of Proposals

A common way to classify proposals reflects the CMAPP elements of message and audience. Consider the following four scenarios.

1. Gilles Radisson, RAI's president, has come to believe that the morale of senior managers in all seven dealerships has been declining, to the detriment of the company as a whole. He asks the company manager, Céline Robillard, to look into the matter and submit to him a proposal for raising morale.

Since Radisson has requested the proposal, we classify it as *solicited*; since Radisson and Robillard are part of the same company, Robillard's proposal is termed *internal* and would likely be introduced by means of a transmittal memo.

2. Jack Lee, the functions coordinator for MU's Student Association Executive, has thought of a way for MUSAEx to make extra money once the new Student Association Building opens. He envisages subletting some of the MUSA space to campus clubs. He decides to create an implementation plan and submit it to the MUSAEx president, Dorothy Palliser.

Because Palliser has not been expecting Lee's proposal, we would call it *unsolicited*; because both individuals are part of the same organization, Lee's proposal is *internal*. Being relatively short, it would likely take the form of a memo.

3. Cal Sacho, GTI's senior facilities manager, has been charged with effecting a geological and geotechnical study regarding potential construction of an Engineering Annex. Seeking a competent consulting firm for what promises to be a major undertaking, he places in the local papers a call for tenders, often referred to as an RFP (request for proposals) or an IFP (invitation for proposals). Always on the lookout for interesting contracts, Mitchell Chung, the AEL senior associate in Vancouver, notices the tender call and submits AEL's proposal for the study.

In this case, Sacho requested bids; thus, we can label Chung's proposal *solicited*. Since two separate organizations are involved, the proposal is *external*. Chung would most likely use a letter of transmittal to introduce his proposal.

4. Nicolas Pleske, a junior associate with AEL in Edmonton, has experience in marketing and advertising. He has heard through personal contacts in Ottawa that RAI is considering opening a dealership in Alberta's capital. Eager to drum up new business, he obtains the name of RAI's president, Gilles Radisson, and creates and submits to him a proposal for bringing RAI's name to the attention of Edmonton's car-buying public.

Since RAI has not requested anything, we would classify Pleske's proposal as *unsolicited*; since AEL and RAI are different organizations, the proposal would be *external*. Pleske would frame his proposal either as a letter or as a document introduced by a letter of transmittal.

Based on the above scenarios, we can classify proposals as being:

- solicited internal
- unsolicited internal
- solicited external
- unsolicited external

In the next section, we consider the CMAPP implications for each of the four scenarios.

CMAPP Implications

One might assume that insider knowledge and easy access to information would make a solicited internal proposal the easiest to formulate, and that, conversely, an unsolicited external proposal would entail the greatest difficulties. For the proposal writer, however, the realities of workplace context and audience can upset that expectation.

Scenario 1: Solicited Internal

As the head office company manager, Robillard knows all the RAI senior managers, and has ready access to all relevant information. You would expect that these advantages would make it easier for her to construct her proposal.

But imagine for a moment the reaction of the senior managers when Robillard begins asking questions. Many are likely to be suspicious of her motives; some may even feel threatened. Their relationships within RAI are thus likely to be affected, regardless of the eventual proposal she develops. As well, the accuracy of the information the senior managers provide—and thus of Robillard's proposal—may be compromised by their speculations about the use to which she will put that information.

Having asked Robillard to propose a solution, Radisson is obviously aware of a problem. Thus, Robillard need not overcome audience skepticism that one in fact exists. What will she do, however, if her research determines that morale has been in decline because of Radisson's own overbearing management style and his unwise operational decisions? In such a case, her own familiarity with her audience, and the fact that it is her boss who asked for the proposal, might run counter to her desire to be factual and objective.

Scenario 2: Unsolicited Internal

Because his proposal is unsolicited, Lee must first convince Palliser that there is a problem to be solved. Thus, his audience's initial skepticism may be high. However, his knowledge of his audience and his own position within MUSAEx may well increase his credibility and thus his ability to persuade her.

As a member of the MUSAEx and a MU student, Lee will benefit from specialized knowledge of audience and context. He can use this knowledge to make his proposal more precise, relevant, and convincing. On the other hand, if his relationship with Palliser is not a good one, he will face an uphill battle. Palliser may not be able to react objectively to his proposal, and might feel that he is making use of his insider knowledge to undermine her position as president.

Scenario 3: Solicited External

Because he is responding to an RFP, Chung need not convince his audience of the existence of a problem; he can concentrate instead on finding a workable solution. However, he is likely unaware of—and thus will not respond to—specific GTI in-house concerns. Further, despite the public tender call, Sacho's decision might be influenced by internal politics. For example, GTI's board of governors might have decided that small, local firms should be given priority, thus leaving AEL—a large, cross-Canada concern—at a hidden disadvantage.

Scenario 4: Unsolicited External

As an outsider, Pleske must first persuade his audience that a problem exists. Radisson, not having requested anything and confident of the strengths of his own business plan, is likely to be highly skeptical and might even take offence. Not being part of RAI, Pleske cannot be certain that RAI is thinking of opening an Edmonton dealership. Further, he needs to convince Radisson not only to undertake marketing and advertising, but to hire AEL to develop and implement the program. In fact, he cannot even be sure he has chosen the appropriate audience: Radisson might be annoyed that a promotional proposal was not directed to Céline Robillard.

On the other hand, Radisson, who might regard an unsolicited proposal from one of his own employees as presumptuous, may be intrigued by an outsider's perspective.

Unencumbered by RAI's corporate culture, Pleske may be able to generate ideas whose originality will appeal to his audience.

Informal and Formal Proposals

Internal proposals are sometimes referred to as *informal*. An example of such a proposal would be furnishing your supervisor or a colleague with a solution to a specific, work-related problem. Most informal proposals of this kind will run no more than a few pages, and will take the form of a memo. If the issue is complex, a longer informal proposal might be framed as a separate document, introduced by a transmittal memo.

External proposals may also be termed *formal*. Whether occasioned by a tender call or some other stimulus, formal proposals tend to be longer than informal proposals and more complex. Although some may be included within a letter, most will be documents introduced by transmittal letters.

There is no prescribed structure for a proposal: its content and organization will be determined by the results of a CMAPP analysis. But informal proposals will typically include the following elements (notice the similarity with the deductive approach to persuasion discussed in Chapter 7):

- *Introduction* Provide sufficient background for your audience to appreciate the rationale for your proposal.

- *Recommendations* Provide a concise list of the steps or actions that you are proposing.

- *Justification* Discuss in detail the arguments supporting your recommendations. Don't forget to consider potential costs and potential benefits, as well as some kind of implementation timeline. Remember that this section is the heart of your attempt at persuasion.

- *Summary* Briefly recapitulate your proposal. Include a call to action: as in any persuasive communication, you must specify what you want your audience to do next.

If your informal proposal is more complex, or if you are preparing a formal proposal, you might use the following structure (again, note the deductive approach):

- *Introduction* Indicate the background. If the proposal is solicited, specify the request to which it is responding. If it is unsolicited, explain the rationale for your proposal.

- *Proposed Solution* Describe precisely the steps or procedures you are suggesting. Indicate the benefits that should derive from implementing your solution.

- *Budget* If appropriate, you might use heads such as *Costs, Staffing, Personnel,* or *Requirements,* either instead of the level head *Budget* or in addition to it. Present the details of the budget clearly and precisely.

- *Benefits*   Specify the benefits to your audience of implementing your proposal. Use your CMAPP analysis to help define your content.

- *Schedule*   If your proposal incorporates several sequenced steps, specify when each step should be accomplished. If, as will usually be the case, timeliness is important, indicate the deadlines you think are necessary.

- *Authorization/Action Request*   If appropriate for your context and your audience, request approval to begin. In all cases, include a clear call to action.

If Jack Lee were to follow through on his proposal to Dorothy Palliser, his informal, unsolicited internal proposal might look like the one shown in Figure 9.1.

General Considerations

Whether your proposal is internal, external, solicited, or unsolicited, you should bear in mind several things.

1. A proposal offers a solution to a problem. If you cannot clearly and precisely describe both the problem and your solution to it, your likelihood of persuading your audience to pay for implementing your solution will be negligible at best.

2. When preparing your proposal, think of ways to counter the inevitable audience skepticism. If your proposal is unsolicited, your audience will probably question the very existence of the problem you are claiming to be able to solve. If your proposal is solicited, you will have to combat concerns about such things as the cost of your solution. In this case, you will normally have to convince your audience that your solution is superior to those proposed by others.

3. Work through your solution in sufficient detail to permit your audience to make an informed decision. Remember that you are targeting your audience's intellect, and must thus provide thorough, cogent arguments. Conversely, you must be brief and concise: extraneous detail tends to prompt a negative response.

4. Ensure that your solution is reasonable. If Céline Robillard had determined that the cause of RAI's morale problem was Gilles Radisson, would it have been reasonable for her to propose to her boss that he remove himself from the company?

5. Ensure that your solution, particularly your costing, is feasible. If Nicolas Pleske had suggested a $5-million dollar marketing and advertising program for RAI, it is unlikely that Radisson would have considered the budget practical. However effective Pleske's proposal might otherwise have been, it would probably have been rejected out of hand.

6. Pay careful attention to the accuracy of your entire message. Numerical errors, faulty terminology, verifiably false assertions, and misspelled names will cause loss of credibility for both you and your proposal.

Figure 9.1: Lee's Informal Proposal

MUSAEx Memo

Dominion 243   Mississauga University Student Association Executive   Local 4334

From:	Jack Lee, Functions Coordinator *JL*
To:	Dorothy Palliser, MUSAEx President
cc.	
Date:	Monday, October 18, 1999
Subject:	Profitable utilization of new MUSA premises

Introduction

As you know, the new Student Association Building (SAB) is scheduled to open in January 2000. Despite its name, the building will not be owned by MUSA, but by the university; MUSA has, however, committed to leasing most of the main floor.

MUSAEx members remain aware of the possibility of financial difficulty in the light of our contracted lease payments, particularly since we have been averse to raising Student Association fees for MU students.

I would like to propose what I believe would be an effective solution, one that I feel would bring social as well as financial benefits.

Proposed Solution

1. We obtain permission from MU administration to sublet part of the premises that we have contracted to lease;
2. We subdivide this section into five club rooms and contract with MU clubs to lease them from MUSA.

Costs

1. What has so far been set aside as the general purpose room comprises some 11.5 m x 10.2 m (117.3 square metres). Since we will be leasing space from MU administration at $1.50 per square metre per month, the prorated cost to us of the general purpose room will be approximately $176 per month.
2. Robust Construction has given me an informal estimate of approximately $4000 to convert the general purpose room into five club rooms, each of approximately 23 square metres: divider walls, doors, electrical renovations, etc. Prorated over one year, this would entail a cost of $333 per month.
3. From my informal discussions with the Engineering Club, the Foreign Students Association, and the Athletics Club, I predict that each of the five club rooms could be rented at $85 per month. Since MU operates on a standard trimester system, the five rooms should be occupied for 11 months per year, providing a total annual income of $4675, and thus a yearly prorated income of $389 per month.

Figure 9.1 (continued)

4. The financial implications would thus be:

First Year		Subsequent Years	
Item	**Amount**	**Item**	**Amount**
Monthly Rental to MU	(175.95)	Monthly Rental to MU	(176.95)
Monthly Renovation	(333.33)		
Sublet Income	389.58	Sublet Income	389.58
Monthly Total	(119.70)	Monthly Total	212.63
First Year Total	**(1436.40)**	**Yearly Total**	**2551.56**

5. From the above table, you can see that
   (a) the first year would show a loss of $1436.40 that could readily be covered by our "rainy day" fund, which currently stands at $2000;
   (b) the second year would show a profit of $2551.56 – $1436.40 = $1115.16;
   (c) subsequent years would show annual profits of $2551.56.

Benefits
1. MUSA would actually begin to see financial benefits before the end of the 3rd quarter of the second year of operation, by which time the renovation costs would have been paid off.
2. Subletting of the space to campus clubs would foster greater intermingling of both clubs and individual students, and would likely result in greater cooperation between MUSA and independent campus clubs.
3. Student members of the clubs that sublet from MUSA would be able to accomplish "one-stop shopping" when they came to the SAB.

Schedule
1. We should attempt to receive sublet approval from MU administration before December 1, 1999.
2. Immediately upon securing this approval, we should begin contacting the respective presidents of campus clubs, and should attempt to have contracts with them signed by December 15, 1999. Such contracts should be for a minimum of one year.

Authorization
I request that within the next week you give me your approval to begin implementing my proposal, so that I may initiate contact with both MU administration and MU club presidents.

Please respond by return memo or by e-mail (leej@mu.on.ca)

7. When developing your proposal, consider each of the complementary attributes of the CMAPP model that were discussed in Chapter 5. To succeed, your proposal must be an effective "total package."

Proposal to AEL from Superlative Design

Situation

In 1999, Leila Berakett, AEL's senior associate in St. John's, hired a small, local design firm called Superlative Design to remodel the company boardroom. Within months of the job's completion, Berakett began to receive complaints from office personnel about the quality of the workmanship. She conceded that her choice of designer had been an unfortunate mistake. At the same time, she recognized that Superlative Design had fulfilled the terms of what she now realized had been a vaguely worded contract.

This year, AEL decided to renovate the consultants' offices. Berakett asked three St. John's design firms to submit proposals. Through a chance conversation with an acquaintance, Jessica Greyland, a partner with Superlative Design, learned about the AEL project; she decided to submit her own proposal, which is shown in Figure 9.2.

Issues to Think About

1. If you were Leila Berakett, what would be your first reaction to this proposal in light of your previous dealings with Superlative Design?

2. Evaluate Greyland's proposal in terms of the following:
   (a) letterhead
   (b) inside address
   (c) salutation
   (d) grammar
   (e) proofreading

3. How would you assess the format of Greyland's proposal? In your answer, consider her use of document visuals and the extent to which she follows (or fails to follow) the business letter conventions discussed in Chapter 8.

4. How might Berakett respond to Greyland's reference to Frank Nabata and Berakett's secretary?

5. How would you evaluate the proposal in terms of (a) level of discourse, and (b) level of technicality?

6. What type of proposal organization do you think Greyland was trying to use? How well did she succeed?

Figure 9.2: Greyland's Proposal

Superlative
Design, Ltd.

Ms. Leila Berakett, Consultant
ACCELERATED ENTERPRISES
101 Signal Hill Road St. John's NF A1B 9A7

#105–321 Prince Philip Drive
St. John's NF A1J 1A6 528-7475
Fax: 528-7476

April 20, 2000

Dear L. Berakett,

We have heard of your call for proposals of the 3rd inst., this kind of short proposal is our response. Thank you for giving Darrell and I the opportunity to submit this proposals. AEL is a firm we are always happy to have good business relations with.

The quality and excellence of every office facility that we design reflects our commitment to our clients. Our innovations are often cited as excellent. All ready this year we have won an award. We pride ourselves in our ability to quickly and efficiently design well engineered systems. We have yet to miss a deadline in our many years of operation, our ten-year anniversary was celebrated last year.

We are familiar with your staff's needs due to the fact that we worked with you in 1998 on the boardroom project. If you may recall, that interior, which Darrell actually designed, required less changes and cost less than expected. And Darrell is confident he can achieve similar results on current project.

Our Human Factors study report (we did one in absentia so to speak) shows that the absolute best use of your office space is to divide that humungous room into nineteen cubicles, 4 cute private offices, and 2 shared offices. We'll get great affects from the high-res chromatography analysis, the shades and tints and hues will be awesome and Statistics indicate that most workers prefer private spaces that are in close proximity to the people they work with. It is clear that the same principal applies to managers and chief executives. According to our research, the number of Worker Compensation claims among employees who suffer from a form of repetitive motion syndrome is greatly reduced by using high-quality, adjustable chairs and desks.

We have forwarded a copy of this proposal to Frank Nabata in Winnipeg who I remember your secretary said really makes all the big decisions. We will be very interested in what he recommends.. If you have any questions, please feel free to contact me whenever. You can either reach me at my office or can call me at my home number, (709)5330099.

We look forward to starting soon. Thank you for taking the time to review this proposal.

Very sincerely yours,

Jessica Greyland

J. Greyland, Human Factors Consultant
SUPERLATIVE DESIGN
JG/jg

7. Greyland has made several assumptions in this proposal. One appears in her first paragraph, another in the action request. What are the assumptions and how do you think Berakett would react to them?

8. How would you evaluate the proposal in terms of brevity, precision, and persuasiveness (targeting the intellect)?

9. Is Greyland's proposal solicited or unsolicited? Justify your answer.

Revision

Had Greyland been more professional, her unsolicited proposal would have looked more like the one shown in Figure 9.3. You'll note that

- Greyland recognizes that her letter might not be warmly received, and thus chooses an inductive strategy and a formal level of discourse;

- her emphasis on the changes at Superlative Design is implied acknowledgment of AEL's likely dissatisfaction with the company's earlier work;

- Greyland understands that she does not have the information required to produce a formal proposal and has thus formulated her letter as a request to submit one;

- Greyland has tried to create a "total package" by paying attention to the complementary CMAPP attributes covered in Chapter 5.

EXERCISES

9.1 Identify and briefly describe the four types of proposals discussed in this chapter.

9.2 Using examples, describe the CMAPP implications for each type of proposal identified in question 9.1.

9.3 Distinguish between informal and formal proposals.

9.4 Explain why proposals employ primarily a persuasive communication strategy.

9.5 Explain why proposals target the intellect rather than the emotions.

9.6 Indicate whether proposals employ the *direct* strategy or the *indirect* strategy (introduced in Chapter 6), and explain why.

9.7 Assume that you and several of your classmates believe it would be more beneficial for your education in a particular course you are taking to work on a term project rather than take the currently scheduled final exam. Construct a CMAPP analysis for the proposal you would submit to your professor.

9.8 Using the guidelines provided in Chapter 3, construct a formal multi-level outline for your term project proposal.

9.9 Write your term project proposal.

Figure 9.3: Greyland's Revised Proposal

Superlative Design Limited

105–321 Prince Philip Drive St. John's NF A1J 1A6
Phone: 709-528-7475 Fax: 709-528-7476

April 20, 2000

Ms. Leila Berakett, Senior Associate
Accelerated Enterprises Ltd.
101 Signal Hill Road
St. John's NF A1B 9A7

Dear Ms. Berakett:

Since our contract with you last year, Superlative Design has undergone a number of changes: a new management structure, new quality control and quality assessment procedures, the addition of two highly experienced, accredited interior designers, and a renewed and more clearly articulated commitment to client satisfaction. I am pleased to report that over the last several months our efforts have brought us compliments from both private- and public-sector clients, including Bentley Industries, WireCo, and the Department of Municipal and Provincial Affairs.

Our policy is to work closely with our clients. Listening carefully to client concerns and consulting with clients on a regular basis are helping Superlative Design to provide accurate estimates, competitive pricing, quality design, and strict adherence to budgets and deadlines.

It has come to my attention that you are planning further renovations to AEL's St. John's offices. Although I recognize that you have not gone to public tender, I would appreciate your giving Superlative Design the opportunity to submit a detailed bid. I am certain that we would be able to meet your needs quickly and effectively.

I hope you will allow us to discuss your requirements, and I would ask you to call me to arrange a meeting at your convenience.

Thank you for taking the time to consider the new Superlative Design.

Yours truly,

Jessica Greyland

Jessica Greyland
Partner

EXPLORING THE WEB

Here are some Web sites you might wish to investigate.

URL	DESCRIPTION
http://www.bus.orst.edu/faculty/ shawd/tutorial/proposals.htm	The Proposals page (maintained by Donna Shaw of Oregon State University) offers advice on writing proposals, as well as links to pages that provide information on other aspects of business and technical communications.
http://www.opticalresolution.com/free.htm	Optical Resolution, a communications consulting firm, offers a free newsletter with simple tutorials on effective writing.
http://library.hilton.kzn.school.za/English/ english.htm	The English Resources page (maintained by Hilton College in Durban, South Africa) provides links to sites dealing with technical writing and related topics.

Common Products (3): Reports and Summaries

In this chapter, we examine two often interrelated CMAPP products: reports and summaries. Oral reports, or presentations, are dealt with in Chapter 11.

Characteristics of Written Reports

As a student, you have probably had to read books and then write about them, or to complete application forms for course transcript requests or club memberships. At some point, you'll likely have to submit an income tax return to the Canada Customs and Revenue Agency, sign up for a medical or dental plan, keep track of sales statistics, record experiments you conducted, or list your company's activities over the last year. Each of these documents is a report. Every report, whether written or oral, can be defined as an organized set of information created in response to an expressed need; in other words, you create a report specifically because a particular audience has requested one.

Written reports can be grouped into two broad categories:

- informal reports, also called short reports; and

- formal reports, also called long reports.

The terms *short* and *long* do not refer simply to length. (In fact, a long short report may be longer than a short long report.) The distinction relates more to the report's structural conventions.

Let's now look at some common characteristics of written reports, both formal and informal.

Response to Need or Request

So far as I know, no one gets up in the morning exclaiming, "I want to write a report today! Now, what should I write about?" You produce a report because someone has asked for it. A report is thus an audience-driven document. As such, it requires you to focus particular attention on your audience and your context.

Rationale

The needs met by written reports are virtually limitless. For example, a report can

- keep others informed of developing situations (e.g., consecutive reports on traffic accidents at a particular corner);

- maintain a permanent record of events (e.g., a scientist's or an engineer's detailed description of a series of experiments);

- reduce errors stemming from faulty recollections or confused interpretations (e.g., witness statements concerning a laboratory accident);

- facilitate planning and decision-making (e.g., a comparison of the Linux and Windows computer operating systems);

- fulfill legal requirements (e.g., a corporation's annual report, an income tax return, or a workers' compensation report on an injury or accident on the job); or

- fulfill administrative requirements (e.g., a company's pay and benefits records, or a medical expense claim form).

The transcript that appears in Figure 10.1 is an example of a report that fulfills administrative requirements.

Hierarchy

If you are the originator of a report within an organization, one of your primary CMAPP considerations should be that organization's hierarchy. In general, you can consider your report as being either *lateral* or *vertical*.

- *Lateral*   Suppose that you are the manager of the steel-detailing group in an engineering firm and have been asked to produce a report on your staff's progress on a particular job. If your primary audience is the manager of the structural drafting section, you are writing for an audience at approximately the same level in the organization, and your report is therefore *lateral*. Your audience, another manager, will have concerns similar to your own with regard to day-to-day activities, level of detail, and so on. These factors, part of the *context*, will influence not only your purpose, but your message (including the report's organization and the language you use).

- *Vertical*   If the principal audience for your report is the vice-president of the design division, someone above you in the organizational hierarchy, your report will be vertical. The VP will likely be interested less in the minutiae of your staff's accomplishments than in the big picture (e.g., the effects on the bottom line). In fact, the VP may very well not have the technical expertise to appreciate the finer points of detailing. By tailoring your report to the results of your CMAPP analysis, you will create a product quite different from the lateral report.

Level of Technicality

Because the level of expertise of your primary audience will dictate the language of your report, the level of technicality is not necessarily dependent on whether the report is lateral or vertical. For example, your primary audience in the first example above

Figure 10.1: Transcript

Mississauga University Transcript of Student Academic Record

Name: Rosalind Rebecca Greene **Student Number:** 1123835988 **Page #** 1

Date of Birth: 69-03-15 **Current Program:** General Studies **Date of Issue:** 99-08-17

Envelope Issued To:
Rosalind Rebecca Greene
#1802–2889 Don Mills Road
Toronto ON M4J 2J5

CONFIDENTIAL COPY
Not valid if removed from sealed
envelope before delivery to
requesting institution.

Mississauga University

R.M. Concorde

Signature of Registrar

Course		Title	Crd	Grd	GPA	Course		Title	Crd	Grd	GPA
Fall Semester 1996						**Fall Semester 1997**					
CMNS	220	App. Bus&TecComm	3.00	B+	3.33	ANTH	320	Advncd Rsh. Tchnqs	3.00	A–	3.67
LITR	210	19th Cent Can. Survey	3.00	B+	3.33	PHIL	150	Survey	3.00	A–	3.67
POLS	245	Early 19th Upper Can.	3.00	B	3.00	SOCI	220	Histor.Ovrview	3.00	B	3.00
POLS	255	Party Systems Anal.	3.00	B	3.00	SPAN	100	Intro	3.00	A–	3.67
SOCI	200	Intro Part 2	3.00	C+	2.33	TCWR	200	MISY Reports	3.00	B	3.00
			Semester: 2.99						**Semester: 3.40**		
Spring Semester 1997						**Spring Semester 1998**					
MISY	214	System Design	3.00	C+	2.33	ENGL	352	Short Story	3.00	A	4.00
MISY	225	System Devel.	3.00	C+	2.33	ENGL	355	Drama Survey	3.00	A	4.00
MISY	229	System Eval.	3.00	C	2.00	MISY	300	LAN connctns	3.00	C+	2.33
PSYC	210	Intro. Statistics	3.00	C+	2.33	MISY	320	Advncd Design	3.00	C+	2.33
TCWR	110	Intro.Tech.Writing	3.00	B+	3.33	MISY	330	Advncd Develop	3.00	B–	2.67
			Semester: 2.46						**Semester: 3.07**		
Summer Semester 1997						**Summer Semester 1998**					
COMP	200	Basic Hrdware Design	3.00	A–	3.67	MISY	350	Intro OS Langs	3.00	B	3.00
COMP	210	Intr. Hrdware Trblshoot	3.00	A	4.00	MISY	355	Intro SysTech	3.00	B	3.00
COMP	215	Intro LAN/WAN	3.00	A	4.00	FRNC	200	Lang & Lit	3.00	A–	3.67
COMP	218	Intro System Recog.	3.00	B+	3.33	PHIL	200	Ethics	3.00	A	4.00
PHYS	110	Intro Physics 2	3.00	A	3.67	TCWR	300	Manuals	3.00	A	4.00
			Semester: 3.73						**Semester: 3.53**		
			YEAR:	**3.07**					**YEAR:**	**3.29**	

might be the personnel manager, whose knowledge of steel detailing is negligible. Although your report in that case would be lateral, you would try to avoid technical jargon. Conversely, if the primary audience for your vertical report were a vice-president who is a practising structural engineer, you would likely support some of your points by using the appropriate technical terminology.

But consider the following situation. Your supervisor, the drafting director, has requested your report and is thus your primary audience. Your supervisor can be considered a technical audience, but you've been told your report will also go to the vice-president of public relations, a lay (nontechnical) audience. Common practice would be to write your report at a high level of technicality for your primary audience (your supervisor) and to append to your report a brief, nontechnical document (often in the form of an executive summary, discussed later in this chapter) for your secondary audience, the VP.

Informal Reports

Characteristics

Informal reports share a number of common characteristics having to do with focus, format, length, and content.

Single Focus   An informal report normally addresses a single issue. Note that "single" does not mean "simple." For example, Melinda Shaw, RAI's VP in Regina, might submit to Gilles Radisson in Ottawa a seven-page report with the *Subject* line "Decline in Sales of Global Minotaur, Regina Dealership, 1996–1999." Her report would certainly include sales statistics. But it might also examine related areas such as supply of new cars, service department concerns about deficient Minotaur components, parts availability, and customer complaints following a Minotaur recall notice. Because the report is a short report with a single focus, however, Shaw would not include an analysis of general advertising budgets for her dealership, or her reaction to the RAI reorganization.

Varied Product Format   Like proposals, informal reports can take the form of a variety of other CMAPP products, including the following:

- *Letter*   Noam Avigdor, an AEL Toronto senior associate specializing in civil engineering, might use a letter as the format for the report on seismic upgrading to the Plumbing and Electrical Building at GTI he is preparing for Cal Sacho, GTI's senior facilities manager.

- *Memo*   Before creating her report to Gilles Radisson, Melinda Shaw asked her manager of new car sales, Caroline Pritchard, to give her biweekly updates on both

Minotaur sales and customer comments. As well, she asked Dean Wong, her service manager, to report every two weeks on Minotaur service incidents. Because both reports were written communications within an organization, Pritchard and Wong appropriately used the memo format.

■ *Report*   Whether *internal* or *external* (as defined in Chapter 9), an informal report may be a document titled "Report on ..." For example, Avigdor might have chosen as his product a document headed "Report on Seismic Upgrading Requirements for the Plumbing and Electrical Building at Grandstone Technical Institute." Similarly, Shaw might have produced a document entitled "Report on Decline in Sales of Global Minotaur, Regina Dealership, 1996–1999." Such a product is typically introduced by a transmittal memo or letter.

■ *Prepared Form*   Many informal reports are communicated through prepared forms. Examples might include the last speeding ticket you received on your way to campus, the transcript in Figure 10.1, the purchase order in Figure 10.2, your income tax return, a magazine subscription form, and the federal government Census Information form that you or your family were required to complete. Such prepared forms proliferate in our society. Whatever their intended use, they allow information to be recorded in a standard, well-organized format.

Length   Short reports normally do not exceed a few pages, although some may actually be longer than some long reports. Consider the following examples:

■ When you receive a parking ticket, the official who fills out the form is, in effect, completing a short report: information with a single focus recorded on a prepared form. Such a report typically runs to no more than half a page.

■ The income tax return you prepare for the Canada Customs and Revenue Agency deals with a single issue: your income tax situation in a particular year. Running some four to eight pages, your tax return is also a short report.

■ AEL submits an income tax return as well. The complexities of the firm's operations are such that the return runs some 77 pages. Nonetheless, AEL's return has a single focus (just as yours did); despite its length, it qualifies as a short or informal report.

Content   The content of an informal report may consist of the following:

■ *Text only:* for example, several paragraphs, perhaps with one or more bulleted lists, or a prepared form such as a parking ticket.

■ *Text and visuals:* for example, Shaw's report to Radisson, which consists of tables of sales figures integrated into several pages of text.

■ *Visuals only:* for example, the table of registration figures, shown in Figure 10.3, that was submitted to Roger Concorde, the Mississauga University registrar.

Figure 10.2: Purchase Order

Radisson Automobiles Inc.

Purchase Order

Quality and Service for Over 50 Years

Radisson Automobiles Radisson

6134 Bank Street
Ottawa ON K2A 2B3
613.433.9888 Fax 613.433.0826

Ensure that Purchase Order Number
immediately below appears on ALL documentation.

GST Reg./Business #: R455000999348

P.O. NUMBER:

To: Ship To:

P.O. DATE	REQUISITIONER	SHIP VIA	F.O.B. POINT	TERMS

QTY	UNIT	DESCRIPTION	UNIT PRICE	TOTAL

SUBTOTAL	
SALES TAX	
SHIPPING & HANDLING	
GST @7%	
OTHER	
TOTAL	

1. This invoice is your official notification.
2. No changes to specifications may be made without
   the express, written permission of Radisson Automobiles.
3. Immediately notify the company officer if you are unable to
   ship as specified.
4. Direct inquiries to:
   George Finlay, General Manager
   Radisson Automobiles Inc.
   6134 Bank Street Ottawa ON K2A 2B3
   613.433-9888 (direct); Fax 613.433-0826
   Head Office: 613.433-9800

Authorized by
_____

Date
_____

Figure 10.3: Registration Figures

1995–1999 Registration by Discipline

	1995	1996	1997	1998	1999	Total
Anthropology	98	88	80	81	77	424
Engineering	105	220	209	231	240	1005
English Literature	224	201	222	219	214	1080
Medicine	255	305	321	350	362	1593
Philosophy	243	222	285	345	385	1480
Psychology	398	421	445	449	512	2225
Geology	111	108	100	120	102	541
Sociology	176	114	101	99	77	567
Totals	**1610**	**1679**	**1763**	**1894**	**1969**	**8915**

Classification

One way of looking at informal reports is to classify them according to the main function they serve. The most common types include the following:

■ *Incident Report*   An incident report documents what happened in a particular situation. It also assumes that the incident is not likely to be repeated. Examples of incident reports would include a safety officer's report on an accident in a large industrial operation, a report on the installation of a new telephone exchange, or the transcript shown in Figure 10.1.

■ *Sales Report*   A sales report presents sales figures for a particular business. Sales reports may consist entirely or almost entirely of visuals, often a table or a graph, as evidenced by the registration data in Figure 10.3 or the sales report (shown in Figure 10.4) prepared by Caroline Pritchard and submitted to Melinda Shaw.

■ *Progress Report*   A progress report indicates the extent to which something has been completed. Examples might include the state of your investment portfolio, the progress of a construction project, the condition of a hospital patient, or your midterm marks.

■ *Periodic Report*   A periodic report appears at regular intervals and focuses on the same issue. Periodic reports might range from daily updates on the results of drilling an oil well to the annual *Maclean's* magazine report on universities in Canada. If Caroline Pritchard were to produce regular reports on RAI Regina sales, they too would constitute periodic reports.

Figure 10.4: Sales Report

RAI Regina: 1st Quarter Sales 2000

	Jan. 1 to Jan. 15	Jan. 16 to Jan. 31	Feb. 1 to Feb. 14	Feb. 14 to Feb. 29	Mar. 1 to Mar. 15	Mar. 16 to Mar. 31	Totals
Chevrolet Impala	12	10	15	13	14	9	73
Ford Windstar	15	18	22	15	19	20	109
Global Minotaur	49	55	56	58	21	15	254
Global Whirlwind	53	65	34	48	22	18	240
Jeep Cherokee	22	25	28	25	29	32	161
Pontiac Sunfire	18	22	15	35	22	32	144
Totals	169	195	170	194	127	126	981

■ *Trip Report*   A trip report might include a site inspection by an engineer to determine the condition of a building site, a field trip by a mining engineer seeking appropriate sites for test holes, a hydro crew member's report on the repair of downed cables, or a professional's report on a recently attended conference.

■ *Test Report*   Tests reports are often completed on prepared forms or according to strict format and wording guidelines. Such reports might include a research biochemist's report on the testing of certain pharmaceuticals, a software engineer's report on debugging and recompilation of operating system subroutines, or an advertising executive's report on the results of a focus group session.

There is considerable overlap among the six types of reports. For example, a biweekly report on car sales would be both a sales report and a periodic report, while a series of regularly scheduled reports covering the various stages of developing a new antidepressant drug would be test reports, progress reports, and periodic reports.

Categories

Your CMAPP context and purpose will lead you to construct a report that falls into one of two general categories: informative (or content) reports or analytical (or persuasive) reports.

Informative Reports   "Just the facts, ma'am." An informative, or content, report should comply with Sergeant Joe Friday's request: it should provide, as objectively and as precisely as possible, the facts.

Leaving your opinion out of a report is no easy task. Suppose that a recent fee increase at your school has left you and your fellow students incensed. But suppose also that you are writing an informative report on the issue. If you refer in your report to "the unreasonable and unjustified hardship imposed on the unsuspecting student body by this untimely and disproportionate fee increase," you are not adhering to the rules for writing informative reports, because the connotation of your words expresses your own opinion. Rather, you might have stated, "Approximately 35% of the students interviewed believed that the $275 per term fee increase will have an adverse effect." Such wording is objective and verifiable: it is informative.

You should organize the body of your report clearly and logically. Common organization patterns include the follow:

- chronological (e.g., a student council meeting);
- spatial or geographical (e.g., the building of a new campus);
- topical (e.g., transportation options around your school);
- importance—from highest to lowest or vice versa (e.g., the impact of turning recreation space into new classrooms).

When completing a prepared form, you will probably be required to follow the organization pattern of the form itself, be it a student loan application, a personnel record form, or a marketing survey report.

Analytical Reports   Variously called analytical, evaluative, or persuasive reports, these reports require you to narrate the "facts" and then comment on them. You voice your opinion through your analysis and/or recommendations. Suppose that you are asked to suggest ways for your student council to respond to an announcement of raised fees. You might create an analytical report that would examine the issue, analyze its ramifications, offer alternatives for the student council, and, probably, indicate which option you prefer.

Normally, you will organize an analytical report in one of two ways. Very common in business settings, the *deductive* or *direct pattern* attempts to provide as quickly and clearly as possible the recommendations that the audience has requested. The following sequence of elements is typical.

1. *Problem* or *Introduction:*   very briefly sets out the reason for the report.

2. *Recommendations:*   precisely and concisely states the recommendations resulting from the analysis.

3. *Background* or *Facts:*   presents relevant details concerning the issues.

4. *Discussion* or *Solution(s):*   discusses the issues, develops the arguments, analyzes the aspects of the problem, and demonstrates evidence for the report's assertions.

In the example described above, you would likely have organized your report so that the student council could quickly note the topic of your report and immediately examine your recommendations; reading the rest of your report, and thus determining how you reached those recommendations, would be optional.

Note the CMAPP implications: your audience is already aware of the subject, and, having requested your recommendations, will respond positively to receiving them, even if their content raises concerns.

If your audience is unfamiliar with the issues or is likely to react negatively to receiving recommendations, you should choose the *inductive* or *indirect pattern.* It follows the steps you often use when you are thinking something through: you prepare the audience for your recommendations by first explaining your route. The inductive pattern incorporates the same elements as the deductive pattern, but the sequence is as follows:

1. Problem or Introduction
2. Background or Facts
3. Discussion or Solution(s)
4. Recommendations

The success of your analytical report will depend in large part on how well you organize items 2 and 3, the background and discussion segments. Suppose that the provincial government has asked you to make recommendations on the issue of post-secondary fees. You could organize the background and discussion segments by *option* or *issue,* as illustrated in Figure 10.5.

Figure 10.5: Organization by Option or Issue

Option	Issue
Raise Fees	**Impact on Students**
Impact on Students	Raise Fees
Impact on Taxpayers	Maintain Fees
Impact on Education	Lower Fees
Maintain Fees	**Impact on Taxpayers**
Impact on Students	Raise Fees
Impact on Taxpayers	Maintain Fees
Impact on Education	Lower Fees
Lower Fees	**Impact on Education**
Impact on Students	Raise Fees
Impact on Taxpayers	Maintain Fees
Impact on Education	Lower Fees

The first column shows organization by option. For the first option—raising fees—you would look at each issue:

- the effect on students, since they will have to pay the fees;
- the effect on taxpayers, since they will also be affected;
- the potential effect on the education provided at the institution.

You would repeat the process for the second and third options, maintaining and lowering fees. By looking at the same issues for each of the options, you are in effect comparing apples with apples, not with oranges.

The second column shows organization by issue. The three issues are the impact of fees on students, taxpayers, and education. For each of the three issues, you would "compare apples with apples" by examining the same options: raising, maintaining, or lowering fees.

How do you decide which organization pattern to use? Conduct a CMAPP analysis. In our scenario, your audience is provincial bureaucrats. Because that audience would likely want to focus on financial implications, you would probably select the organization pattern that places emphasis on raising, maintaining, or lowering fees: organization by option.

But suppose that your audience is members of the student council who want to stimulate public opposition to higher fees by focusing on the negative impact on students and (if they could make the argument) on taxpayers and education as well. Such an audience might well prefer a report organized by issue.

Formal Reports

Formal, or long, reports need not run hundreds of pages, although some—the annual reports of large businesses such as Ontario Hydro, for example—might well do so. Generally, their length is dictated by their content and structure. As Figure 10.6 shows, the body of a formal report mirrors the three-part structure of other technical communications.

Formal reports differ from informal reports in the following aspects:

1. *Multiple Focus*   The report deals with the interrelationships of a number of issues.
2. *Complex Content*   The message is complex and thus requires considerable analysis and synthesis. Not only will a secondary message almost inevitably complement the primary message, but a long report frequently harbours a secondary purpose as well. Often, the primary message will be informative, while the secondary message will be persuasive—for example, convincing shareholders how well management has run the company.
3. *Detailed Organization*   A multi-level outline (see Chapter 3) is used to develop the multiple focus and complex content.

Figure 10.6: Structure of Different Types of Communications

Formal Report	Other CMAPP Products	Business Presentation	Traditional Prose Paragraph
Front pieces			
Body • Introductory information • Discussion • Conclusion	• Introductory topic summary • Body text • Concluding summary	• Introduction • Body • Conclusion	• Topic sentence • Supporting sentences • Concluding sentence
End pieces			

4. *Format*   The long report never takes the form of a letter, a memo, or a prepared form; rather, it accompanies the transmittal memo (internal) or letter (external) that introduces it.

5. *Content*   The long report will always contains substantial text, often enhanced by visuals; it can never consist of visuals alone.

Structure

Most formal reports follow a three-part structure consisting of front pieces, body, and end pieces.

Front Pieces   Also referred to as *front pages* or *front matter*, front pieces assist the audience in dealing with the complexities of the report. They are numbered separately from the body of the report, usually with lowercase roman numerals.

Standard front pieces include the following:

1. *Transmittal Letter* or *Transmittal Memo*   The transmittal letter or memo introduces the report to the audience; it may also direct the audience's attention to particular passages or recommendations. A transmittal letter or memo that runs longer than one page is numbered separately from the other front pieces.

2. *Title Page* or *Cover Page*   The title or cover page typically presents the title of the report, the name of the author, the identity of the primary audience, and the submission date. The title page is not numbered.

3. *Abstract*   The abstract (discussed later in this chapter) is a brief description and assessment of the report. Most abstracts appear on a separate, unnumbered page.

4. *Executive Summary*   The executive summary presents the main points of the report, often for the benefit of a nontechnical secondary audience. The executive summary always begins on a new page.

5. *Table of Contents*   The table of contents lists the level heads of the report and the page number on which each appears. It provides a clear picture of the organization of the document, and allows the audience to easily locate particular sections.

   The table of contents always begins on a new page and is typically the first numbered page in the front matter.

6. *List of Figures*   The List of Figures (also titled List of Illustrations, Table of Figures, or Table of Illustrations) indicates the page numbers on which the illustrations appear. It serves as a secondary table of contents in a report whose message relies significantly on its visuals (e.g., one that emphasizes comparisons and contrasts among tables of costs).

Body   The body constitutes the bulk of the formal report. When roman numerals are used in the front matter, the body begins with arabic number 1. Mirroring the three-part structure of *introduction, body,* and *conclusion,* the body begins with an overview, proceeds to a description and analysis of the issues, and concludes with a short summation and, in some cases, a set of recommendations.

End Pieces   Also called *end pages* or *end matter,* end pieces furnish relevant information not included in the body. The end matter typically picks up the arabic numbering where the body left off.

Standard end pieces include the following:

1. *Appendix*   A report may include one or more appendixes. (An alternative plural is *appendices.*) An appendix contains material not essential to an understanding of the report but of potential interest to the audience. Examples would include a table that is too long or cumbersome to be included in the main body of the text, a transcript of an interview, or the full text of a document referred to in the report.

2. *Endnotes*   Like a footnote, an endnote provides additional information about a particular part of the report. Unlike a footnote, an endnote is placed at the end of the report rather than at the bottom of the page. If you use endnotes in your report, you should follow the note form outlined in your chosen style guide.

3. *Glossary*   Sometimes used as a front piece, a glossary is an alphabetized list of words or phrases that the report's author believes may require definition or explanation.

The choice of glossary items should depend on the results of a CMAPP analysis, particularly with respect to level of technicality.

4. *Works Cited*   If your report contains quoted material, you may use a works cited page to present the bibliographic credits for your citations. The format you use will, once again, depend on your style guide.

5. *Bibliography*   More comprehensive than a works cited page, the bibliography lists research sources such as books, periodicals, interviews, and Web sites. The sources are typically arranged alphabetically, by the last names of authors. Again, consult your style guide.

6. *Index*   An index is a list of alphabetically arranged entries (consisting primarily of key words and concepts) that appears at the very end of the report. Whether you include an index will depend on the nature of your report. An index is particularly appropriate in the case of a report that is long, complex, and technically oriented. When developing an index, you should take care to ensure that it does not simply replicate the listing of level heads in the table of contents. You should also conduct a CMAPP analysis to determine which key words and terms your audience is most likely to want to look up.

Summaries

If you were asked to tell someone what you've done over the last 24 hours, it's unlikely you'd describe in detail every activity you could recall. (Such an account would be excruciating for your audience.) In all likelihood, you would select the activities you consider most significant and briefly recount them. You would, in effect, be creating a summary.

In the context of technical communications, a written summary is a concise document that conveys the original document's important ideas and, in some cases, its significant details. What are significant details? The answer lies in a CMAPP analysis. For example, imagine that you had to summarize a complex, technical report on weather conditions in the Toronto area over the past 10 years. If the audience for the summary (not necessarily the same audience as that for the report) were a group of graduate students in a meteorology program, they would likely think significant such things as the annual mean temperature and the average yearly snowfall. If the audience were a company that staged outdoor events, however, the significant details would likely include the amount of precipitation on holidays such as Canada Day.

Categories

Summaries can be grouped into two broad categories: content summaries and evaluative summaries. *Content summaries,* also known as *informative summaries* or *informative abstracts,* sum up the important elements of the original document. Objectivity is crucial in a content summary, which should not contain embellishment, opinion, or highly connotative vocabulary.

Two special types of content summaries are minutes and executive summaries. *Minutes* are the record of what occurred at a meeting; they document decisions made, actions to be taken, and, on occasion, comments made. As mentioned earlier, an *executive summary* is a summary found in the front matter of a formal report. An executive summary often targets a secondary audience that is less technical than the primary audience. Executive summaries typically do not exceed a single page.

Evaluative summaries, also known as *analytic summaries* or *assessment summaries,* provide not only the essential ideas of the original document, but also the author's opinions, often in the form of recommendations.

Two special types of evaluative summaries are descriptive abstracts and abstracts. Most common in an academic context, the *descriptive abstract* (generally no longer than a few lines) presents a synopsis of the original documents, followed by a brief indication of the document's value or applicability to the project at hand. A descriptive abstract that follows an entry in a bibliography is often called an *annotation*— hence the term "annotated bibliography."

If you had written a report on the use of Windows NT versus UNIX in your company, and your bibliography included the book *UNIX for Dummies,* your annotation for that title might resemble the following:

> Part of the popular series of "Dummies" books, this is a 360-page primer on the operating system that still underlies a large part of the World Wide Web. Though the book is at times self-consciously populist and facetious, its 30 chapters provide a useful (and relatively nontechnical) introduction to UNIX.

A standard front piece in reports is the *abstract,* which presents a brief description of the report and offers the reader (typically the secondary audience) an evaluation of it (usually a very positive one). Abstracts tend to be shorter than executive summaries. Figure 10.7 shows examples of an executive summary and an abstract.

Content and Length

What you should include in, and exclude from, a summary depends on whether it is a content summary or an evaluative summary. In most cases, you can apply the criteria listed in Figure 10.8.

How long should a summary or abstract be? The answer is *as short as possible* and *as long as necessary.* As you saw in Chapter 5, technical documents often require you to balance the need for precision against the need for brevity and concision. The more information you provide, the more you impose on your audience's time; the less information you provide, the more likely it is that your audience will not receive everything necessary.

Summaries typically run anywhere from 5 to 15 percent of the length of the original. However, keep in mind the inverse proportion rule, whereby the longer the

Figure 10.7: Executive Summary and Abstract

Personnel Strategies for RAI Toronto Dealership

Executive Summary

In January 2000, RAI requested that AEL identify personnel strategies for a potential RAI expansion into the Toronto market. That investigation has yielded two potential strategies:

1. Senior staff to be drawn from RAI's Head Office in Ottawa. This strategy would involve the relocation to Toronto of Vice-President Alberto Chavez, General Manager George Finlay, and Sales Manager Mariela van Damm, with concomitant backfilling.

2. Senior staff to be drawn from (a) RAI's Montreal dealership (involving the relocation of General Manager Michel Gagné, who would become Toronto Vice-President, and Sales Manager Maurice Duclos), and (b) RAI's Winnipeg dealership (General Manager Carole Schusterman), again with concomitant backfilling.

Abstract

AEL recently identified two strategies for effectively staffing RAI's planned Toronto dealership. Both meet RAI's budget provisions and take excellent advantage of local conditions. While either is likely to prove successful, one relies primarily on nearby RAI in-house expertise in Ottawa, while the other would draw on RAI's Montreal and Winnipeg locations for the necessary expertise.

original document, the smaller the percentage of its length that will be required for a summary. For example, a summary of a three-page report might be just over half a page (close to 20 percent), while a summary of a 200-page report might run two full pages (only 1 percent). Remember, too, that most executive summaries still do not exceed a single page, regardless of the length of the original document.

Content Summary Process

Creating an effective content summary can be a complex and painstaking undertaking. Following are suggestions for each of the stages of that process.

Figure 10.8: Content of Summaries

Content Summary		Evaluative Summary	
Often Includes	**Typically Excludes**	**Often Includes**	**Typically Excludes**
• Overall theme or goal	• Opinion	• Overall theme or goal	• Since the purpose here is evaluation or assessment, it is impossible to identify any *a priori* exclusions.
• Main points	• New information	• Main points	
• Significant details	• Insignificant details	• Assessment / evaluation of original's content	
• Reference to any conclusions in the original document	• Embellishments		
	• Technical jargon (if possible)	• Assessment / evaluation of original's effectiveness	
• Reference to any recommendations in the original document	• Supportive examples or illustrations		
	• Visuals		
	• Quotations		
	• Citation credits		

1. *Familiarization*   First, become thoroughly familiar with the original text. Doing so involves much more than the one cursory reading you might prefer. If you are the author of the original document, the rule still applies: writing something is not the same as reading it. When familiarizing yourself with a document you have written, approach it as though you were not the author.

2. *Identification and Marking*   Identify the main points and significant details. While you will want to be as objective as possible, you are in a position not unlike that of a television news director who has to choose which items to broadcast, how much time to devote to each, and how to present each one. Selection is by definition a subjective process.

   You can make a concerted effort to *try* to be objective by making use of verbal cues in the original document. You can look, for example, for words or phrases that suggest importance in the mind of the document's author. These include:

   ▪ Pointers: 1st, 2nd, 3rd, next, last, etc.

   ▪ Causes: thus, therefore, as a result, consequently, etc.

- Contrasts: however, despite, nonetheless, etc.
- Essentials: moreover, in general, most importantly, furthermore, etc.

As you identify the points you need to include, mark them (you can star, underline, or highlight) *on your own copy* of the document. (You should not, of course, mark up other people's materials.) Try to identify single words or very short phrases; if you mark whole sentences, your task later in the process will be much more difficult.

3. *Collection and (Re)organization* If you write out all the words and phrases you have identified, you will be faced with something that looks much like the results of the data collection that you examined in Chapter 3. You must now organize that data into usable information. In effect, you will be creating a multi-level outline for what will essentially be a *new* document. This is an important point. A summary is an original document—not merely an abridgment. As such, it will not replicate phrasing used in the original document.

   As you develop your outline, you may sometimes find that in order to make your summary "flow" effectively, you have to reorganize some elements. Such reorganization is acceptable provided that your summary would not confuse an audience that is familiar with the original document, and that it does not take on a slant or bias not apparent in that document.

4. *Draft* Now that you have an outline, write your first draft, treating it like any other technical communications product you would create.

5. *Revision and Final* Review, edit, revise, proofread, and check again. Remember that your summary, like every other CMAPP product, reflects on you and your credibility.

CASE STUDY

RAI Report on Participation in GTI Internship Program

Situation

In 1998, Radisson Automobiles participated in Grandstone Technical Institute's Internship Program. Several students in GTI's Automotive Mechanics and Electronics programs secured work placements with Radisson's Vancouver dealership. Upon graduating in the early summer of that year, most of these students applied for positions with Radisson and a number were hired. In 1999, as a result of union-related and financial issues, Radisson declined to participate in GTI's Internship Program. In the summer of 1999, Angelos Methoulios, the Internship Program coordinator, wrote to Howard Blumen, Radisson Vancouver's vice-president, requesting (a) that Radisson Vancouver report on its reaction to its 1998 participation, and (b) that the company consider participating again in the Internship Program in early 2000.

Blumen asked Corinne Chin, Radisson Vancouver's general manager, to take care of the matter. Chin consulted company records and sought additional input from both Larry Cornetski, the service manager, and Emily Cardinal, the personnel manager. Having concluded that their 1998 participation in the program had been worthwhile, and that it would be in Radisson Vancouver's interest to take part again, Chin created for Methoulios the report that appears in Figure 10.9.

Issues to Think About

1. How would you describe the context at the outset of this case study?

2. Why do you think that Blumen chose to have Chin deal with the matter instead of dealing with it himself?

3. From your answer to question 2, what can you infer about the relationship between Blumen and Chin?

4. Is Chin's report formal or informal? What are the criteria that led you to your answer?

5. How would you summarize Chin's primary message? Can you see a secondary message? If so, what do you think it is?

6. What do you think of Chin's choice of product? Would you have chosen a different one? If so, why?

7. How would you describe her primary purpose? Can you discern a secondary purpose? If so, what might it be?

8. The primary audience is Methoulios. Do you see a secondary audience? If so, who is it?

9. Does the report reflect a deductive or inductive strategy? Did Chin make the right choice? (Give reasons for your answers.)

10. How would you describe the report's organization pattern?

11. What "call to action" has she used to close her letter? How effective is it?

12. How do you think Methoulios will react to the report? What would you expect to happen next in this scenario?

13. Do you think Chin has made effective use of document visuals? (Support your answer with examples.)

EXERCISES

10.1 Give a brief definition of a report, and explain why a report is an audience-driven document.

Figure 10.9: Chin's Report on Internship Participation

Radisson
Fine Automobiles
927 East Broadway Vancouver BC V1N 2H8
604. 348-7256 Fax: 358-6443 Email: radiss.van@cars.com

Your file: IP98-RA1
Our file: CC970909.1

September 13, 1999

Mr. Angelos Methoulios
Coordinator, Internship Program
Grandstone Technical Institute
9999–2011th Street
Langley BC V1V 0M0

Radisson Participation in Grandstone Internship Program

Dear Mr. Methoulios:

Thank you for your letter of August 16, 1999, to our Vice-President, Mr. Howard Blumen. He has asked me to reply.

Your letter made two requests:

1. That we give you our views on our 1998 participation in your Internship Program;
2. That we consider participating again later this year.

First, here are our overall reactions.

Conclusions

1. As a whole, Radisson Vancouver staff regard the internship experience as having been positive for the company.
2. Recorded feedback from the students who interned with us suggests that for the most part they too found the experience productive and valuable.
3. Upon graduating, several students applied for full-time work with our company; three are now employees of Radisson Vancouver.
4. Although we foresee little opportunity for full-time hiring in 2000–01, we would be pleased to participate in the Internship Program in early 2000.

Let me now deal with each of your queries in detail.

Figure 10.9 (continued)

Methoulios, page 2

1998 Participation

In November of 1997, 14 students applied for internship positions with Radisson Vancouver. As a result of the subsequent interview process, and in the light of our own projected needs, we accepted eight for placement for the period of January 5, 1998, through March 6, 1998.

The students were assigned a variety of tasks and their progress was monitored by assigned Radisson personnel, who then provided our management with written feedback. The following table summarizes the information collected.

Student	GTI Area	RAI Work Sector	Comments From Staff
Peter Bennett	Automotive	Repair Shop Floor	Knowledgeable; conscientious; enthusiastic; learned quickly; good interpersonal skills; good communication skills; required little supervision. **Hired as apprentice mechanic, May/98.**
Penni Melele	Electronics	Administration	Excellent understanding of MIS electronics; broad operating system background; worked very quickly; thorough and meticulous; some difficulty accepting criticism; average interpersonal but excellent written communication skills.
Francine Orti	Automotive	Repair Shop Floor	Good independent worker; got along very well with mechanics and with customers; eager to learn; enthusiastic worker; intent on finding solutions to problems; excellent mechanical diagnostic sense; good interpersonal and communication skills. **Hired as apprentice mechanic, May/98.**
Jason Parakh	Automotive	Parts Dept.	Competent worker but rather unenthusiastic; argued at times with supervisor and with mechanics; seemed very keen on coffee/lunch breaks; often unwilling to accept personal responsibility for errors, problems, etc.

Figure 10.9 (continued)

Methoulios, page 3

Student	GTI Area	RAI Work Sector	Comments From Staff
Shiraz Ram	Electronics	Parts Dept.	Eager worker; quick learner; enthusiastic; punctilious; dealt extremely well with customers; always calm under pressure; sent thank-you notes to his supervisor; stayed in touch with company until graduation. **Hired into Parts Dept., May/98.**
Dana Rowan	Automotive	Repair Shop Floor	Good worker; good practical and diagnostic skills; good communicator; likable personality; good sense of responsibility; did not seek employment here.
Ahmed Sala	Automotive	Repair Shop Floor	Excellent worker; liked and respected by supervisor and mechanics; well above average expertise—had worked as mechanic for three years before coming to Canada; did not apply for employment here, despite supervisor's encouragement to do so.
Katie Wing	Electronics	Repair Shop Floor	Excellent theoretical knowledge; very conscientious; excellent interpersonal skills; well liked by all; made interesting comment: glad she had chance to work here—learned she prefers programming; did not apply for position.

2000 Participation

After discussions with appropriate personnel, I am pleased to inform you that Radisson Vancouver will have five internship openings for the spring of 2000:

(a) two Automotive Mechanics students in the repair bays;

(b) one Electronics student in the automotive service area;

Figure 10.9 (continued)

Methoulios, page 4

(c) one Electronics student in our expanding Parts Department;
(d) one Plumbing & Welding student in our Facilities Management area;

The placement period will be from January 3, 2000, through April 28, 2000.

Our lead-hand contact with Grandstone Technical Institute will be our personnel manager, Ms. Emily Cardinal, who can be reached by phone at 348-7256 and by fax at 358-6443.

Final Remarks
We are pleased that you kept Radisson Vancouver in mind when planning your Internship Program for the coming year. It is our conviction that partnerships of this kind between post-secondary educational institutions and established businesses are of enormous value. They provide capable students with the practical experience that allows them to enter the work force better prepared, and they confer on businesses such as ours the opportunity to get to know the people who often become the key to our own continued success. Believing programs such as yours to be essential to the growth of the provincial economy, Radisson Automobiles remains committed to them.

Thank you again for your interest in Radisson Automobiles. Ms. Cardinal looks forward to receiving your call over the next couple of weeks.

Yours sincerely,

C.R. Chin

Corinne Chin
General Manager

c.c. H. Blumen
　　　L. Cornetski
　　　E. Cardinal

10.2 Briefly describe four or more needs that are met by written reports.

10.3 Explain the difference between a lateral and a vertical report, and relate that difference to level of technicality.

10.4 Identify and describe at least three of the six types of informal reports discussed in this chapter, and give an example of each.

10.5 Describe the differences between informal and formal reports with respect to focus, format, length, and content.

10.6 Distinguish between an informative report and an analytical report.

10.7 Identify at least two of the four common organization patterns found in informative reports.

10.8 Describe the organizational difference between the deductive pattern and the inductive pattern used in analytical reports. Explain the CMAPP implications for each pattern.

10.9 Identify and briefly explain the two approaches to organizing the background and discussion segments of an analytical report.

10.10 Assume that you have been asked to write an informal analytical report on possible changes to the parking situation at your institution. Identify the two organizational approaches you might use. Explain which approach you would choose if your primary audience were:
(a) the senior administration of your institution
(b) the student association executive

10.11 Name the three main parts of a formal report. Identify and describe at least two elements in the first part and two elements in the third part.

10.12 Review Chin's report on Radisson participation. Imagine that her investigation had led her to conclude that RAI's experience with GTI's Internship Program had been of no benefit to the company. Rewrite the report accordingly, paying particular attention to the information you provide about the students, the wording you use to do so, and your concluding segment and call to action.

10.13 Distinguish between a content summary and an evaluative summary.

10.14 Briefly describe each of the following types of summaries:
(a) abstract (as front piece in a report)
(b) annotation
(c) executive summary

10.15 Summarize the article that appears in Box 10.1. Your summary should not exceed 150 words.

Box 10.1 Poorer Not Richer

Those of us lucky enough to reside on the south coast of British Columbia tend toward climatic snobbery. Unlike the typical Canadian, we need not dread (nor welcome, as do some peculiar individuals) the months that caused Samuel de Champlain, one of the first Europeans to attempt settlement in this country, to spurn the land as "quelques arpents de neige"—a few acres of snow. In this spring of 1989, however, we can look fondly back to a season in which even we occasionally participated in the great Canadian winter (by our standards, at least).

Among last winter's cruel tribulations was the embarrassment it engendered. In late February, Eastern Canadian visitors arrived on my doorstep expecting the crocuses and daffodils of which I had earlier boasted. They then smiled smugly through the cold and snow that seemed to make a sham of our much-vaunted lotus land. I suppose we must now work harder to bridge the credibility gap that this last Alaskan winter created. (Notice how using the innocent adjective "Alaskan" subtly shifts responsibility to a foreign power.)

Not long ago, Kathleeen Logan of CFMI Radio interviewed me for her *In Touch* program. Our conversation dealt with some of the peculiarities of English speech. Among the issues she raised was the widespread use of colloquialisms such as *kind of*. As Kathleen pointed out, it's not uncommon to hear a radio personality say "John's a really compassionate *kind of* guy" or "This portable TV is a high-tech *kind of* item." As words or expressions gain popular currency, they eventually assume a place in the lexicon of the educated speaker and writer. By way of example, critics once looked askance at the use of the word "hopefully" to mean "it is hoped" or "let us hope." In all but very formal speech, however, *hopefully* is now considered quite acceptable. In effect, English gained a new word to fill a recognized gap. But does the introduction of *kind of* really add to the language?

One may argue, I suppose, that *kind of* does convey information: it directs our attention to generalities rather than details; it suggests overall qualities rather than specific traits. But is its message really pertinent? Does it have the semantic wherewithal to command our linguistic respect? Or is it, rather, a cop-out in that it allows us to abrogate our responsibility to think when we speak or write?

Had the radio personality stated "John's compassionate," we would have formed a definite picture of John's character. Had the statement been "John's a compassionate guy," we would have been aware (however unconsciously) of the informality of the language used. The radio personality might have had to exercise greater discipline of thought to say, "Overall, John's a compassionate person." But we could then have inferred that John's behaviour does not always suggest compassion. In other words, *kind of* may add a little to the language, but I believe it subtracts even more, since it deters us from taking advantage of our language's superb ability to provide nuances of meaning.

Kathleen also noted that many people make almost exclusive use of the verb *go* to introduce direct quotations. Particularly in the speech of teenagers and young adults, *he goes* and *she went* replaces *he says* and *she said*. Does this reflect, Kathleen wondered, a desire to make speech active rather than merely descriptive? Certainly *going* evokes a more dynamic image than *saying*. But is the phenomenon a useful addition to the language? Once more, I suspect that what we're observing is a case of linguistic lassitude rather than inventiveness. And I would reiterate that its result is the depletion rather than the expansion of our language's resources.

In certain fields of human endeavour, it may well be highly efficient to replace five similar (although not necessarily identical) items with a single, generic one. Language, however, should not be forced to march to the same expedient drummer. Throughout the development of English, words have entered the language and words have disappeared from use. Fortunately, immigration has always exceeded emigration; thus, English boasts a cornucopia of vocabulary that delights articulate speakers as much as it dismays many of those who must learn the language. Nothing of value would be gained, I submit, were *go* to supplant *announce, confirm, cry, decry, denounce, deny, expostulate, imply, suggest, utter, whisper*, and a hundred other words. Rather, much would be lost.

Last summer the local media carried a human interest story that soon appeared on national television. A farmer on Vancouver Island had for years been offering free meals to eagles roosting near his field. The magnificent birds had grown accustomed to feasting on the unwanted beef carcasses that he had been leaving out for them. Then a small tragedy struck. Unwittingly, the farmer had given his feathered guests a toxic meal. A carcass he had given them contained high levels of a drug whose ingestion killed at least one eagle and sickened others. Luckily, the problem was discovered before more damage was done, and veterinarians were able to cure most of the afflicted eagles.

How does this story relate to language use? Initially in the West Coast media, and later on CBC's *The Journal*, reporters described the offending drug as a *barbituate*. Today's pharmacopoeia does contain a group of powerful (and not infrequently abused) medications known as *barbiturates*. To date, however, I have been unable to find a listing for *barbituate*.

National press and broadcasting exert a strong influence on our language. As a result, for example, many people have come to associate *scrum* with the anarchic questioning of a politician, rather than with the game of rugby. It would not be gross exaggeration to suggest that the media have become New Age lexicographers. If the word "barbituate" is repeated often enough, it may well take the place of its more legitimate predecessor.

Indeed, about a year after the afflicted-eagle story first appeared, a reference in the local newspaper caught my attention. It referred to the abuse of *barbituates*. Tune in a quarter-century from now for the conclusion to the *barbiturates/barbituates* saga.

EXPLORING THE WEB

Here are some Web sites you might wish to investigate.

URL	DESCRIPTION
http://www.annualreportservice.com/	The online Public Register's Annual Report Service provides links to hundreds of online company annual reports.
http://www.ifi.uio.no/~inint/Gamle/ H1997/report.html	"Writing Technical Reports: An Introduction for Computer Scientists," a 1997 article by Gisle Hannemyr of the University of Oslo, provides comprehensive technical report guidelines.
http://www.coop.engr.uvic.ca/engrweb/ WTR.HTML	The Work Term Report Guidelines of the University of Victoria's Engineering Co-op Program provide a detailed examination of the creation of long reports according to a particular house style. An appendix presents samples of basic report elements.
http://www.colostate.edu/Depts/ WritingCenter/references/documents/ execsum/page2.htm	Maintained by the Writers' Center at Colorado State University, this page offers guidelines on writing executive summaries, as well as links to a variety of useful resources for writers.
http://www.hodu.com/	Maintained by Hodu Winning Documents, a team of professional writers, researchers, and consultants, this page offers a subscription to a free e-zine (electronic magazine) called *Effective Communication,* as well as links to the e-zine's archives.

Inevitably, you will have to speak in public. Whatever your course of studies at college or university, whatever your career, occasions will arise on which you will be required to deliver a presentation or a speech to an audience consisting of classmates, colleagues, clients, or strangers. In your personal life, you might be asked to propose a toast at a wedding, act as MC at a social function, or deliver a eulogy at a funeral. In college or university and in the workplace, you might be required to present reports or projects, or demonstrate your company's product or service.

The first group of activities are examples of speeches. Speeches are designed to amuse, console, persuade, or entertain. Their function is primarily social rather than pragmatic, and though they might be constrained by the rules of etiquette, their approach is fundamentally casual. The second group of activities are examples of presentations. Here you will be concerned with the characteristics of technical communications introduced in Chapter 1: necessity for a specific audience, integration of visual elements, ease of selective access, timeliness, and structure. Further, your effectiveness as a presenter will derive from your judicious use of the CMAPP approach.

The CMAPP Approach to Presentations

You can look at your presentation in terms of the CMAPP components, which might include the following elements:

Context

1. The reasons for your being the presenter

2. The physical conditions, including:
    (a) the size of the room and the distance between you and those members of your audience seated farthest from you
    (b) the size of your audience
    (c) the necessity for a microphone or sound system
    (d) the length of time you have been allotted
    (e) the technology available for integrating visuals

3. The expectations your audience has of you and vice versa.

4. The relationships that exist between you, your audience, and anyone else involved (instructor, classmates, boss, colleagues, etc.).

5. The impact you think your presentation will have.

Message

1. Your words (recall the effect of both denotation and connotation)

2. Your visuals (recall the impact of both information and impression)

3. Your delivery (think about the paralinguistic considerations discussed later in the chapter)

Audience

1. The type of audience you are addressing, including:
   (a) their level of technicality
   (b) their likely bias toward you (whether positive or negative) before you even begin

2. The expectations of your audience:
   (a) what they likely already know
   (b) what they likely need to know
   (c) what they likely want to know

Purpose

1. What you are trying to achieve by delivering your presentation.

2. How you want your audience to react to your presentation.

Product

1. Which of the four types of presentations (discussed later in the chapter), you will use:
   (a) manuscript
   (b) memorized
   (c) impromptu
   (d) extemporaneous

Audience Analysis

When considering your audience as part of your CMAPP analysis, you should take into account the following seven factors.

1. *Age Range*   A group of twenty-somethings will respond differently than a group of seniors; their interests will be different, as will the cultural referents to which they will likely relate.

2. *Cultural Background*   Different cultures respond differently to particular stimuli, references, topics, types of humour, presentation approaches, and so forth. When developing your presentation, you should take into account the cultural background of your audience.

3. *Educational Level*   The reactions and expectations of a highly educated audience will likely be different from those of a less-well educated group; your levels of discourse and technicality should vary accordingly.

4. *Occupation*   An audience composed of neurosurgeons will be different from an audience composed of loggers. You should be sensitive to the interests and expectations of whichever audience you address.

5. *Political and Religious Affiliation*   There are many hot-button issues associated with politics and religion. To be effective, your CMAPP analysis should take into account the potential views and affiliations of your audience.

6. *Sex*   A group of women is likely to have different interests, preferences, and expectations than a group of men. This general observation refers not to women or men as individuals, but rather to commonly observed tendencies among groups.

7. *Socioeconomic Status*   People from different income groups tend to have different priorities, interests, and expectations. For example, as groups they are likely to respond quite differently to such issues as taxation, employment insurance, and subsidized housing.

Purpose

You must have a solid idea of what you wish your presentation to accomplish, of how you want your audience to react, and of what you want from them. For example, imagine that you are to deliver a presentation whose overall topic was an upcoming provincial election. You should choose as your primary purpose one of the four purposes described below.

- *Descriptive Purpose*   If your primary purpose is to describe, you will want your audience to see (in their mind's eye) something they have not seen before, or to see something more clearly than before. Therefore, you might talk about the pressure of being a candidate on the hustings, the emotionally charged atmosphere in a riding headquarters on election night, or the enthusiasm of the myriad volunteers who work to help elect a member.

- *Informative Purpose*   If your main purpose is to inform, you will want your audience to know or understand something they did not before. You might discuss the province's constituency system. You might explain how a party that receives only 30 to 40 percent of the popular vote can come to hold a majority of provincial seats. Or you might talk about the Canadian parliamentary system in general and then apply your observations to the province in question.

- *Instructive Purpose*   If you want primarily to instruct, you will want your audience to know how to do something that they could not do before. You might teach them how to determine whether they are eligible to vote, how to verify if their names are on the official voters list (and what to do if they're not), how to find out the location of their appointed polling place, and how to fill out a ballot so that it will remain valid.

■ *Persuasive Purpose*   To persuade, you must effect a change in your audience, normally in terms of belief, attitude, or behaviour. You might try to persuade an undecided audience to vote for a particular political party. You might encourage a partisan audience to volunteer in a candidate's riding association, or even to espouse the policies of a different party (usually an uphill battle indeed!). You might simply want to persuade your audience not to remain among the more than 50 percent of eligible voters who customarily do not even bother to exercise their franchise.

It is impossible to describe without informing, to instruct without describing, and so forth. Inevitably, your presentation will incorporate elements of more than one purpose. Nonetheless, in order for your message to be effective, you must choose a single purpose as the foundation.

Conquering Stage Fright

In popular surveys, people often rank fear of speaking in public above fear of dying. (There are no documented cases of anyone actually dying of stage fright!) Dealing with that fear is important. Your presentation will not be effective if you don't appear calm and confident. Note my use of the word "appear." In the context of a presentation, what counts is not how you actually feel but rather how you *appear* to feel. Your heart may be thudding, but your audience can't hear it; nor can it see the perspiration on your sweaty palms or feel the dryness in your throat. As far as your audience is concerned, if you *appear* to be in control of yourself and your presentation, you *are* in control.

There's some truth to the old saw, "Fake it till you make it!" Each time you "fool" an audience by *appearing* confident, you fool yourself a little too. Do this often enough and you will find that you are actually *becoming* more confident. Remember another cliché: nothing succeeds like success.

Here are some tips for dealing with stage fright:

■ *Avoid stimulants.*   Someone might have told you that the best way to conquer stage fright is to have a stiff drink. Don't! It may make *you* feel better, but it won't make *your audience* feel better when your performance inevitably suffers as a result. The same advice applies to other chemical crutches, from pot, to uppers, to high doses of caffeine (whether in coffee or soft drinks).

■ *Practise breathing and visualization techniques.*   Get into the habit of taking several slow, deep breaths just before you walk up to deliver your presentation. Long before you reach that point, you can use a technique known variously as visualization, self-visualization, positive visualization, or positive imaging. Fundamentally, it involves imagining yourself—as vividly as you can—delivering a successful presentation and reaping the rewards of having done so. Taken seriously and practised assiduously, it works for most people.

- *Imagine the worst-case scenario.* From time to time, even the best presenter bombs. Accept the fact that, despite your best efforts, you are occasionally going to flop. Then consider what is the worst that could possibly happen if you did? The answer could be anything from feeling hopelessly embarrassed to losing a coveted contract. So, imagine the worst possible result, think of how you will deal with it, and—almost always—watch it not happen. And if it *does* happen? Those of us who have had the experience have somehow managed to survive. So will you.

- *Be prepared.* As with most things in life, proper preparation pays off. If you are lazy about developing your presentation, your lack of effort will be evident in your presentation and your audience will be alienated. Take or make the time to prepare thoroughly: conduct a CMAPP analysis and apply its results long before you stand before an audience.

- *Maintain a positive attitude.* If you believe that you're going to do poorly, that your audience will dislike you and your presentation, that the experience will be frightening and uncomfortable, and that you have no chance of success, then in all likelihood all those things will likely come to pass. On the other hand, if you can convince yourself that you're going to do well, that your audience wants you to succeed (and that is usually the case), that the experience will be rewarding for both you and your audience, and that success is within your grasp, your convictions will likely come true. Remember that your attitude toward a task has a lot to do with how well you accomplish that task.

The Development Process

Over the years, people have constructed various processes for developing speeches and presentations. Deciding which process to use is less important than actually using one.

In the context of technical and business communications, the process outlined below is both simple and effective. Note that you will often work on steps 1 through 4 simultaneously, since these steps tend to be interdependent. Steps 4 through 6 are a direct reflection of the multi-level outlining process you learned in Chapter 3.

1. Conduct your *CMAPP analysis.*

2. Decide on the *specific topic* you wish to cover. If you are not able to express your topic in a short phrase, you have not got it firmly fixed in your own mind.

3. Formulate the *thesis statement.* The thesis statement is a single sentence that encapsulates your purpose and topic. It will serve as the foundation for step 6.

4. Conduct your *research.*

5. Determine your goals or objectives—the *main points* of your presentation. These will turn into the level-one heads you create in step 6.

6. Construct a *multi-level outline*. It should contain sufficient detail (e.g., references to quotations and visuals you will be using) to permit you to develop a new set of speaking notes months later, should you need to do so. If you are preparing for a manuscript or memorized presentation (discussed later in this chapter), your outline will serve as the skeleton for your text. For an extemporaneous presentation (also discussed later in the chapter), you will "contract" your outline into the speaking notes described in the next step.

7. Develop your *speaking notes* (also called *speaker's notes*) for your extemporaneous delivery. Speaking notes are what you actually use while delivering your presentation. They are designed to remind you of the issues you will discuss—issues with which you are already very familiar. Unlike your outline, speaking notes are brief and concise, often to the point of being cryptic. If you were to look at them several months after your presentation, you might well fail to understand them.

   Because you want your audience's attention focused on you rather than on your notes, you will want the notes themselves, as well as your use of them, to be as inconspicuous as possible. Here are some suggestions:

   (a) Write legibly and in large, clear letters: you want to be able to glance quickly at your notes and find your next point without difficulty.

   (b) Use single words or very short phrases; clauses or sentences take longer to "find" when you are trying to glance at your notes without drawing your audience's attention to the fact. You might make use of symbols—for example, a $ to remind you to discuss financial issues, or a symbol character such as 🔒 to prompt you to mention security concerns.

   (c) Use white space generously: you will be able to find your points more readily.

   (d) On letter-size paper, write on one side only. This will allow you, during your presentation, to move from page to page without making your audience constantly aware that you are doing so. Many presenters put speaking notes on small cards (3" x 5" index cards cut in half, for example) and hold them in the palm of their hand while delivering. If you decide to use cards, you should allow for plenty of white space (put only three or four items on each card), print on one side only, and number your cards so that they can be quickly reordered if dropped.

8. *Rehearse* your presentation. I know of no better way to find out whether your presentation is likely to work. Among other things, rehearsal allows you to test your arguments and your visuals, and to verify your time and timing. While rehearsing can feel a bit awkward, most presenters would tell you that the private discomfort of rehearsal is preferable to the public embarrassment of a flawed presentation.

Types of Presentations

Broadly speaking, there are four types of presentations. Each has advantages and disadvantages. Which you choose will depend on the results of your CMAPP analysis.

Manuscript Presentation

A manuscript presentation is the delivery of a carefully prepared text that you refer to while presenting. The main advantage of this delivery type is that your presentation can be meticulously crafted: you can take pains to ensure that you always have the right word and visual in the right place at the right time. Another advantage is that should you have to deliver the presentation again, you can do so accurately and with a minimum of effort.

The main drawback of manuscript presentations has to do with the differences between written language and spontaneous, spoken language. It's difficult to write a presentation that, upon delivery, does not sound recited—and thus potentially boring to your audience. (Through a combination of training and experience, a good TV news anchor has learned to surmount this problem. Most of us, of course, are not professional news anchors.)

Another disadvantage of manuscript presentations is that it is more difficult to interact with an audience while referring to a written text. A presenter who never or rarely strays from the written text runs the risk of becoming monotonous.

Memorized Presentation

A memorized presentation is the delivery of material that you have composed and memorized. Like manuscription presentation, this delivery type allows you to craft your presentation carefully. At the same time, it allows for greater interaction with an audience because it removes the barrier of written text that exists between you and your audience during a manuscript presentation. On the negative side, it's no easy task to make memorized text sound spontaneous and natural, as opposed to rehearsed and recited. Repeat presentations can exacerbate the problem: like actors in a long-running play, presenters may find their delivery becoming increasingly stale.

Impromptu Presentation

The least formal of the delivery types is the impromptu presentation. You will use it when you are (more or less) unexpectedly called upon to speak. In class or in the workplace, you may be asked for your opinion or your analysis. Although you might have guessed that you would be called upon, and although your audience will expect you to have some familiarity with the topic, you will not have had the opportunity to thoroughly prepare what you are going to say.

An obvious advantage of the impromptu presentation is that, because you are given little, if any, time to prepare, your audience is disposed to cut you some slack: their expectations are relatively low. Further, since you are likely to have no notes, your presentation will appear to be what it is—spontaneous. In addition, you are free to interact extensively with your audience.

The main disadvantage is the flip side of the first advantage: because you have negligible time to prepare, your success is much more dependent on your ability to think on your feet. The more complex your arguments, the greater your risk—and your audience's—of becoming confused. Remember the KISS principle!

Extemporaneous Presentation

The extemporaneous presentation is the most widely used of the four delivery types. It involves diligent preparation and the delivery of what appears to your audience to be a spontaneous presentation.

The extemporaneous presentation allows you to prepare carefully, tailoring your presentation (including any visuals) to your context, audience, message, and purpose. Moreover, since you will be making use only of speaking notes, you will be able to talk spontaneously and interact extensively with your audience. On the negative side, inadequate preparation will be painfully obvious to both you and your audience. As well, should you lose your focus during the presentation, you will have only the cryptic content of your speaking notes for support.

When preparing your extemporaneous presentation, you should follow the development process outlined earlier in the chapter. Never write out, word for word, any part of your intended presentation. Doing so will make your presentation as a whole sound uneven, and make parts of it sound recited.

Elements of the Presentation

Here is a three-part rule for perfect presentations:

1. Tell 'em what you're gonna tell 'em.

2. Tell 'em.

3. Tell 'em what you told 'em.

In developing your presentation, you will use the same kind of tripartite structure found in all technical communications: an introductory segment, a body, and a concluding segment.

Introductory Segment

The introductory segment should normally include all but the second of the following elements (not necessarily in the order given):

- *Attention-Getter* You'll want to start things off by gaining your audience's full attention. To get it, don't explode firecrackers or do or say anything else that is totally unrelated to your presentation. If your topic were the upcoming provincial election referred to earlier in the chapter, and if your purpose was to inform, you might gain your audience's attention by saying something like, "Did you know that most so-called majority governments in this country are actually voted into office by a minority of eligible voters?"

- *Self-Introduction* If someone introduces you to your audience, you need not reintroduce yourself. Otherwise, you should clearly state your first and last names and, if appropriate, your position or title as well.

- *Initial Summary* The initial summary serves as a road map to your presentation. You prepare your audience for what is to come by stating your purpose and your main points (typically the level one heads in your multi-level outline).

- *Speaker Credibility* Tell your audience why you are the right person to talk about the topic. The fact that you are the leader of a famous rock band does not automatically mean that your views on the state of postsecondary education will be taken seriously. Your credibility as a speaker has to be renewed each time you give a presentation. You might mention your experience in the field, your credentials and/or qualifications, your research on the topic, and so forth.

- *Audience Relevance* Indicate why the topic should be of interest to the audience. (Rely on your CMAPP analysis.) Audience relevance is not necessarily obvious or straightforward. For example, suppose that you are speaking to a group of urban condominium owners and your topic is the possibility of an NHL franchise team locating in the downtown core. Talking about the excitement of the game will likely score no goals with this group. A better strategy would be to focus on things like construction jobs, tax revenues, parking, and street noise.

Body

The body of your presentation is the bulk of your CMAPP message. Its content will depend on your context, audience, purpose, and product (your delivery type). Here are some elements typically found in the body:

- *Rhetorical Questions* A rhetorical question is a question that is intended to produce an effect rather than solicit an answer. An example is the sample attention-getter in the preceding section. Within your presentation body, rhetorical questions can be used to focus your audience's attention on a particular point.

- *Signposts* Signposts indicate to your audience where you intend to go, and thus what they can expect. Signposts include such words and phrases as *first, second, on the other hand, however, correspondingly,* and *conversely.*

- *Transitions* Related to signposts, transitions indicate a change from one point or idea to another. They include such phrases as: *now that we have...*, *let us turn to...*, and *having looked at..., I will now...*

- *Emphasis Markers* Emphasis markers are used to focus an audience's attention on a particular point. They include such phrases as *most importantly, I'd like to draw your attention to...*, and *it cannot be stressed enough that...*

- *Repetition Markers* Repetition markers are used to introduce the reiteration of a point made earlier in the presentation. They include such phrases as *let me repeat [the point that]...* and *as I've already mentioned...*

- *Segment Summaries* If you are giving a long presentation, you should provide your audience with brief summaries of the individual segments. A segment summary includes a transition into the next segment. For example, at some point in your informative presentation on the upcoming election, you might have said, "So far, we have talked about how ridings are determined by governments, how a party nominates a candidate, and how a candidate is selected to represent the party in an election. Let's now look at the current election campaign."

Concluding Segment

Your concluding segment should include the following four elements (in the order shown):

- *Closure* This element lets your audience know that you are going to finish soon. However fascinating your presentation might have been, your audience's attention will perk up when you make it clear that you have almost concluded. You can signal closure by using a phrase such as *in conclusion,...* or an emphasis marker such as *I'd like to make one final point before I finish.* Never indicate closure prematurely: if your presentation continues for more than a few minutes after you have signalled closure, your audience will likely tune out.

- *Final Summary* At this point, you will sum up the main points of your presentation. A final summary is essentially a paraphrase of the initial summary. (Note that it does not include a statement of purpose.)

- *Call to Action* Most technical communication products conclude with a call to action (also known as an action request). If your presentation's main purpose is persuasive, your call to action is likely to be very direct, as in "Cast your ballot for the candidate you know will work hardest for you!" If your purpose is informative, descriptive, or instructive, your call to action will be more subtle. It may be a personal statement or an indication of your hopes. In your informative presentation on the upcoming election, you might say:

One of the responsibilities of citizenship is exercising our franchise. Personally, I believe that our decisions should be educated ones, and that the more we know about our electoral process, the more informed our ballot choices will be. I hope my presentation has helped you come to the same conclusion.

- *Close* Sometimes your call to action will be sufficient to let your audience know that you have finished. Most of the time, though, it is a far better idea to indicate more explicitly that your presentation is over. You might do so by saying something like, "Thank you for your time today. I've appreciated the opportunity to speak with you."

Paralinguistic Factors

Many experts feel that at least 60 percent of what your audience assimilates and uses to assess you and your presentation has nothing to do with the words you use. Rather, their judgment is based on their perceptions of your appearance, your bearing, and your vocal qualities. All these factors can be termed *paralinguistic* (beyond language). Although your audience might not be consciously aware of them, you, as an effective presenter, must be.

Dress

We do judge people by the clothes they wear. That might not be right, but it's true. Dress appropriately. You wouldn't wear jeans and an old sweatshirt at a formal wedding. Nor would you put on a tux or evening gown before taking your car to an auto repair shop. Decide what's appropriate in light of your CMAPP analysis, consider the kind of image you want to present, and dress accordingly.

Confidence and Presence

Successful people tend to look successful, and confident people tend to look confident. Such people have what is often called "presence." Presence is an attribute that is difficult to define, although most of are quick to recognize it. As I pointed out in my earlier discussion of conquering stage fright, if you *look* confident, your audience will likely believe that you *are* confident, and over time you will likely *become* confident. Self-confidence appears to be one aspect of that mysterious thing we call presence.

Eye Contact

In one-on-one conversations, we naturally make eye contact with each other. When you're presenting, your audience appreciates confirmation that you know that they're there. Making eye contact with your audience is crucial to a successful presentation. Here are some suggestions:

- When dealing with a small audience, try to make eye contact randomly with everyone several times during your presentation. If one or more audience members will not give you the opportunity to do so, don't force the issue.

- If the audience is large, mentally divide the room into segments and look at each segment several times in the course of your presentation.

- Limit the eye contact to a second or two; otherwise, people may feel you're staring and become uncomfortable and/or resentful.

Posture and Movement

Good posture is an indication of self-confidence—don't slump. And stimulate your audience's interest (at least on an unconscious level) by moving around a bit. You don't have to do a breakdance: just avoid remaining motionless.

Facial Expressions and Gestures

Your presentation will be more effective if you show some facial animation. Don't get carried away: just as in person-to-person conversations, simply allow your face to show your emotions.

Gestures, like facial expressions, should be expressed naturally. If you use a pointing gesture, make sure you're not pointing at someone in your audience; most people don't like even the appearance of being singled out.

Volume

Vary your volume for effect. Some highly competent presenters use everything from a stage whisper to a shout. Even if you avoid extremes, you should also avoid the monotony of unchanging volume: it is ineffective and may well put your audience to sleep.

Speed

A metronome keeps time by ticking at unvarying speed. A lack of variety in the speed with which you speak causes the same monotony, and a loss of audience interest.

Tone, Pitch, and Intonation

In face-to-face conversations, you automatically vary your tone, pitch, and intonation. When you ask a question, for example, you tend to end on a rising tone. When surprised, you tend to use a higher pitch. As you converse, your intonation changes to show emotion, emphasis, and so on.

Natural variations in tone, pitch, and intonation add interest and lustre to your presentation and help keep your audience attentive. If you speak with little or no variety of tone, pitch, and intonation, you will sound as though you are reciting something of no interest to you. Computer-generated voices often do that, but effective presenters should not.

Enunciation and Pronunciation

Ensure that you speak clearly and that you have mastered the pronunciation of whatever terms or names you intend to use. If you slur or mumble, or if you falter or err in the pronunciation of words you yourself have chosen, your audience is unlikely to request a repetition; they will, however, judge you.

Hesitation Particles

You may have noticed that some inexperienced speakers seem to say *um* or *uh* every second word. Just as unconsciously, others may say *you know* or *like* with irritating regularity. Such "fillers," as they are sometimes called, eventually draw your audience's attention away from your message. Avoiding them is, for most of us, difficult; doing so requires a conscious awareness of our words while we are speaking. Gaining that facility, however, will make you a more effective presenter.

In most cases, it is better to pause—briefly. Your audience will usually accept such pauses as the mark of thoughtfulness. Frequent hesitation particles, however, will inevitably work against you.

Time Management

Pacing your presentation takes practice and experience. Ensuring that you have left enough time for all of your points is just as important as making certain that you do not run out of message halfway through your allotted time. Your audience expects you to take the time you have—not much less and certainly not much more. Probably the best way to test your time management is to rehearse.

Visuals and Visual Aids

Visuals are playing an increasingly important role in effective presentations. As you discovered in Chapter 4, visuals should:

- illustrate, not overpower;
- explain, not confuse;
- enhance, not detract;
- simplify, not complicate;

- fulfill a CMAPP purpose, not merely decorate;
- be visible to all;
- be intelligible to all.

In the discussion that follows, we will look at some widely used presentation visuals and visual aids.

Handouts

Handouts are one of the most popular forms of presentation visuals. They allow your audience to take a more active part in the communication; as well, many audiences appreciate being able to take away information for future reference.

You can distribute handouts before, during, or after your presentation. Here are some advantages and disadvantages of each strategy:

- *Before* Distribution will not create interference during your presentation, and you can refer to any part of the handout at any time. *But* your audience will likely continue to examine (and perhaps rifle through) the material until their curiosity has been satisfied—not just until you want to begin.

- *During* You can retain your audience's attention until you distribute the material, and you can refer to your handouts from the moment they have been distributed. *But* every means of distribution will be an interruption: people will be looking to find their copy, and will begin to examine what they have received.

- *After* You have your audience's attention throughout your presentation. *But* you cannot effectively refer to material in your handout, because your audience does not yet have it.

How you design your handouts and time their distribution should be determined by the results of your CMAPP analysis.

Props

Props is a generic term that can refer to a variety of visuals, including the ones listed below.

- *Maps* You could use a map to illustrate the changes in weather patterns as one traverses the Rockies.

- *Models* You could use a scale model to explain the workings of the Rideau Canal locks.

- *People* You could use a person to demonstrate first-aid techniques.

- *Photos* You could use a photo to illustrate the architecture of Toronto's Queen's Park legislature. Note that any photo (or printed item) can be scanned and used in the computerized preparation of a visual, as I did with the 1970s photo of my parents (see Figure 11.1).

■ *Samples* You could explain how an overhead projector functions by using a real projector. Avoid passing around a single example of a prop. Only the person actually holding the item will be able to relate it to what you say; the attention of the rest of your audience will be divided between listening to you and tracking the prop's progress around the room.

Figure 11.1: Creating an Acetate

Creating Projected Visuals

This simple visual was created using a word processor.

This slide took about 5 minutes.

1. Plan your visual (CMAPP)
2. Formulate text
3. Add graphics
4. Decide on colour (if colour printing)
5. Print directly onto acetate (check type!)

Overhead Projectors

An overhead projector is still one of the most common visual aids used in presentations. Here are some of its advantages:

■ It works well even with normal ambient lighting (with the lights on in a classroom, for example).

- You need not (and should not) turn your back on your audience: what you see on the overhead's plate is what your audience sees on the screen behind you.

- If you are standing at the overhead, you can draw your audience's attention to any item on your acetate merely by pointing at it with a pen or even your finger.

- Anything you can print on a sheet of paper can be quickly, easily, and cheaply turned into an overhead visual of decent quality. You can photocopy or print directly onto an acetate, in black and white or in colour. (Note that there are three common types of acetates: for overheads only, for photocopiers and laser printers, and for ink-jet printers. Run through a laser printer or a photocopier, an overhead acetate is likely to melt inside the machinery! Using an ink-jet printer on a non-ink-jet acetate will likely result in little but smudges.)

- By using a computer application, you can experiment with any number of possibilities before deciding to print. Even if you then dislike the result, creating a new one is relatively easy and inexpensive.

- An audience tends to turn their eyes to the screen when you switch on the overhead; they tend to look back to you when you turn it off but continue talking. Thus, you can control the direction of your audience's attention.

Here are a couple of disadvantages:

- Screens usually hang vertically, while the overhead projects its image toward the screen at an angle. The result, termed *keystoning*, is a distortion of what is called *aspect ratio*: the top of the image becomes horizontally stretched.

- The further the overhead sits from the screen, the larger the image it projects. At the same time, however, the larger the image, the lower its quality. Thus, overheads are not usually effective for a very large audience in a very large hall.

35mm Projector and Slides

You've likely had snapshots developed as 35mm slides. When used as presentation visuals, they offer the following advantages:

- Excellent colour, legibility, clarity, and resolution are retained even when the slides are projected from considerable distance onto a large screen.

- Using such snapshots is easy and relatively inexpensive.

Here are some disadvantages:

- Creating a 35mm slide from a computer-generated visual generally means sending your computer file to a service bureau: few people have the specialized equipment (a slide imager) at home. At the moment, you will likely pay about $7 per slide. If you don't like the product, revising requires another file sent to the service bureau.

- Use of a 35mm projector normally requires a darkened room; you and your audience cannot see each other well, and your audience cannot easily take notes, for example.

- Finding that a slide has been inserted in the tray backward or upside down is common, and correcting the problem makes for a significant interruption in your presentation.

Computer Presentations

You can use a computer to display almost any visual, from a slide show created with presentation graphics software, to a real-time illustration of word processing, spreadsheet development, database programming, or AutoCad design, to a demonstration of Internet search engines. The larger the monitor and the crisper its resolution, the more effective your visuals will be. Specifications aside, computer presentations should be used only when your audience is very small (no more than five people).

Software packages such as Microsoft PowerPoint and Lotus Freelance Graphics allow you to integrate text with graphics, and to add sound, video clips, and animation. You can use PowerPoint to design, create, and edit *presentations*, defined in this context as a set of screens (also known as slides) that you present to a small audience. The software allows you to produce a dazzling array of special effects. While you may be tempted to include every eye-catching multimedia effect that your software permits, you should not forget the KISS principle. Don't allow form to take precedence over content: if a special effect doesn't support your message, and thereby benefit your audience, you should probably leave it out of your presentation.

Data Projectors

The use of data projectors is becoming increasingly common in the business world. The data projector receives the signal from a computer and projects it onto a screen, often while "piping" a copy to a computer monitor. Here are three advantages:

- Data projectors work well even in normal ambient light.
- They can incorporate a computer's sound and video capabilities, or connection to the Internet.
- Many can be connected to other input sources such as VCRs.

One drawback is that they remain relatively expensive (currently in the $6000–$10,000 range). Also, since they must interact with the computer hardware and software, incompatibilities are not uncommon.

Question Period

Before your presentation begins, you should let your audience know whether or not you will field questions once it concludes. Here are some suggestions for dealing with questions from the audience:

- If you don't get any questions, don't allow a long and potentially embarrassing silence to develop. Rather, say something like, "Well, since there don't seem to be any questions at this time, I'd just like to thank you again for your attention"—and consider your presentation over.

- When you are challenged to clarify or justify a particular point, don't go on the defensive; rather, look on your answer as an opportunity to reinforce your message.

- When you are asked a question that requires a lengthy response, try to organize your answer so that it reflects the three-part rule (introductory segment, body, and concluding segment).

- Don't let yourself be drawn into an argument. Whatever the provocation, remain calm.

- Don't let any one questioner monopolize the floor. Politely but firmly suggest that someone else be given a chance to speak.

- It is often a good idea to repeat or paraphrase a question before answering it. By doing so, you not only ensure that the question is heard by all members of your audience (especially important if the questioner is soft-spoken), but you buy yourself time to gather your thoughts and mentally prepare your answer.

CASE STUDY

AEL Presentation to Students

Situation

AEL's senior partners, Sarah Cohen and Frank Nabata, have for some years had a social relationship with Carole Schusterman, RAI's general manager in Winnipeg, and her husband, Ben. Over supper one evening, Carole mentions Radisson Vancouver's highly positive assessment of its participation in Grandstone Technical Institute's Internship Program. Intrigued, Cohen and Nabata consider over the next few weeks how AEL might benefit from a similar involvement with GTI. They conclude that while AEL would not be able to accommodate GTI students in the context of an internship or co-op program, the company would have much to gain from an organized effort to attract bright young people into the business. With this in mind, they arrange for Noam Avigdor, a senior associate in AEL's Toronto office, to deliver presentations to students in each of the cities in which AEL maintains offices: St. John's, Toronto, Winnipeg, Edmonton, and Vancouver.

Avigdor has his office contact universities in each of those cities and arrange for him to deliver 30-minute presentations to groups of fourth-year students in the areas of particular interest to AEL: chemical, civil, and geological engineering, and software design and development. The preparatory work Avigdor does for his presentations can be seen in Figures 11.2, 11.3, 11.4, and 11.5.

Figure 11.2: Avigdor's CMAPP Analysis

Recruitment Presentation: CMAPP Analysis

Context:

- Students likely interested in available employment after graduation

- Many may not have heard of AEL: probably necessary to establish relationship

- Top students likely to hear several recruiters and have several options

- Others likely there because of few possibilities: important for me to present AEL as top firm looking only for best students

- Presentations likely to be in classrooms, small conference rooms, etc.; will probably vary from university to university

- Technology available: data projector only a possibility; therefore, prepare visuals for overhead projector—almost certainly available

- Probably groups of 10–50 students: will vary according to institution and how well recruitment presentation is publicized

- Length of presentations: about 30 minutes, including question period at end

- Some students may expect me to be signing recruitment offers; if so, I must try to maintain their enthusiasm but temper it with patience

- AEL hopes to receive applications from at least 50 students

Message:

- AEL's reputation

- Outline of AEL's organization and activities

- Opportunities for postgraduation placement in the various fields: What? Where? When? Starting salaries?

- Typical career advancement opportunities at AEL

- Means to indicate interest: statement of interest forms

- "AEL is interested in *you*"

Audience:

- *Education*: impending graduation in technical specialty areas (at least 4 years' university education)

- *Age range*: 21–24

- *Attitude*: Most likely to be enthusiastic; some skeptical and/or unmotivated

Figure 11.2 (continued)

- *Sex*: Likely even M/F split, although possible preponderance of males

- *Cultural background*: extremely varied

- *Economic status*: most likely to be from middle- to upper-middle-class backgrounds; as students, a significant number may be experiencing financial difficulties

- *Political bias*: most likely to be sympathetic to conservative/neoconservative platform

- *Know*: most likely aware of current entry-level job market in their fields; likely have idea of type of position/company they are looking for

- *Need to know*: what opportunities available, how to contact us, how to apply

- *Want to know*: whether AEL's opportunities are really of interest to them (type of work, benefits, corporate culture, cost of living in respective cities, travel opportunities, etc.); how to find out more

Purpose:

Persuasive—I want to:

- obtain a sense of numbers and types of potential employees

- present AEL as modern, energetic, ethical, profitable, exciting, etc.

- stimulate interest of the best students

- convince students to follow up with AEL offices in respective cities

Product: extemporaneous presentation with overheads as visuals

Figure 11.3: Avigdor's Topic, Thesis Statement, and Objectives

Topic: Working with AEL

Thesis Statement: If you are a qualified, ambitious graduate in a relevant field, you should apply to AEL for excellent entry-level opportunities.

Objectives:

1. Description of AEL
2. What we are looking for
3. Who we are looking for
4. Next steps

Figure 11.4: Avigdor's Multi-Level Presentation Outline

I. **Introduction**

    (A) "Career success won't come by itself!"   *Visual #1: AEL logo/building photo*

    (B) My position

    (C) Relevance to you as impending graduates

    (D) Why AEL is interested in you

II. **Description of AEL**

    (A) History

        (1) Engineers in Winnipeg   *Visual #2: photos of Cohen & Nabata*

        (2) Growth of consulting activities

        (3) Opening of offices   *Visual #3: Map showing cross-Canada offices*

    (B) Organization   *Visual #4: Organization Chart*

        (1) Senior partners and partners

        (2) Senior associates and associates

        (3) Senior consultants and consultants

        (4) Junior consultants

        (5) Staff associates

    (C) Locations   *Reprise: Visual #3: Map*

        (1) St. John's

        (2) Toronto

        (3) Winnipeg (Head Office)

        (4) Edmonton

        (5) Vancouver

    (D) Areas of Endeavour

        (1) Civil engineering   *Visual #5: Vanier Place project, Mississauga U.*

        (2) Chemical engineering   *Visual #6: MicroGen Test Labs*

        (3) Geological engineering   *Visual #7: Martini Falls Dam Project*

        (4) Software design   *Visual #8: HelioTech "Vivacious" brochure cover*

Figure 11.4 (continued)

(5) Software development

Visual #9: HelioTech Software Test Lab

(6) Now investigating:

    (a) Environmental engineering

    (b) Industrial safety

    (c) Urban planning

III. **What we are looking for**

  (A) Demonstrated attitudes

    (1) Cooperation

    (2) Team spirit

    (3) Enthusiasm

    (4) Desire to succeed

    (5) Client satisfaction

  (B) Qualifications

    (1) Only the best of the best!

    (2) Appropriate degree (see #II, D above for list)

    (3) Marks

       (a) At least 85% average in relevant subjects, AND

       (b) At least 80% average each term throughout degree program

  (C) Experience

    (1) Not mandatory but an advantage

    (2) Internship/Co-op is desirable if in appropriate field

    (3) Extracurricular if relevant

IV. **Who we're looking for**

  (A) Entry-level candidates for:

    (1) St. John's

    (2) Toronto

    (3) Winnipeg

    (4) Edmonton

    (5) Vancouver

  (B) People willing to relocate

  (C) People willing to travel

  (D) People looking for self-motivated work

Figure 11.4 (continued)

      (1) Senior firm members seek contracts

      (2) Other consulting staff often work independently

    (E) People able to work under little or no supervision

    (F) People who take pride in their own work and want the company's name to be recognized for quality and integrity

      (1) You represent the company and it represents you

V. Next Steps

    (A) Take brochures   *Visual #10: Show sample brochure*

    (B) Think over what I've said

    (C) Send letter of application to senior associate in city of interest according to handout   *Visual #11: List of senior associates*

    (D) If no word within three weeks, follow up with phone call

VI. Conclusion

    (A) Brief summation of points

    (B) Recommendation to act immediately: competition becomes stiffer

    (C) Question period

    (D) Thanks and hope to see you again   *Reprise Visual #1: AEL logo/ building photo*

Figure 11.5: Avigdor's Speaking Notes

1.		2.	
(a) CAREER SUCCESS ◯ #1		(a) COMPANY ORG. CHART	◯ #4
(b) ME + YOU + AEL		(b) CURRENT LOCATIONS	◯ #3 (bis)
(c) START & GROW ◯ #2		(c) CIVIL	◯ #5 (Vanier)
(d) OFFICE OPENINGS ◯ #3		(d) CHEMICAL	◯ #6 (MicroGen)

Figure 11.5 (continued)

<table>
<tr>
<td>

3.

(a) GEOLOGICAL   ○ #7 (Martini)

(b) S-DESIGN   ○ #8 (Vivacious)

(c) S-DEV   ○ #9 (Helio)

(d) POTENTIAL EXPANSION

</td>
<td>

4. ATTITUDE:
- Cooperation
- Team
- Enthusiasm
- Positive
- Success
- Clients

(b) QUALIFICATIONS:
- Cream of crop
- Degree 85% topic + 80%
         overall

</td>
</tr>
<tr>
<td>

5.

(a) EXPERIENCE:
- Advantage + Co-op + Other

(b) WHO:
- Entry: ALL CITIES

- Moves

- Motivation>> <<Supervision

- Pride>>>Mutual Recognition

</td>
<td>

6.

(a) BROCHURES   ○ #10
                (brochure)

(b) CONSIDER!

(c) APPLY   ○ #11 (list)
- Follow-up

(d) QUESTIONS/THANKS ○ #1
                 (close)

</td>
</tr>
</table>

Issues to Think About

1. What is your overall impression of Avigdor's CMAPP analysis (Figure 11.2)? Justify your answer in terms of the complementary CMAPP attributes you studied in Chapter 5.

2. What important element is missing from each component of the analysis?

3. How well do you think Avigdor has planned for his presentations? Justify your point of view with examples.

4. How would you deal with the problem of multiple audiences that Avigdor faces?

5. How accurately do you think Avigdor's topic and thesis statement (Figure 11.3) represent his ideas? How might you rephrase both?

6. Look at Avigdor's multi-level presentation outline in Figure 11.4. How might you explain the absence of visuals to illustrate sections III and IV?

7. Has Avigdor adhered to the principles of subordination, division, and parallelism in his outline? What changes would you suggest?

8. What can you say about the relationship between Avigdor's outline and his speaking notes (Figure 11.5)? What changes might you make to the speaking notes?

11.1 Distinguish between a presentation and a speech.

11.2 Briefly explain how each of the five CMAPP components applies to presentations.

11.3 Identify and describe five factors considered in audience analysis.

11.4 Identify the four main types of presentations and indicate the principal advantages and disadvantages of each.

11.5 Identify and describe at least three strategies for dealing with stage fright.

11.6 Identify and describe the four types of purpose discussed in this chapter.

11.7 Describe the purpose and physical makeup of speaking notes, and explain the relationship of those notes to the multi-level outline.

11.8 Identify and describe at least three elements found in each of the following:
(a) introductory segment
(b) body
(c) concluding segment

11.9 Identify five paralinguistic considerations discussed in this chapter, and briefly explain the importance of each to an effective presentation.

11.10 Briefly describe the advantages and disadvantages of each of the following visual aids:
(a) overhead projector
(b) 35mm projector
(c) data projector

11.11 Explain the advantages and disadvantages of distributing handouts
(a) before the presentation
(b) during the presentation
(c) after the presentation

EXPLORING THE WEB

Here are some Web sites you might wish to investigate.

URL	DESCRIPTION
http://www.ukans.edu/cwis/units/coms2/ vpa/vpa.htm	The Virtual Presentation Assistant is an online tutorial devoted to helping users improve their public speaking skills. The site is maintained by the Communication Studies Department at the University of Kansas.

http://www.toastmasters.org/	The home page of Toastmasters International offers links to information about Toastmasters and tips on successful public speaking.
http://www.intranet.ca/~jwaisvisz/index.htm	The Speaker's Coach Web site offers free articles and tips on public speaking, along with the option to purchase books and tapes that deal with business presentation skills.

12 Seeking Employment

Seeking employment is the subject of a vast number of books—enter the keyword *résumés* in the search window at *www.chapters.ca* and you may be presented with a list of over 600 titles! So, what can you expect from this short chapter, apart from a few bromides? You will find recommendations and tips designed to point you in the right direction. How far you progress will be up to you. My own experience, and that of countless others, suggests that there is no sure-fire recipe for success; rather, you need determination, hard work, and tenacity.

Despite what the self-help gurus might say, you also need a certain amount of luck: being in the right place at the right time. Sending off cover letters and résumés is, in some ways, like gambling—playing the horses or betting on the hockey pool. Admittedly, the more you know about the subject, the better your chances of winning; however, unless you expect to be hired by a relative or a friend who wants *you* regardless of anything else, the element of chance still plays an inevitable role.

The good news is that knowledge and skills will invariably help you land that dream job. At the very least, they will help you to create a winning employment application package. The five elements of this all-important package are:

1. preparation—doing your homework before you send out your application;

2. cover letter—using an effective CMAPP analysis to compose the best application for the occasion;

3. résumé—tailoring your content, form, and format as needed;

4. interview—saying the right things at the right time;

5. follow-up—remembering that you're probably not the only player in the game.

Preparation

Unless your sole employment goal is wealth, don't try to get into a field and then try to find a way to like it. Rather, decide what you enjoy and are good at, and then try to find a way to make a living at it.

Once you've identified your dream job, you should disabuse yourself of any illusions you might have about how easy it will be to land it. What follows is a reality check:

- Don't believe that your credentials, qualifications, experience, and enthusiasm make you unique. However good you are at whatever you want to be paid to do, you can count on there being a great many others of equal or better merit, trying to make sure that they, rather than you, get the position.

- Don't believe the fairy tale that if you want a job enough, it will drop into your lap. Doing, not wanting, brings results.

- Unless you are graduating top of your class from a prestigious institution, in a field currently in extremely high demand, don't believe that employers are desperately seeking you. They are more likely to be searching for ways to keep their businesses profitable—with or without you.

- Many employers have indicated that their hiring is based 90 percent on aptitude, and their firing based 90 percent on attitude. The moral of that story is that if you look for employment on the assumption that you can always "take the course again" or submit a "rewrite" for better marks, or that a potential employer has a responsibility to help you obtain what you want, you are likely to be cast aside before you are even hired.

Having dismissed your illusions, you can take action. Here are some suggestions:

1. *Network.* Probably the majority of career positions are not filled through newspaper ads. People know people who know people who know people; therefore, get to know people. Use personal contacts, libraries, and Internet resources to obtain the names of people who work in companies that operate in the area that interests you. Ask for a bit of their time, stressing that you are *not* trying to obtain a job— you are trying to find out more about the industry and what it values. Most people will be quite accommodating if you specify that you want no more than half an hour—and then stick to it. Thus, when you do apply for a job, you are likely to have—and be able to demonstrate—greater familiarity with the field. That knowledge gives you an added edge.

2. *Read ads carefully.* Notwithstanding the previous point, it is likely that you will at times respond to an advertised position. If so, treat the text of that ad as a combination of explicit and encoded information. Pay attention to what the ad says and to what it likely implies. For example, if it says, "No phone calls, please," it is likely that your deciding to call anyway will be treated as an unwillingness to accept direction rather than as initiative. Similarly, if the ad asks for specific remuneration expectations, the employer may be trying to find out whether you are already sufficiently familiar with the field to know typical pay and benefits.

3. *Judge yourself.* If you aren't thoroughly familiar with all the terminology in the ad, perhaps you'd best not apply. If an ad mentions Java and Active X programming, the Kepner-Tregoe process, or Monte Carlo simulation for molecular modelling, the potential employer presumes that qualified candidates know and use the jargon.

4. *Research your topic.* Research the fields that you think might interest you. Although you're unlikely to really know what's involved until you're working there, you can likely form at least a preliminary opinion by investigating the literature, and by talking to people who are already in the field. You can also look at texts on seeking

employment, although you should remember that their authors were also seeking to sell their books.

5. *Don't procrastinate.* Murphy's law implies that things left to the last minute *will* fail. So, several months before you expect to graduate, start investigating the job market in the fields that interest you.

Cover Letters

You'll recall from Chapter 7 that much persuasive communication targets the intellect rather than the emotions. That's what a cover letter should do.

Rationale

Why bother using a cover letter? After all, isn't the résumé the important thing? The rationale for taking the trouble to create an effective cover letter is as follows.

- Analogous to a report's transmittal letter, a cover letter introduces both you and your résumé.

- It is your opportunity to use the letter's content, form, and format to your advantage in selling your résumé and yourself.

- It is an expected convention; thus, its absence would be jarring.

Content

An effective cover letter should incorporate well-reasoned points to press your case.

1. Refer precisely to what you are applying for. If you are responding to an advertisement, be specific. For example, your referring to "your recent ad in the local paper" is worse than vague; alluding to "Competition #99-A343, described on page F8 of the Careers Section in the April 8, 2000, edition of the *National Post*" does two things: it allows the reader to know what you are talking about, and it suggests to the potential employer that you will be specific and precise in your work.

    Avoid superfluous information. For example, beginning with "Let me introduce myself. My name is [your name], and I would like to apply for ...," leaves your reader thinking, "I know that from the letterhead; don't waste my time." Putting serious effort into your initial CMAPP analysis for your cover letter will help you ensure it is precise, accessible, and concise.

2. Focus explicitly on what you can do for the company, not what the company can do for you. Remember: they are quite rightly looking to *their own* benefit, not yours.

3. Reiterate any specific points in your résumé that you feel should be of particular interest.

4. Include a clear call to action. Again, think of your CMAPP analysis, and consider the language you are using. A very weak (though unfortunately common) action request is, "If you have any questions, please don't hesitate to call me at ...." In effect, you are telling your reader *not* to call you unless he or she has *questions*— even, for example, if the audience were considering offering you an interview.

Form

If you can obtain next-to-no information about your specific audience, how can you determine the appropriate levels of discourse and technicality? Your CMAPP analysis will help you decide. For example, if the context is that of a specialized, technical position, you should probably assume that your audience has certain technical expectations. If the context is more generalist, that factor too should influence the construction of your letter. In all cases, you should be careful to keep your writing as clear, concise, and precise as possible.

Format

Beyond a requirement for professional appearance, a cover letter need follow no prescribed format. You should, however, follow certain guidelines.

1. Do not exceed a single page.

2. Use letterhead stationery. (All good word processors now enable you to produce your own.)

3. Your letterhead should include your first name and surname, your address, any phone numbers you think would be useful to your audience, and (if you have one) your e-mail address. If you maintain a Web site, include it *only* if its existence would be relevant to the employer.

4. Make effective use of appropriate document visuals as outlined in Chapter 4.

5. As much as possible, follow the business letter conventions discussed in Chapter 8. If you cannot identify your audience appropriately, you might consider the *simplified* letter format, since it requires neither an honorific nor a salutation.

Résumés

A résumé (spelled with or without the accents) is often called a *curriculum vitae* (abbreviated as *c.v.*), Latin for *life's path*. Irrespective of terminology, you might consider your résumé:

- a short analytical summary (Chapter 10) of your salable credentials and qualifications;

- a short analytical report (Chapter 10) on the relevant aspects of your background;

- a short persuasive document (Chapter 7) targeting the intellect and functioning as a complementary attachment to your cover letter;

- introduced by its cover letter, a short, external, probably solicited, proposal (Chapter 9) for assisting the organization to which you are applying.

Your résumé is, in effect, all of the above. Furthermore, it is one of the most important documents you will ever create: it is a reflection of you that you want examined by people from whom you hope to obtain substantial, long-term benefit.

Message

A common mistake of many people looking for employment is to carefully construct a résumé, and then use it when applying for a variety of positions. Doing so, however, violates the principles of good CMAPP analysis. Each application necessarily involves a different context and a different audience; the individual résumé's message, therefore, must be specific to that context and audience. Although your background, of course, remains the same, as might the basic elements of your product—your résumé—you must tailor your document. This means you must create a "new" résumé each time you make an application; you will want to highlight certain experience, stress particular accomplishments, use your format to convey specific impressions, and so on.

Professional Objective   Very common at the beginning of a résumé is an elliptical clause or a single sentence indicating your professional objective. An example might be:

> **Professional Objective**: To apply my accounting skills and experience in a large, well-respected firm that offers the potential for career advancement to senior management ranks.

Should you include a professional objective in your résumé? One school of thought advocates including a professional objective, maintaining that it demonstrates forethought and long-term commitment. Another advises against including one, pointing out, first, that should you be interviewed, a manager will prefer to discuss the issue directly, and, second, that if your stated objective does not match that of the employer (to you, a poorly known audience), it will likely work against your candidacy.

Since there is an element of gambling involved here too, you should conduct the most accurate CMAPP analysis you can, and decide in which basket to place this particular egg.

Audience

Although the situation may well vary, you are likely to have both a primary and a secondary audience when you submit a résumé to an organization.

Primary Your primary audience is probably a personnel or administration officer. Remember that this person's customary role is *not* to choose you from among the likely numerous applications received. Rather, it is to find reasons (indicated within your résumé and/or your cover letter) to *exclude* your application. Thus, your résumé and letter must be persuasive enough to convince this primary audience *not* to exclude you.

Secondary Your secondary audience will likely be a line manager—one who has authority over the position in question. That individual's role likely includes reviewing the primary audience's "inclusions" (but *not* the excluded applications) and deciding which *few* candidates are most suitable for interviews. Thus, your résumé must persuade your secondary audience as well.

Purpose

Another frequent but mistaken assumption is that your résumé's purpose is to get you a job. It won't. Its purpose is to obtain you an interview; *that* is your opportunity to convince your audience to offer you the position.

Product

You should consider several CMAPP issues in particular.

Form Brevity, precision, and concision are crucial. Avoid wasting words and space. For example, using the headings *Name* and *Address* to introduce your name and address is counterproductive: your audience *recognizes* the information.

Choose action verbs in preference to weaker, roundabout constructions: *apply* not *make application*, *ensure* not *make certain that*, *guided* not *looked to the guidance of*, *created* not *established the creation of*, and so forth.

Résumés make use of phrases or elliptical clauses rather than complete sentences. Remember, however, to observe the principle of parallelism (Chapter 3) rigorously; otherwise, your text is liable to lose cohesion, coherence, and consistency.

The levels of discourse and technicality you should use will depend on your context and your audience; your choice should derive from your CMAPP analysis.

Finally, typographical, grammatical, or structural flaws lessen credibility, and thus your audience's interest.

Format The appearance of your résumé reflects your abilities. Make effective use of level heads. Commonly, these appear as though in the left-hand column of a table, complemented by the "information" that appears in a wider right-hand column. (See Figure 12.1 for an example.) Remember accessibility: you want your audience to extract salient items without having to pore over every word.

Length How long should your résumé be? Again, there are two schools of thought:

1. Your résumé should never exceed a single page. The rationale is that the audience will not be inclined to take the time or trouble to read more than one page. After

all, the résumé will merely identify candidates for the next step in the selection process. This point of view is valid.

2. Regardless of the number of pages, your résumé should include everything relevant to the application. The rationale is that the audience will be trying to exclude applications, and is likely to do so if the sparse contents of a single page do not provide enough information to permit a confident decision. Your audience will inevitably exclude a résumé of uncertain value rather than take the trouble to contact you for further information. This point of view is also valid.

Here is further evidence of the "crap shoot" nature of submitting applications. Unless you know your audience well enough to decide which of the two points of view they favour, you are gambling. You can try to boost your odds by using a third option. Create a one-page "summary" résumé; at the bottom, indicate *Details Attached,* and include a more comprehensive version, perhaps titled *[Your name]—Detailed Résumé.*

Do the best CMAPP analysis you can, make your decision, and create the most professional document possible. With the bit of luck that always plays a role, you should be successful.

Type   Broadly speaking, you can organize your résumé in one of two ways:

- to reflect *when* events occurred (this is usually referred to as a *chronological* résumé);

- to group information according to its *function* (this is customarily called a *functional* résumé).

Chronological Résumés

Since the ordering of employment information is typically from most recent to earliest, the chronological résumé is often referred to as being in reverse chronological order. (An example is Rick Vanderluin's c.v. in Figure 12.1.) Skills and accomplishments are integrated within each employment segment. This is viewed as a traditional format, and is probably the most common—and thus the most commonly expected on the part of your likely audience.

The chronological résumé is particularly effective for illustrating an improving career path. On the other hand, it tends to draw attention to any lack of career progress (if you are just beginning, for example) and to any chronological gaps (if you were unemployed for a protracted period while caring for a family, for example).

Functional Résumés

The functional résumé focuses on your skills and accomplishments. You organize your background information around the practical benefits you can offer your potential employer. Functional résumés are very effective for highlighting *what you can do* rather than *when you did it.*

Figure 12.1: A One-Page Reverse-Chronological Résumé

Rick Vanderluin, a senior employee with the Ottawa marketing firm of Avery and St-Georges, heard through the grapevine that RAI might be looking to create a marketing department. He decided to apply to Céline Robillard, RAI's company manager. Here is the one-page curriculum vitae he attached.

Richard (Rick) Vanderluin

1151 St. Jerome Crescent Orleans ON K2A 2A6
(613) 732-4438 Fax: 732-7878 E-mail: vanderl@rite.com

Academic	MBA (1985) University of Toronto
	BA (1983) York University

Career

1995 to Present	**Senior Associate**: Avery and St-Georges (Kanata, Ontario) • Report to Senior Partner. • Supervise staff of six. • Develop promotional strategies for several large clients, including Loblaws, Steinberg, and CIBC. • Assess and recommend new target opportunities: generated $2.5 million in new business in 1999.
1992–1995	**Director of Marketing**: Rawlinson Hotel (Kingston, Ontario) • Reporting to General Manager, set up Hotel's marketing department. • Supervised marketing staff of two. • Developed new marketing strategies: increased Hotel revenue by 27%. • Secured profitable linkages with out-of-town business and government, including Toronto Chamber of Commerce, Belleville Board of Trade, Upper Canada Dentistry Association, and Ontario Federation of Municipal Regions. • Actively pursued convention and meeting business: from 1993–1995, secured a minimum of five association AGMs.
1990–1992	**Sales Director:** FastService Hotels Ltd. (North Bay, Ontario) • Exercised full line responsibility for all company sales staff in North Bay, Sudbury, Elliott Lake, and Sault Ste. Marie. • Coordinated corporate-sponsored functions for all four FastService Hotels. • Actively solicited tourism business: received FastService's "Most Successful Manager" award in 1994 and 1995.
1987–1990	**Sales Associate:** Auto Qualité Legrand (Montreal, Quebec) • Reported to Sales Director • Recommended and developed marketing campaign for *Autos de grande qualité / Cars of Superior Quality*, increasing sales by 13% in 1990. • In both English and French, sold new and used Cadillacs and Lincolns.
References	Available on request.

Note, however, that they remain less common than chronological résumés; consequently, some audiences still tend to look askance at them, suspecting that they are designed to obscure unflattering information. In making your choice, therefore, you must effect as accurate a CMAPP analysis as possible—and then cast your dice. Figure 12.2 shows Vanderluin's c.v. reworked as a functional résumé.

To examine the situation of someone with little career experience, contrast the chronological and functional résumés of Rosalind Greene, the Mississauga University student whose transcript appeared in Chapter 10 (as Figure 10.1). They are shown in Figures 12.3 and 12.4.

Relevant Information

There are no certainties in choosing the information to incorporate in a résumé. Obviously, the better you know your context and your audience, the more effectively you can decide what to include or exclude. Here are a few general guidelines:

1. Include only relevant employment experience. If you are applying for a job as a research technician, and have paid experience as a technical assistant and as a nightclub bouncer, the former is pertinent—the latter is not.

2. Remember that you may have acquired relevant, transferable employment skills even though you were not being paid at the time. Rosalind Greene, for example, was a volunteer lifeguard at a children's camp; thus, she can lay claim to organizational, communication, and supervisory skills, and to the assumption of substantial responsibility—the lives of the children she supervised. A potential employer is primarily interested in the assets you can bring, not in how much you were paid to acquire them.

3. Under a separate heading in a chronological résumé but within the appropriate "function" in a functional résumé, include hobbies only if they furnished you expertise useful to the potential employer. If, for example, you have gained a high standing in one of the martial arts, your accomplishment could be relevant to an application with a police force or a security firm; your valuable baseball card collection would not be.

4. If you are looking for a summer job or just starting out in your career, or if a position has a particular academic requirement, your grades, degrees, diplomas, scholarships, or academic awards will probably be taken as evidence of commitment and accomplishment. Otherwise, they are likely superfluous.

5. Job awards such as salesperson of the month or highest record of accuracy in test results are likely to be worthwhile inclusions.

6. Use your CMAPP analysis to decide how far back to go. Again, if you have a very short employment history, you may want to include even relevant summer jobs

Figure 12.2: A Functional Résumé

Richard (Rick) Vanderluin

1151 St. Jerome Crescent Orleans ON K2A 2A6
(613) 732-4438 Fax: 732-7878 E-mail: vanderl@rite.com

Academic	MBA (1985) University of Toronto
	BA (1983) York University

Marketing Skills
- Developed promotional strategies for several large clients, including Loblaws, Steinberg, and CIBC.
- Assessed and recommended new target opportunities: generated $2.5 million in new business for the Ottawa marketing firm of Avery and St-Georges.
- Developed new marketing strategies that increased Rawlinson Hotel (Kingston, Ontario) revenue by 27%.
- Secured profitable linkages with out-of-town business and government, including Toronto Chamber of Commerce, Belleville Board of Trade, Upper Canada Dentistry Association, and Ontario Federation of Municipal Regions.
- Recommended and developed marketing campaign (*Autos de grande qualité / Cars of Superior Quality*) for Auto Qualité Legrand of Montreal, increasing sales by 13% in 1990.

Sales Skills
- For Rawlinson Hotel, secured a minimum of five association AGMs in each of two years.
- Actively solicited tourism business for FastService Hotels, receiving their "Most Successful Manager" award in 1994 and 1995.
- In both English and French, sold new and used Cadillacs and Lincolns.

Administrative Skills
- Set up and managed Rawlinson Hotel's marketing department.
- Coordinated corporate-sponsored functions for all FastService Hotels across Northern Ontario.
- Exercised full line responsibility for staff of up to six sales and marketing professionals.

References Available on request.

Figure 12.3: Greene's Chronological Résumé

Rosalind Rebecca Greene
#1802–2889 Don Mills Road Toronto ON M4J 2J5
(416) 487-9873 Cell: (416) 709-1837 E-mail: rgreene@britenet.com

Education

1999	**BIS** (Bachelor of Information Science): Mississauga University
	Major: Systems Design Minor: Political Science
	Overall GPA: 3.47
1995	High School Graduation: Fitzgerald Collegiate (Toronto)

Employment

Fall 1998–present
Senior Server (part-time): La Champagne Restaurant, Toronto
- Provide table service to clientele in a four-star downtown restaurant
- Maintain own table and tip accounts for restaurant management
- Supervise work of two other part-time servers

April–September, 1998
Supervising Server (full-time): La Champagne Restaurant, Toronto
- Trained all new regular servers
- Supervised work of four servers and three bussers
- Provided table service to clientele
- Maintained own accounts and oversaw those of the four servers and three bussers

1995–1998
Server (part-time): La Champagne Restaurant, Toronto

Volunteer Work

May–September, 1995–Present
Lifeguard (C.L.A. certified): Camp Harnessy, Toronto
- Every Sunday, held full-shift responsibility for lifeguarding at Olympic-sized pool at children's day camp
- Supervised swimming activities of up to 52 children, aged 6–8
- Submitted shift reports to Camp management
- In July 1997, received Lifesaver Hero award after resuscitating and providing first aid to a ten-year-old who had fallen and knocked himself unconscious against the diving board support.

Hobbies
Competitive swimming, track and field

References
Available on request

Figure 12.4: Greene's Functional Résumé

Rosalind Rebecca Greene
#1802–2889 Don Mills Road Toronto ON M4J 2J5
(416) 487-9873 Cell: (416) 709-1837 E-mail: rgreene@britenet.com

Education

1999	**BIS**	(Bachelor of Information Science): Mississauga University
		Major: Systems Design Minor: Political Science
		Overall GPA: 3.47
1995		High School Graduation: Fitzgerald Collegiate (Toronto)

Training and Supervisory Skills
- Over a period of four years, trained a total of fourteen servers at La Champagne, one of downtown Toronto's four-star restaurants
- Regularly supervised the activities of four servers and three bussers
- Supervised the swimming activities, and was responsible for the pool safety, of up to 52 children, aged 6–8, at Camp Harnessy in Toronto

Organizational and Financial Skills
- Working as Server, Senior Server, and Supervising Server at La Champagne, maintained my own table and tipping accounts and oversaw those of other servers and bussers

Interpersonal and Communication Skills
- Dealt regularly with clientele at one of Toronto's four-star restaurants
- As lifeguard at Camp Harnessy, provided regular shift reports to Camp management
- Dealt effectively with up to 52 children during their swim times

Awards
- As CLA-certified Lifeguard at Camp Harnessy in July 1997, received Lifesaver Hero award after resuscitating and providing first aid to a ten-year-old who had fallen and knocked himself unconscious against the diving board support.

Hobbies
Competitive swimming, track and field

References
Available on request

held during high school. If you have been working for several years, include only what is of particular relevance to the position for which you are applying.

7. If you have been led to understand that you should include referees or letters of reference, do so. Otherwise, it's usually sufficient to include the phrase "References available on request." Note, however, that if you receive an interview, you must make sure to have the information with you at the time. Interviewers become impatient with candidates who apologize and offer to forward reference details later.

Electronic Résumés

More and more North American organizations are permitting—and in some cases encouraging or even requiring—electronic copy of résumés. A number of clearing houses for potential candidates and employers now occupy large Web sites, and are searched regularly by some organizations. Because such searches operate very differently from the traditional process, you have to approach the composition of your résumé differently as well.

Conventions for electronic résumés are still far from universal; thus, the "crap shoot" factor is higher. If you are looking to file your résumé electronically, however, you should bear in mind a few generalities.

1. Your wording will remain of crucial importance: not only must it persuade your audience, but it must be effective in terms of being flagged by whatever electronic search engine the employer uses. Remember that no one is likely to actually read all of the résumés in the posting bank; rather, a search engine will cull for those that match the criteria (the *keywords*) chosen by the employer.

2. Don't assume that your ability to simply file your résumé electronically necessarily gives you a real advantage. Just as with more traditional job searches, you will be competing with many other skilled candidates.

3. Learn as much as you can about creating electronic résumés. You can get a good start by looking at the Web sites offered at the end of this chapter.

Ethics

It is undeniable that some people have submitted successful applications that contain deliberate and inaccurate exaggeration. While your résumé must be persuasive, and while you should try to word it in a way that casts a favourable light on you and on your activities, I strongly recommend you not cross the bounds of truth. You will recall the earlier comment regarding aptitude and attitude. Consider how you would be viewed if, for example, your résumé specified that you were an expert user of the UNIX operating system, and, after a few weeks' employment, your lack of expertise became obvious. An old proverb states, "The truth will out." In most cases, that is what does happen. Therefore, don't compromise your integrity by untruthfully exaggerating your worth.

A profitable way to look at an employment interview is as a series of rapid impromptu presentations (see Chapter 11). Therefore, consider the following.

1. Your CMAPP analysis, part of your preparation before submitting your application, is crucial.

2. Your overall purpose at this stage is to convince your audience to hire *you* rather than someone else.

3. Each time your audience asks a question, or asks you to play a role in a scenario, you can benefit from the impromptu presentation skills you have learned.

4. Take advantage of the effective use of the paralinguistic factors and of the three-part rule introduced in Chapter 11.

5. Your audience will likely want to see how well you can think on your feet (even though you're probably seated...).

6. Before you submitted your application, you would have had the luxury of broad preparation; at the least, you should now have a good idea of the company's main functions.

7. This same preparation, coupled with the on-the-spot audience analysis, should allow you to ask intelligent, relevant questions of your own—an opportunity commonly afforded applicants. What you ask will depend on your context and audience. Nonetheless:

    (a) Avoid seeming flip: what you consider humorous, your audience may find cavalier or disrespectful; thus, for example, the question "So, did I do OK?", might be asked with a smile but received without one.

    (b) There may be a fine line between laudable self-assurance and apparent arrogance or conceit. Unless you are negotiating for a senior position, concluding your interview by asking about stock options is not likely to sit well with your audience.

    (c) It is acceptable to ask how long it might be—in ballpark terms—before they make their decision, and whether there is anything else you can offer that might help them reach it. Be careful of connotation here: you should not be asking whether you can now "correct" something you think you did poorly during the interview; you are diplomatically offering to help *them*.

    (d) If you have been successful in doing your homework about the organization, and if you're sure of the accuracy of your information, you can ask about company operations. Make sure, however, that what you mention is public knowledge: this is *not* the time to try to impress the audience with your ability to ferret out confidential information about them! Similarly, name-dropping is unlikely to impress your audience. In both cases, you're courting the consequences of the aptitude/attitude issue mentioned earlier.

Questions and Answers

Your audience is there to assess you—not only to find out about your likely ability to do the job, but probably to decide if they would like to work with you. Thus, thinking back to Chapter 1's discussion of ethics in technical communications, you should be honest and forthright.

With certain exceptions, Canadian law generally prohibits your being asked questions regarding your sex, age, religion, or ethnic background. If your interviewer does refer to them, you should consider politely indicating that you feel the question is inappropriate, tactfully avoiding it, or diplomatically stating that you might be agreeable to answering if your interviewer can demonstrate how the information is relevant to performing the job.

If you feel that you are being unfairly pressed, consider whether you are seeing a reflection of the working environment. Ask yourself if you would really like to be a part of such an organization. Remember that unethical interview questions likely reflect how the employer treats employees.

Follow-up

Some authorities specify a standard follow-up to your interview: a short letter, addressed to at least one of the interviewers, expressing your appreciation for their time, and reiterating your interest in the position. Often, that is an excellent strategy. It shows your continued involvement, stresses your interest, and may well be what distinguishes you from other candidates.

Unfortunately, however, some audiences react to such letters negatively. They see them as meddling or as an inappropriate attempt to influence their decision. While you may think this perspective unproductive, it is not one you should ignore. You might even wish to conclude your interview by asking whether you could take the liberty of following up within the next few days. Unless the response is a clear and definitive "no," writing the follow-up letter is probably to your advantage.

Make sure you do not allow reasonable follow-up to become pestering. Unless your interviewers have clearly indicated otherwise, they are unlikely to welcome repeated queries about their decision. Remember that your peace of mind, however important to you, is probably not the first priority in their working lives.

CASE STUDY

Cover Letters from MU Students to AEL

Situation

Wally Strong, a fourth-year electrical engineering student at MU, and George Nagmara, a civil engineering M.Sc. student there, both heard Noam Avigdor's presentation regarding employment with AEL. (See Chapter 11's case study.) Despite having grown up in Toronto, Strong has always wanted to live for a time in Newfoundland, and decides to submit an application to AEL's St. John's office. His cover letter appears in Figure 12.5. For his part, Nagmara senses an opportunity to return to his home town of Winnipeg; the cover letter for his application appears as Figure 12.6.

Issues to Think About

1. Strong and Nagmara attended the same presentation, and created cover letters addressed to the same company, albeit to offices in different cities. What can you say about the two letters in terms of the following CMAPP components?
   (a) Audience:
      (i) examination of sources to determine a specific audience (if necessary, review Chapter 11's case study);
      (ii) response to what the audience knows, needs to know, and wants to know.
   (b) Message: content of the letter to fit the context and the audience.
   (c) Form: language appropriate to the context and the audience.
   (d) Purpose: clear indication to the audience of the purpose of the letter.
   (e) Product:
      (i)   credibility deriving from the quality of the product;
      (ii) impression of author as potential employee;
      (iii) specific format issues.

2. What do you think might have been Strong's principal error or errors?

3. Why do you think that Strong did not attach a résumé? Why do you think Nagmara did?

4. How would you describe Strong's action request? How would you formulate it? How does it differ from Nagmara's?

5. How would you account for the differences between the two letters?

6. What would you presume to be the likely reactions of Frank Nabata and of Leila Berakett (AEL's senior associate at the St. John's office)?

EXERCISES

12.1 What are the five elements of the employment application package discussed in this chapter?

12.2 On what attributes do many employers seem to base their hiring and firing decisions?

12.3 Briefly explain the value of networking before you apply for jobs.

12.4 What are the principal reasons for using a cover letter with your résumé?

12.5 How do you decide on the appropriate level of technicality for your cover letter?

Figure 12.5: Strong's Cover Letter

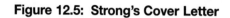

#1225–1356 Davenport Road Toronto ON L3L 2A8
354-0908 Cell: 879-3435
03/03/00
Employment Manager, AEL
101 Signal Hill Road
St John NF A1B 9A7

Dear Employment Manager,

Hello. My name is Wally Strong and I live in Toronto but I have been going to Mississauga U for a while in engineering. I'd like to apply for any of the positions that your person talked about when he visited where I was at school near Toronto.

My studies were completed when I finished my forth year at MU near here in Mississauga. I took a lot of different courses but really majored in engineering, most of my marks were pretty good but I did get a couple of not so good ones too, but I'm sure what I learned in engineering can be applied practically to whatever kind of engineering you do there in Nfld, where I've always wanted to live. That's the reason why I'm applying to you way out there rather than trying to get a good offer closer to home here.

I'm sure you'll be able to make really good use of all my engineering and communication skills in St Johns because I know you do a lot of consulting and my specialty is in electrical engineering, I hear in the papers that Nfld is looking to lay some new electrical grids with Labrador. Yes I do try to keep up with the news, that's another reason why you'll probably want me in your St. Johns office not on the Mainland.

I'm not married and don't have any responsibility which would make it easy for me to move whenever you'd need me to start. (Actually, I have a camper van and I don't have a lot of stuff, so I can move myself pretty easily and save you the money.)

I sure hope you'll at least interview me for this job because I'm sure that when you see my credentials and background in detail (I can send a copy right away if you want to see them before you speak to me) you'll think I'm worth it.

Thanks for taking the time to read this and think of me. If you have any questions at all just call me anytime, even on my cell at 879-3435, though that's probably long distance, hope you don't mind.

Thanks again, it'll be really great to meet you!

Wally Strong
Wallace (Wally) Strong

Figure 12.6: Nagmara's Cover Letter

George Nagmara

March 6, 2000

Mr. Frank Nabata
Senior Partner
Accelerated Enterprises Ltd.
352 St. Mary Avenue
Winnipeg MB R2R 1M8

Dear Mr. Nabata:

I am writing in the light of Mr. Noam Avigdor's February 23, 2000, presentation to students at Mississauga University (MU) in Mississauga, Ontario.

You will note from my enclosed curriculum vitae that I am currently completing my M.Sc. degree in Civil Engineering here at MU, for which I expect to maintain my current GPA of 4.00. You will likewise note that I returned to university to undertake my graduate degree after a hiatus of three years, during which I was employed as an Engineer Trainee at the firm of Lather and Frumm in Winnipeg, my home town. Mr. William Frumm has kindly agreed to offer me a reference, should you wish to speak to him. He may be reached at his office at 548-1435.

I would be keenly interested in the possibility of a civil engineering career with Accelerated Enterprises. I expect to be in Winnipeg from May 2 through May 12, following my thesis defence here in Toronto. Therefore, I would be grateful if you could spare me an hour of your time during that period, so that we might discuss how my education and experience could be of benefit to Accelerated Enterprises.

Could you perhaps have your office contact me as soon as possible at the address, phone, fax, or e-mail shown below, so that we might arrange a time convenient to you.

Thank you for your consideration. I look forward to meeting with you.

Yours truly,

George Nagmara

George Nagmara
Encl.

#512–478 Bloor Street Toronto ON L3R 4B5
Tel: 416 322-0907 Fax: 416 787-1421 E-mail: nagmara@torcity.com

12.6   What are the principal format aspects that you should consider for your cover letter?

12.7   What is another term for a résumé?

12.8   A résumé could be considered a combination of which four CMAPP products?

12.9   How long should a résumé be and why?

12.10   What is the principal advantage and what is the main possible disadvantage of including a statement of professional objective?

12.11   What are the two basic types of résumés?

12.12   In what principal way do they differ?

12.13   What are the principal advantages and disadvantages of each?

12.14   Create an effective résumé that might accompany a revised cover letter from Wally Strong (see Figure 12.5). Use the type of résumé shown in Figure 12.1 on page 221.

12.15   Create the résumé that George Nagmara might have enclosed with his cover letter (Figure 12.6). Use the type of résumé shown in Figure 12.2 on page 223.

12.16   Contact at least two people from different companies or organizations, who are authoritatively involved in the hiring process. Ask them individually for a few minutes of their time to help you in your project. Ask them to tell you what are the most important things they look for in a cover letter, a résumé, and an interview. In a short oral or written analytical report (perhaps to your class), compare and contrast the answers you received and draw conclusions from them.

EXPLORING THE WEB

Here are some Web sites you might wish to investigate.

URL	DESCRIPTION
http://www.monster.com/	Monster.com is one of the largest sites for electronic résumés, linking employers and employment-seekers.
http://www.headhunter.net/	Headhunter.net is another large site, comparable to Monster.com.
http://www.career.com/	Career.com bills itself as the "World's first recruitment site." Its function is similar to that of Monster.com and Headhunter.net.
http://webx.contactpoint.ca/scripts/webx.exe	The Contact Point Discussion Forum provides questions and answers, discussion groups, and information links related to the creation of electronic résumés.

http://www.provenresumes.com/reswkshps /electronic/electrespg1.html	The ProvenResumes.com site offers tips and hints on scannable electronic résumés, e-mail résumés, Internet résumé posting banks, and Web home page résumés.
http://www.careerowl.ca/	CareerOwl is a Canadian "electronic hiring hall" that offers information and links for job-seekers, particularly graduating postsec-ondary students.

Index

Abbreviation, definition of, 81
ABC (accuracy, brevity, clarity), as CMAPP attribute, 83
Abstract, in long/formal reports, 173, 175
Accelerated Enterprises Ltd., introduction to, 11
Accessibility, as CMAPP attribute, 86
Accuracy
    CMAPP attribute, 83
    ethical issue, 5
    proposal element, 153
Acronym, definition of, 81
Action, as part of AIDA strategy, 116
Action request, as proposal element, 153
Administrative requirement, as rationale for reports, 162
Advertisement, 215
AEL. See Accelerated Enterprises Ltd., introduction to
Age range. See Audience, analysis, in presentations
AIDA (Attention, interest, desire, action). See Persuasion
Alphanumeric numbering. See Multi-level outline
Analysis, tips for CMAPP model, 18–19
Analytical reports, 169–71
Analytic summaries, 175
APA (American Psychological Association) style, 57
Appeal to the intellect, in persuasion, 110
Appendix, in long reports, 173
Assessment summaries, 175
Asterisk, for emphasis in e-mail, 135
Attention-getter, in presentations, 196
Audience
    analysis, in presentations, 189
    benefits, in proposals, 153
    definition of, in CMAPP model, 17
    relevance, in presentations, 196
    in résumés, 218–19
Audience-driven, definition of, 2
Author-driven, definition of, 2
Authorization, as proposal element, 153

Bad news strategy, 96
Bar charts, 62
Bibliography, in long reports, 174
Block format. See Letter
Body text, 51
Box, as document visual, 56

Breathing, before presentations. See Presentations, conquering stage fright
Brevity, as CMAPP attribute, 83
Budget, as proposal element, 152

Call to action
    AIDA strategy, 116
    cover letters, 217
    presentations, 197
    proposals, 152
Canadian Press, 57
Canadian Style guide, 57
CAP (concise, accessible, precise), as CMAPP attribute, 86, 88–89
Causes, for creating summaries, 177
CFF (content, form, format), as CMAPP attribute, 84–85
Charts, 60–65
Chicago style, 57
Chronological pattern, in reports, 169
Clarity, as CMAPP attribute, 83
Classification of reports, 167–68
Clip art, 67–68
Close, in presentations, 198
Closure, in presentations, 197
CMAPP, 14–31
    analysis tips, 18–19
    audience, definition of, 17
    bad news strategy, 97
    context, definition of, 17
    deductive strategy for persuasion, 111
    general application of, 21
    good news strategy, 95
    interrelationships among elements, 20–21
    introduction to model, 16–18
    message, definition of, 17
    neutral news strategy, 99
    product, definition of, 17
    purpose, definition of, 17–18
    technical description, 99
Colour, in visuals, 58
Complimentary close, in business letters, 127
Concision, as CMAPP attribute, 86
Concluding segment, in presentations, 197–98
Conclusion, in syllogism, 114
Confidence. See Paralinguistic factors
Content
    CMAPP attribute, 84–85
    long/formal reports, 172
    short reports, 165

Context
    definition of in CMAPP Model, 17
    presentations, 188
Contrasts, for creating summaries, 177
Costing, as proposal element, 153
Cover letters, 216–17
Cover page, in long reports, 173
Cultural background. *See* Audience, analysis, in presentations
Cultural preferences, 6
Cultural referents, 6

Data collection, for creating summaries, 178
Data organization. *See* Multi-level outline
Data projector, 204
Data versus information, 38
Date format, in business letters, 124
Decimal numbering. *See* Multi-level outline
Decorative fonts, 55
Deductive strategy, in persuasion, 111
Delivery, speed of. *See* Paralinguistic factors
Descriptive abstract, 175
Desire, as part of AIDA strategy, 116
Detail, level of, in visuals, 59
Dictionaries, use of, 44
Directness, as cultural preference, 7
Direct strategy, for good news. *See* Good news strategy
Division, principle of, in outlines, 42
Document visuals, 51–56
    body text, 51
    boxes, 56
    definition, 51
    fonts, 54
    footers, 51
    headers, 51
    justification, 52
    level heads, 51
    line spacing, 52
    lists, bulleted and numbered, 56
    margins, 52
    paragraph spacing, 52
    reverse or inverse text, 56
    rules, 56
    white space, 52
Dress. *See* Paralinguistic factors

Electronic communications, 132–36
E-mail, 123, 134–36
Emoticons, 135
Emphasis markers, in presentations, 197
Employment, seeking, 214–28
    advertisements, 215
    cover letters, 216

    interviews, 227
    networking, 215
    preparation, 214–16
    procrastination, 216
    research, 215
    résumés, 217–26
    self-assessment, 215
Endnotes, 173–74
End pieces, in long reports, 173
Enhancement, in visuals, 58
Enunciation. *See* Paralinguistic factors
Error reduction, as rationale for reports, 162
Ethics, 3–6
    AIDA strategy, 117
    broadcast fax, 133
    codes of, 3
    definitions, 4
    logical fallacies, 115
    résumés, 226
Evaluative summaries, 175
Exaggeration, as ethical issue, 5
Executive summary
    content summary, 175
    front piece of long report, 173
Extemporaneous presentation, 195
Eye contact, 7–8. *See also* Paralinguistic factors

Facial expression. *See* Paralinguistic factors
False dichotomy. *See* Logical fallacies
Familiarization, in creating content summaries, 177
Faulty consequence. *See* Logical fallacies
Faxes, 123, 133–34
Feedback, in transactional model, 14
Figures, list of, in long reports, 173
Fillers. *See* Paralinguistic factors, hesitation particles
Final summary, in presentations, 197
5WH (who, what, where, when, why, how), as CMAPP attribute, 81–82
Focus, in short reports, 164
Fonts, as document visual, 54–55
Footer, 51–52
Form, as CMAPP attribute, 84, 85
Formal reports, 171–74
    abstract, 173, 175
    appendix, 173
    bibliography, 174
    cover page, 173
    criteria, 171
    endnotes, 173
    end pieces, 173
    executive summary, 173

figures, table of, 173
front pieces, 172
glossary, 173
index, 174
structure of, 172–74
table of contents, 173
title page, 173
works cited page, 174
See also Executive summary; Summaries;
    Transmittal letter; Transmittal memo
Format
    CMAPP attribute, 84, 85
    résumés, 219
    short reports, 164–65
    technical communications, 87–88
    traditional prose, 87
Front pieces, in long reports, 172–73

Gender
    cultural referent, 8
    honorifics, 128
Geographical pattern, in reports, 169
Gesture. *See* Paralinguistic factors
Glossary, in long reports, 173–74
Good news strategy, 95
Grammar and usage guides, 45
Grammar checker, electronic, 46
Grandstone Technical Institute, introduction to,
    11
Graphs, 60–65
GTI. *See* Grandstone Technical Institute, intro-
    duction to

Handouts, in presentations, 201
Hasty generalization. *See* Logical fallacies
Header, 51–52
Hesitation particles. *See* Paralinguistic factors
Hierarchy, in reports, 162
Honesty, as ethical issue, 4
Honorifics, in business letters, 124, 127
Humour, as cultural preference, 7
Hyperlinks. *See* Technical description

Identification of main points, in creating con-
    tent summaries, 177–78
IEEE (Institute of Electrical and Electronic
    Engineers) style, 57
Importance pattern, in reports, 169
Impromptu presentation, 194–95
Incident report, 167
Index, in long reports, 174
Indirect pattern, in reports, 170
Indirect strategy. *See* Bad news strategy
Inductive strategy, in persuasion, 111

Informal reports, 164–71
    classification of, 167
    content, 165
    length, 165
    organization of body, 169
    prepared form, as short report format, 165
Information *versus* impression, in visuals, 57
Informative reports, 169
Informing others, as rationale for reports, 161
Initial summary, in presentations, 196
Inside address, in business letters, 124
Instructions, 102–4
Interest, as part of AIDA strategy, 116
Interference, in transactional model, 15
Interviews, 227–28
Intonation. *See* Paralinguistic factors
Introductory segment, in presentations,
    195–96
Issue, in organization of evaluative report, 171

Justification, of recommendations in
    proposal, 152
Justification, of text, 52–53

KISS (Keep it simple, stupid) principle, 82–83

Lateral reports, 162
Legal requirement, as rationale for reports, 162
Legibility, in visuals, 58
Length
    résumés, 219–20
    short reports, 165
    summaries and abstracts, 175–76
Letterhead, in business letters, 124
Letters, 123–29
    block format, 124, 125, 127
    business letter conventions, 124, 126
    definition of, 123
    modified block format, 124, 126, 127
    short report format, 164
Level heads, definition of, 51
Line charts, 63–66
Line spacing, 52
List of figures, in long reports, 173
Lists, bulleted and numbered, 56
Logical argumentation, as persuasive strategy,
    110–15
Logical fallacies, 114–15

Manuscript presentation, 194
Maps, as presentation visuals, 201
Margins, 52–53
Memo, 129, 131–32
    short report format, 164–65

Memorized presentation, 194
Message
    definition of in CMAPP Model, 17
    in presentations, 188–89
Minutes, as content summary, 175
Mississauga University, introduction to, 11
MLA (Modern Language Association), 57
Models, as presentation visuals, 201
Modified direct strategy. *See* Neutral news
    strategy
Monospace fonts, 54
Movement. *See* Paralinguistic factors
Ms., as honorific, 128
MU. *See* Mississauga University, introduction to
Multiculturalism, definition of, 6
Multi-level outline, 38–44
    collecting data, 38
    data organization, 39
    numbering systems, 39
    in development of presentation, 193
    principle of division, 42
    principle of parallelism, 42
    principle of subordination, 42
    process and structure, 38
    refining, 40–43

Netiquette. *See* E-mail
Networking, 215
Neutral news strategy, 98–99
Number, in honorifics, 128

Occupation. *See* Audience, analysis, in presenta-
    tions
Option, in organization of evaluative report, 171
Organization patterns, in technical description,
    100
Outlining. *See* Multi-level outline
Overhead projector, 202

Paragraph spacing, 52
Paralinguistic factors, 198–200
    dress, 198
    enunciation and pronunciation, 200
    eye contact, 198
    facial expression, 199
    gesture, 199
    hesitation particles, 200
    movement, 199
    posture, 199
    presence, 198
    speed of delivery, 199
    time management, 200
    tone and intonation, 199
    volume, 199

Parallelism, principle of, in outlines, 42
People, as presentation visuals, 201
Periodic report, 167
Permanent record, as rationale for reports, 161
Persuasion, 110–21
    advertising, 110
    AIDA, 115–18
    cultural preferences, 116
    intellect versus emotion, 110
    logical argumentation, 110–15
    as element of proposal, 149
    targeting emotions (*see* Persuasion, AIDA)
Photos, as presentation visuals, 201
Pie charts, 60–61
Planning, as rationale for reports, 162
Pointers, for creating content summaries, 177
Politics. *See* Audience, analysis, in presentations
Positive attitude, before presentations. *See*
    Presentations, conquering stage fright
Positive imaging. *See* Presentations, conquering
    stage fright
Posture. *See* Paralinguistic factors
Precision, as CMAPP attribute, 88–89
Presence. *See* Paralinguistic factors
Presentations, 188–212
    audience analysis, 189–90
    body, 196–97
    call to action, 197
    CMAPP approach to, 188–89
    concluding segment, 197–98
    conquering stage fright, 191–92
    data projector, use of, 204
    development process, 192–93
    elements of, 195–98
    emphasis markers, 197
    extemporaneous delivery, 195
    handouts, 201
    impromptu delivery, 194–95
    introductory segment, 195–96
    manuscript delivery, 194
    memorized delivery, 194
    multi-level outline, 193
    overhead projector, use of, 202–3
    paralinguistic factors, 198–200
    props, 201–2
    purpose, 190–91
    question period, 204–5
    rehearsal, 193
    repetition markers, 197
    rhetorical questions, 196
    segment summaries, 197
    self-introduction, 196
    signposts, 196
    speaker credibility, 196

speaking notes, 193
thesis statement, 192
three-part rule, 195
35 mm projector, use of, 203–4
transitions, 197
types, 194–95
visual aids, 202–4
visuals, 200–2
Privacy, in e-mail, 135
Process description
definition of, 99
instructions, compared with, 102–3
Product, as CMAPP attribute, 17–18, 189,
219–20
Progress report, 167
Pronunciation. *See* Paralinguistic factors
Proportional-space fonts, 54
Proposals, 149–58
classification of, 149–50
CMAPP implications, 150–52
definition of, 149
formal, definition of, 152
formal, elements of, 152–53
general considerations, 153, 156
informal, definition of, 152
informal, elements of, 152
Props, in presentations, 201–2
Purpose
definition of, in CMAPP Model, 17
of presentations, 189, 190–91
of résumés, 219

Question period, in presentations, 204

Radisson Automobiles Inc., introduction to, 11
RAI. *See* Radisson Automobiles Inc., introduction to
Rehearsal, in development of presentation, 193
Religious affiliation. *See* Audience, analysis, in
presentations
Reorganization of data, for creating summaries,
178
Repetition markers, in presentations, 197
Reports, 161–74
abstracts, 175
analytical, 169–71
categories, 168–71
evaluative (*see* Reports, analytical)
formal (*see* Formal reports)
hierarchy of organization, as audience for
report, 162
informal or short (*see* Informal reports)
informative, 169
level of technicality, 162

organization by issue, 171
organization by option, 171
organization patterns, 169
persuasive, 169
See also Formal reports; Informal reports
Research
employment fields, 215–16
during presentation development process,
192
Response to need or request, in reports. *See*
Reports, rationale for
Résumés, 217–26
audience, 218–19
chronological, 220, 221, 224
definition, 217–18
electronic, 226
ethics, 226
format, 219
functional, 220, 222, 223, 225
message, 218
product, 219–20
professional objective, 218
purpose, 219
relevant information, 222, 226
Reverse text, as document visual, 56
Rules, as document visuals, 56
Running head, 51–52

Sales report, 167
Salutation, in business letters, 127
Samples, as presentation visuals, 202
Sans-serif fonts, 55
Scale, in visuals, 59–60
Schedule, as element of proposal, 153
Self-assessment, for employment, 215
Serif fonts, 55
Sex. *See* Audience, analysis, in presentations
Short reports. *See* Informal reports
Signature block, in business letters, 127
Signature file. *See* E-mail
Simplification and emphasis, in visuals, 58
Size, in visuals, 58
Skepticism, in proposals, 153
Socioeconomic status. *See* Audience, analysis, in
presentations
Solution, as proposal element, 152
Spam, 136
Speaker credibility, in presentations, 196
Speaking notes, 193
Speed of delivery. *See* Paralinguistic factors
Spell checker, electronic, 45
Spelling and vocabulary, as cultural preference, 7
Stage fright, conquering. *See* Presentations, con-
quering stage fright

Stimulants, before presentations. *See*
    Presentations, conquering stage fright
Strategies
    AIDA, 115–17
    bad news, 96–97
    deductive, in persuasion, 111
    good news, 95–96
    inductive, in persuasion, 111
    neutral news, 98–99
    persuasion, 110–18
    simple instructions, 103–4
    technical description, 100–2
Style guides, 56–57
Subordination, principle of, in outlines, 42
Summaries, 174–78
    analytic or assessment, 175
    content or informative, 174
    content summaries, process for creating,
        176–78
    definition of in long reports, 174
    descriptive abstract, 175
    evaluative summaries, 175
    executive summary, 175
    inclusion and exclusion of content, 175
    length of, 175–76
    long report abstracts, 175
    minutes, 175
    as element of proposal, 152
Syllogism, 111, 114

Table of contents, in long reports, 173
Table of figures, in long reports, 173
Tables, 66–67
Tautology. *See* Logical fallacies
Technical communications
    characteristics of, 1–3
    ease of selective access, 2
    integration of visual elements, 2
    necessity for specific audience, 2
    relevance of, 1
    structure, 3
    timeliness, 2–3
Technical description, 99–102
    complex strategy, 102
    computerized hyperlinks, 102
    organization patterns, 100
    simple, strategy for, 100–1
    vocabulary preferences, 100
Technicality, level of, in reports, 162, 164
Test report, 168
Thesaurus, 44–45, 46
Thesis statement, in presentations, 192

35 mm projector, use of, 203–4
Time management. *See* Paralinguistic factors
Title page, in long reports, 173
Tone. *See* Paralinguistic factors
Transactional communication model, 14–16
Transitions, in presentations, 197
Transmission vehicle. *See* Transactional commu-
    nication model
Transmittal letter
    formal reports, 172
    informal reports, 165
Transmittal memo
    formal reports, 172
    informal reports, 165
Trip report, 168

Undisprovable theory. *See* Logical fallacies

Vertical reports, 162
Visualization. *See* Presentations, conquering
    stage fright
Visuals
    bar chart, 62–63
    clip art, 67–68
    colour, use of, 58
    data projector, use of, 204
    definition of, 51
    detail, level of, 59
    emphasis, 58
    enhancement, 58
    handouts, 201
    information versus impression, 57–58
    legibility, 58
    line charts, 63–66
    overhead projector, use of, 202–3
    pie charts, 60–61
    presentations, role in, 200–4
    props, 201–2
    relevance, 58
    scale, 59–60
    simplification, 58
    size, 58
    tables, 66–67
    technical description, 100
    35 mm projector, use of, 203–4
Volume. *See* Paralinguistic factors

Warnings, in instructions, 103
White space, 52
Works cited page, in long reports, 174
Worst-case scenario. *See* Presentations, con-
    quering stage fright

To the owner of this book

We hope that you have enjoyed David Ingre's *Express: A Brief Guide to Technical and Business Communication* (0-17-616758-7), and we would like to know as much about your experiences with this text as you would care to offer. Only through your comments and those of others can we learn how to make this a better text for future readers.

School _____ Your instructor's name _____

Course _____ Was the text required? _____ Recommended? _____

1. What did you like the most about *Express*?

   _____

   _____

   _____

2. How useful was this text for your course?

   _____

   _____

   _____

3. Do you have any recommendations for ways to improve the next edition of this text?

   _____

   _____

   _____

4. In the space below or in a separate letter, please write any other comments you have about the book. (For example, please feel free to comment on reading level, writing style, terminology, design features, and learning aids.)

   _____

   _____

   _____

   _____

Optional

Your name _____   Date _____

May Nelson Thomson Learning quote you, either in promotion for *Express* or in future publishing ventures?

Yes _____   No _____

Thanks!

You can also send your comments to us via e-mail at **college@nelson.com**

PLEASE TAPE SHUT. DO NOT STAPLE.

TAPE SHUT

TAPE SHUT

- - - FOLD HERE - - -

TAPE SHUT

TAPE SHUT

MAIL ⮞ POSTE
Canada Post Corporation
Société canadienne des postes
Postage paid   Port payé
if mailed in Canada si posté au Canada
Business Reply   Réponse d'affaires
0066102399   01

NELSON
✦
THOMSON LEARNING™

0066102399-M1K5G4-BR01

NELSON THOMSON LEARNING
HIGHER EDUCATION
PO BOX 60225 STN BRM B
TORONTO ON M7Y 2H1